THE ROMAN EMPIRE IN 395 A.D.

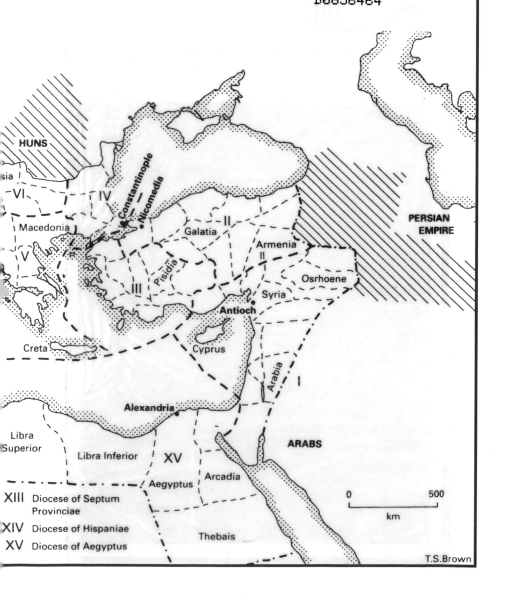

HUNS

sia

VI   IV

Constantinople
Nicomedia

Macedonia

Galatia   II

V   Armenia
II

Pisidia   Osrhoene

III   Syria

Antioch

Creta   Cyprus   Arabia
I

Alexandria

Libra
Superior   Libra Inferior   XV   ARABS

Aegyptus   Arcadia

XIII   Diocese of Septum
Provinciae

XIV   Diocese of Hispaniae

XV   Diocese of Aegyptus

Thebais

PERSIAN
EMPIRE

0   500
km

T.S.Brown

BEYOND THE EMPIRE

Also by Desmond O'Grady:

Eat from God's Hand
A Long Way from Home
Deschooling Kevin Carew
Valid for All Countries
Raffaello! Raffaello!
Marriage Gamblers
Caesar, Christ and Constantine
Correggio Jones and the Runaways
The Turned Card
Rome Reshaped

BEYOND
THE
EMPIRE

*Rome and the Church from
Constantine to Charlemagne*

DESMOND O'GRADY

A Crossroad Book
The Crossroad Publishing Company
New York

The maps on the endpapers have been adapted from Angus Mackay with David Ditchburn, eds., *Atlas of Medieval Europe,* maps copyright © 1997 T. S. Brown. Used with permission of Routledge.

The Crossroad Publishing Company
481 Eighth Avenue, New York, NY 10001

Printed in the United States of America

Library of Congress Cataloging-in-Publication Data
O'Grady, Desmond, 1929-
  Beyond the empire : Rome and the Church from Constantine to
Charlemagne / by Desmond O'Grady.
     p. cm.
  Includes bibliographical references and index.
  ISBN 0-8245-1908-6
  1. Catholic Church – History. 2. Church history – Primitive and early church, ca. 30-600. 3. Church history – Middle Ages, 600-1500.
4. Church and state – Rome – History. I. Title.
BX970 .O35 2001
270.2 – dc21

                                                    2001001543

1   2   3   4   5   6   7   8   9   10   06   05   04   03   02   01

*We are anguished to think that while savage and bar-
barous peoples have found their way to mercy, you who
are called the Merciful One have turned savage and cruel.
The entire West grows rich in faith because holy Peter
leads it.*

—Pope Gregory II (715–731) to the Byzantine Emperor Leo III,
who began a campaign against icons

CONTENTS

ACKNOWLEDGMENTS

My thanks are due to the following for their help: Edmund Campion, Mark Coleridge, Robert Dodaro, O.S.A., Edward Farrugia, S.J. Mario Fois, S.J., Hans Grotz, S.J., Bernhard Kriegbaum, S.J., George Lawless, O.S.A., John Michael McDermott, S.J., Tess Mobilia, John Navone, S.J., Gerald O'Collins, S.J., Philip Salom, Tommaso Stojnic, and my editor, John Eagleson.

INTRODUCTION

A N EQUESTRIAN STATUE of Constantine stands at one side of the atrium of St. Peter's basilica, another of Charlemagne at the other. This book is an exploration of the almost five hundred years separating the two emperors whose statues stand 180 strides apart in the church which unites them.

In *Beyond the Empire* the time between the two emperors is foreshortened as is the space in the atrium. The intention is to evoke a complex period by focusing on key figures who can convey the human drama involved in what otherwise becomes a mere sequence of events.

Although remote, it is a period that has similarities with ours because it saw seismic changes in the social, cultural, and psychic landscapes that produced both alluring prospects and anxiety.

As expectations of an imminent Second Coming faded, Christians grappled for the first time with being members of a recognized church and tried to embody the Gospel in a society initially confident but later in disarray.

Now the proportion of Christians is dropping, whereas the earlier period saw a burgeoning church described by Ambrose of Milan as "a moon waxing." But both periods are marked by acute tensions within the church, and between the church and society, aggravated by the scale and speed of change.

The church was positioning itself in respect to developments that foreshadowed the contemporary world. The contact of the peoples beyond the Alps with the Gospel message mediated through Rome resulted eventually in that Western Europe whose civilization was to outstrip others, such as the Chinese, that were then at a similar level or superior. The contemporary European Union was foreshadowed by the empire of Charlemagne. Among other things, it developed the script whose letters are found on computer keyboards and introduced a common currency that Europe was not to have again until the third millennium.

In the church also there were seminal developments as its members explored the implications of their faith in a society founded on other presuppositions: durable structures and laws were instituted; relations between bishops and Rome and bishops and the laity started to be defined; hermitages and monasteries were founded; confessional and hagiographic writing began, and Christian pilgrimage developed; Christian poetry, art, architecture, and music took their initial steps. The liturgy assumed diverse forms, Marian devotion emerged, and penitential practices became varied. The understanding of Christ and the Trinity was deepened and biblical concepts found expression in metaphysical language.

A strong feature of the period was all-rounders, bishops who were at the same time pastors, preachers, polemicists, and perhaps also monks and judges. Each activity nourished the other, and all enriched their writing. Often they wrote—or dictated—as they ran, using a nonspecialist language which was robust and immediate but could also be poetic. They preceded the age of specialized and academic theology, relying more on Scripture than syllogism. The writers of that time equivalent to Thomas Merton, G. K. Chesterton, and George Bernanos were bishops.

As today, Christians wrestled with the meaning of the body and sexuality. Augustine of Hippo and Julian of Eclanum furnished different responses to dualist ideas that exalted the spirit while despising the body. The church's esteem for consecrated virgins gave a higher status to women who, in various ways, found Christianity liberating. In other words, in troubled periods faith-filled figures produced innovative responses.

Beyond the Empire makes Rome its focus, underlying the ties with the city of people like Jerome and Boniface. Rome had a special role as the see of Peter, the city whose domain coincided with the known world and whose image often outstripped its reality.

The political thread in the story is that Charlemagne substitutes for Constantinople as protector of the territorial autonomy of the Roman see, which enabled it to look beyond the Mediterranean world. The cultural evolution is of more lasting interest. Rome anchored the church while a synthesis was achieved between the initially Jewish awareness of a relationship with God and a Greek conviction that the universe was ordered and hence knowable through rational enquiry. The synthesis enabled development of fundamental concepts such as that of the human person. Christianity modified classical culture but also absorbed elements of it: which tendency prevailed is discussed later. The issue became crucial when the Roman empire in the West crumbled and all seemed lost. The church of Rome, however, pursued its vocation of pulling things together, mediating what it had received from the East to the new peoples beyond the Alps to form the Carolingian core of the West.

The success in welding the Judeo-Christian religious viewpoint with Greco-Roman culture, followed by the Carolingian venture beyond its Mediterranean matrix, gives Rome a continuing weight in the Christian story as long as churches are not simply national and there is a conviction that renewing traditions is an option.

Today, when Rome must find other means to have universal relevance and inspire affection, it is worthwhile looking at its historic role, particularly as the papacy has shown a new willingness to acknowledge its faults. The emphasis of the Second Vatican Council on Scripture influenced religious education positively but needs to be complemented by knowledge of the church when it was first shaping society. As the liturgical movement before the council showed, looking back can see through current pseudo-traditions to discover something more authentic that triggers a rebirth. The interplay between Rome, its image, history, and culture and the church between 313 and 800 reflects a vitality, resourcefulness, and tenacity still needed by both church and society.

– I –

PARTYING IN A TIME WARP

T HE SCENE IS THE RESIDENCE of the Roman senator Vettius
Agorius Praetextatus during the feast of Saturnalia. For
the festivities of Saturn, the god of sowing, business, and
schools, executions and military operations were suspended, slaves
temporarily freed, dice gambling was allowed, and gifts were exchanged. Rowdy plebeian merry-making was the order of the
week (December 19–26), but some Roman patricians, who considered themselves "the best of the best," preferred to hold dinner
parties where literary, philosophical, and antiquarian discussions
predominated.

Quintus Aurelius Symmachus, Virius Nicomachus Flavianus,
and other local aristocrats are joined at Praetextatus's residence by
non-Romans such as a Greek philosopher and an Egyptian doc-
tor of medicine. The host speaks of the origins of the Saturnalia
festival instituted some eight centuries earlier in 497 B.C. and then
compares various pagan religious beliefs, claiming that Roman,
Hellenistic, and Middle Eastern gods are but different names for
the solar god. His talk is an example of the imaginative theories
of the otherworld relished by an elite that saw through the beliefs
of the plebs enjoying Saturnalia.

The discussion moves from this exercise in comparative religion to comments on Virgil and Cicero. Arrival of dessert sparks
a disquisition on nuts and then on different kinds of apples and
pears. There is speculation on the causes of gray hair, baldness,
and blushing, and even a debate on which came first, the chicken
or the egg. The symposium might have seemed an example of the
"idle antiquarianism" that Seneca deplored but, although its tone
was light, many serious subjects including grammar, science, and
ethics were raised.

The meeting was an imaginary one involving real people, explicitly in the style of Plato's dialogues. It was invented by a pagan

scholar, Macrobius, about A.D. 384, but several of the participants' views are confirmed from other sources.

There are convincing contemporary descriptions of senators as vain and frivolous people who kept their libraries shut like tombs. But those depicted at Praetextatus's residence were learned men who represented what came to be called the "Pagan Party."

Originally "pagans" meant country folk in contrast to city dwellers. Christians, who were found mainly in cities, appropriated the word to designate those, except Jews, who did not share their faith. It covered a multitude of beliefs in various gods (polytheism) by those who, as St. Paul said, "do not share our hope" (in the resurrection). Calling others "pagan" was a way for Christians to define themselves in contrast to the traditional culture. The so-called Pagan Party's leader was Senator Aurelius Symmachus, an esteemed administrator and renowned orator, whose immense wealth was indicated by his three mansions in Rome, one of which was later partly excavated on the Coelian Hill, and another twenty-eight outside it. Symmachus seems to have been the epitome of Roman gravity, which verged on stuffiness: he even boasted that, on a summer vacation, his son swam with dignity. His group revered Rome's past and felt a responsibility to preserve its culture and religion. Its members revised and copied the manuscripts of Latin writers such as Apuleius and Livy but also translated Plato, Plotinus, and other Greek authors. In the contiguous forums of Augustus and Trajan, schools of grammar and rhetoric revised ancient manuscripts, as was done also at the patricians' great villas, for instance in Enna, Sicily. Notes at the end of the redactions recorded where they were done. The cultural tradition to which the members of the Pagan Party gave scrupulous care was an underpinning of their social status. Its preservation was a tribute to all that had made Rome great.

Symmachus was solidly traditional in religion, which, in Rome, was intertwined with patriotism. Despite the excesses of some emperors and of some Hollywood travesties, it is simplistic to identify Roman paganism with hedonism. Cicero, Seneca, Marcus Aurelius, and others were eloquent advocates of rectitude and moderation. Wild behavior was to be eschewed in favor of subdued dignity or, as the Romans called it, *gravitas*. Virtues had a civic purpose, while meticulous performance of rites was designed to placate the wrath of the gods. A stern morality was the ideal.

Sturdy Roman religion was fused with that of the Greeks when Hellenistic culture took hold. The two sets of gods were identified, and Rome accepted the more imaginative Greek mythology. What was supposed to be Aeneas's ship was displayed in Rome as proof of its link with Troy.

Symmachus accepted the Roman-Greek pantheon, but his friend and host, Praetextatus, had taken a step further. He too was an eminent imperial official who had been proconsul to Greece and prefect of Rome. A doughty defender of the Senate's prerogatives, he translated Greek literature, preserved Latin texts, and restored the portico of the Decian Consentius building, which stands in the Forum near Vespasian's column and the Temple of Concord. The ideal pagan aristocrat, respected by many he ruled, he even argued that a slave's status was due to misfortune rather than to an inferior nature.

For his aristocratic wife, Paolina, Praetextatus was first and foremost a spiritual guide interested not only in religious history but also in religious experience. He was a priest of no less than ten cults, some Roman such as that of Vesta; others Greek mystery cults; still others Middle Eastern cults. Roman religion was becoming increasingly eclectic and initiation into one cult did not exclude another.

Praetextatus had convinced Paolina to undergo various initiations: she was introduced to the mysteries of Hecate and became a priestess of the Eleusian cult; she underwent the bull's blood ceremony, which a contemporary described:

> The person involved descends into a pit with head adorned by marvelous tasseled ceremonial headbands, temples protected by wraps and crowned with gold. A wooden platform is placed above the pit and then pierced by gimlets. A huge bull, whose shoulders and chained horns are adorned with flowers, is led in and a consecrated knife is plunged into its chest. The person below holds back his head to expose cheeks, ears, lips and nostrils to the bloody shower. From a distance, all admire one who has undergone such a ceremony, convinced that the dead bull's dirty blood has brought about a purification.

With such emotionally charged initiations, Paolina felt she had been reborn to eternal life.

Initiation into the cult of Isis, as described by Apuleius, was less dramatic: "The celebrant, dressed in a garment of new linen, took my hand and led me into the most sacred recess of the holy sanctuary....I approached the borders of death, I stepped upon the threshold of Prosperine. I was borne along through all the elements....I came into the presence of the gods who dwell above the earth and those who dwell below, and I paid them honor."

After accepting Hellenistic religious concepts, Rome had been invaded also by the mystery cults of gods such as Isis, Cybele, Serapis, and Mithra. Often the rites of these cults promised personal salvation rather than the health of society; they were ecstatic or orgiastic, demanding enthusiasm instead of sobriety. Their success showed that the Romans' civil religion did not satisfy all its inhabitants' needs; indeed it had begun to break down at least from the first century A.D.

From 361 until his death in 363 Emperor Julian, who, although raised as a Christian, had come to believe that the various gods were all expressions of solar worship, revived paganism, which earned him the sobriquet "the Apostate." The discussion at Praetextatus's residence echoes some of the ideas of Julian, who had been a friend of Praetextatus and was a hero for traditionalist pagan aristocrats. He had tried to give Neo-Platonic texts a status within paganism similar to that of Scripture in Judaism and Christianity. Another influence was the Greek philosopher Plotinus, who, by interpreting Plato as a philosopher of religion, had given paganism a new intellectual stature. The participants at Praetextatus's residence were convinced that their literature conveyed the deepest spiritual truths and the most humane wisdom, that their education system was irreplaceable, in other words that they held the cultural high ground, which also implied a moral superiority because virtue was identified with learning.

Rome's temples and other pagan monuments stood intact, and new pagan statues had been erected in the Forum after Constantine's death. Since the time of the Caesars its baths, theaters, and stadiums had been among the wonders of the world. The Pagan Party may have considered it inevitable that the capital would eventually revert permanently to the beliefs that had ensured its grandeur. But Diocletian's attempt to prop up paganism at the beginning of the century had been a bloodstained failure, and Julian's reversion to it was a mere interlude. Were the members of the Pagan Party blinded by Rome's past and its monuments, by their own wealth and erudition? Certainly they were proud, and this may have made them smug.

In the lengthy discussion of religion at Praetextatus's residence there was no mention of Christianity. Some participants may have had a particular distaste for Christianity as an outcrop of Judaism. Rome was willing to include in its pantheon the gods of all the peoples it subjugated: it was tolerant provided the worshipers of these gods accepted the totalitarian claims made for the imperial power. But the Hebrew God would not be assimilated.

Romans such as Tacitus had scorned the vain mysteries of the Jews, who built temples to a God with neither face nor form and whose name could be pronounced only once a year. The God of the Jews seemed more an absence than a presence when compared to Rome's array of potent divinities.

For Roman traditionalists, it was unthinkable that widely accepted polytheism should have to give way to exclusivist monotheism, which made nonsense of moderation. When some Jews claimed that a carpenter who had been crucified as a criminal for trying to lead an anti-Roman movement was their Messiah, it was not only abhorrent but also subversive. Instead of the Stoic ideal of serenity, instead of lofty philosophic wisdom, here was a revelation that involved the body as well as the mind in a passionate striving, gave a new sense to existence, and did not distinguish between an enlightened elite and superstitious plebs. Admittedly the new creed had attracted many non-Jews, but members of the Pagan Party could well have been convinced that Rome's innately superior traditions would reassert themselves: if this was their viewpoint, they did not realize how much water had flowed under the Milvian Bridge in the seven decades or so since Constantine had recognized Christianity.

Or perhaps discretion had counseled Praetextatus's guests to ignore Christianity because many of them were imperial officials at a time when the Christian emperors were becoming officially intolerant. In the first three centuries, some Christians had undergone martyrdom rather than fight in Rome's wars, but an edict of Emperor Theodosius in 380 obliged Christians, under threat of excommunication, to serve in the Christian emperor's army, from which pagans were gradually excluded. In this climate of opinion, it was already something that Macrobius, who practiced astrology himself, and his personages were able to present paganism in a favorable light. Other contemporary pagan authors likewise ignored Christianity; perhaps they believed that, if ignored, Christianity might disappear or, simply, that it had no cultural status. But the Christian places of worship in Rome were not just those of another Eastern mystery cult. Constantine himself had built St. Peter's and other huge churches. True they were on the outskirts of the city, because the center retained its sacred significance for pagans, but their scale was imperial.

Already approximately half the inhabitants of Rome were Christian. Praetextatus had commented on the bishop of Rome's wealth. One of the members of the Albani family at Praetextatus's residence had a Christian wife, and the other was almost certainly a Christian.

Toward the end of the fourth century a discussion of religion that ignored Christianity indicated a narrow focus. The time-warp aspect of the discussion at Praetextatus's residence becomes fully evident when one looks at the fortunes of the church in Rome in the seven decades after Constantine had triumphed under the sign of the cross.

– II –

No Small Thing

CONSTANTINE SAW ROME for the first time when he entered the city as a victor. In all, he spent only about five years there. His conquest of Rome was a crucial episode, but only an episode, in a protracted civil war that concluded in the East. After the first wave of barbarian onslaughts, Diocletian had transferred the capital to Nicomedia as part of his reorganization of the empire. Constantine might have brought the capital back to Rome but instead returned himself to the East, where he had grown up as a hostage at Diocletian's court. Near the site of small and pagan Byzantium, where Europe touched Asia, from 324 he built a new Rome, a mirror image of the old, on seven hills again and at the same latitude. The old Rome was tenaciously pagan, but his new Rome, Constantinople, would be Christian. The center of Rome, where the sacred and the civic melded, was administered by the old senatorial families. St. John Lateran had been built at a distance on imperial property abutting the city walls while the other churches such as St. Peter's were outside the walls of the pagan city. In Constantinople, the churches were in the city center.

Constantine's conversion followed closely after Diocletian's persecution, which was the most extensive of all, and his expansion of imperial prerogatives. The first emperor, Augustus (26 B.C.– A.D. 14), had called himself Princeps, or First Citizen, and had at least pretended to respect the Senate, but from Diocletian on there were no limits, even formal, on the power of the emperor.

Diocletian's reorganization of the empire downgraded its proud citizens into mere subjects oppressed by a centralized bureaucracy. Imperial style changed significantly also. Augustus had affected a homespun approach, but, by the beginning of the fourth century, simplicity had been replaced by pomp, dignity by ostentation, the linen toga by silken garments, and the headband by a jeweled crown. The conjunction of the end of persecution and the evolution of imperial style meant that Christians were extremely grateful to a figure who had unrestricted power and pretensions. Not only did Constantine continue to be Pontifex Maximus, head of the Roman pagan priesthoods, but moving to the East he assumed the style of Oriental kings who considered themselves icons of God.

Constantinople, situated between the empire's traditional enemy, Persia, and the Balkans, which were under barbarian threat, was better placed strategically than Rome. The site made cultural sense also: the empire had long been in fact a Roman-Greek empire in which Roman military prowess and organizational ability were wedded to Hellenistic culture. Latin was the language of the administration and the imperial court in Constantinople, whose inhabitants considered themselves Roman, while much of the teaching in Roman schools was in Greek. Plutarch used Greek in writing his *Roman Lives* as did Marcus Aurelius for his *Meditations*. Greek-language culture was more sophisticated, but those whose first language was Latin were intelligent enough to recognize this and assured enough to regard Greek-language culture as enrichment rather than as threat.

The empire embraced the whole Mediterranean basin: at one end it was bound by the Atlantic, at the other by the Persian empire. North Africa was Rome-across-the-sea. Under Julius Caesar, Western Europe had been incorporated into the empire, but Britain was regarded as the world's end: the empire's richest, most populous, and most cultured zone was the East. Constantinople was the capital, but from 394 the western half of the empire was ruled from Milan. Rome had been demoted, although it was still the symbolic capital, the prestigious Senate survived, and, with an estimated eight hundred thousand inhabitants, it remained the most populous city. Moreover, the citizens of the empire considered themselves Romans.

The emperors, who claimed a direct line to God, felt responsible for all aspects of society. They protected the unity of the faith as a basis for social cohesion and repressed its enemies. But, in addition, some wanted to determine questions of faith and were prepared to use violence against popes who, after all, were their subjects. In the early years of Christianity, many bishops were called pope or Father. From the fifth century, the usage began to be restricted to important bishops such as patriarchs and, in the West, was applied only to the bishop of Rome.

Popes and emperors also needed each other. As popes inevitably had relations with civil power, it was convenient that it be well-disposed, but also at a safe distance. Emperors, in turn, could be in difficulty if popes were at odds with them on questions of faith.

Much of the time they respected one another. From the late fifth century, popes sought ratification of their election from the emperors, who could apply pressure by delaying it. Annually popes paid homage to the reigning emperor before his portrait in the chapel of the Byzantine representative's palace on the Palatine. The papal image had a place of honor in religious ceremonies in Constantinople but was omitted when relations were tense. Popes kept a representative, a nuncio or apocrisarius, there; the importance of the post is indicated by the fact that several incumbents later became pope.

From the time of Christ's "render unto Caesar" and the Roman citizen Paul of Tarsus, some Christians had seen the empire as a providential instrument for spreading the message of salvation. This conviction survived even the persecutions and, after Constantine, Christians began to identify Christianity with the empire. When Rome declined the church found itself gradually taking over many civic functions: it replaced the philanthropy of the pagans with charitable initiatives. Its building programs modified the city.

But if the church shaped Rome, Rome also shaped the church. The empire was not identified with a nation but with a city: Rome, which, in the words of the poet and administrator Claudius Rutilius Namatianus, "united all peoples into one nation and made all the world one city." The advantage of the heritage was the incentive for the church to maintain unity and incorporate new peoples. The danger was that the city-empire be identified with the world as a whole and that contact be lost with Christians beyond the empire's frontiers, such as those in Asia, where at this time the presence of Christians is claimed on the west coast of India, and in Africa where the King of Ethiopia was converted to Christianity in 319.

After the departure of Constantine the church in Rome expanded within a culture that, with misgivings and modifications, it accepted. Rome was valued for its organizational genius, its educational system, its law, literature, and technical achievements such as plumbing and a road system that enabled communications not equaled again until the thirteenth century.

Rome's elaborate legal tradition, based on the idea that judicial precision was the basis of rights (Ammianus Marcellinus called laws "the everlasting foundations and moorings of liberty"), combined fairness and firmness. Recognition of the church made it part of this system, and it came to govern through decretals similar to imperial rescripts, which were definitive written replies, with the force of law, to requests for guidance. The Roman education system, adapted from Hellenism, continued for centuries until monastic and episcopal schools were formed, but its influence is still felt. Christians gradually accepted the riches of Roman literature and the wisdom of some of its philosophy. But in the spiritual sphere there were dangers in organization and juridicism suggested by the fact that the Roman terms for Christian concepts tended to be legal whereas the corresponding Greek terms were ontological.

The persistence of the imperial city provided a benchmark for a church that claimed to have a new and higher concept of humankind and its destiny. As the church had inherited an imperial capital, broad perspectives became congenial. But did it assimilate too fully to Rome? It is an issue that will be examined after recounting how the church, perhaps convinced that it had received the keys to history as well as to heaven, was buffeted by its impetuous course. For Christians, classical and pagan Rome was by turns a goal, an oppressor, a challenge, a context, and a heritage. Rome was all these things and more because, even before Christianity, it had been no small thing.

– III –

THE SPLIT

THE CREATION OF CONSTANTINOPLE seemed likely to reduce the importance of the bishop of Rome, but in the long run it proved a blessing. If Constantine had made Rome the capital once more, the city's bishops could have been overshadowed by the emperor's importance, tempted by his blandishments, and involved in his politics. Power moved with the emperor, and Rome was becoming a backwater with Pope Sylvester, whose reign (314–35) coincided almost exactly with Constantine's, keeping a low profile.

Christians in the East were divided by the claims of a Libyan priest, Arius, who had studied in Antioch but lived in Alexandria, where he was pastor of an important church and a popular preacher. A contemporary, Epiphanius, described him as a tall man who dressed habitually in a short cloak and sleeveless tunic. Soft-voiced, he was persuasive, kept his eyes downcast, and, according to the hostile Epiphanius, "like a guileful serpent deceived any unsuspecting heart." For Arius, the Jesus Christ who was tempted, suffered, and died could not be the equal of God the Father. Bishop Alexander of Alexandria excommunicated Arius, expecting him promptly to abandon his ideas, but instead he gathered such support that Constantine summoned a council in Nicaea to avert a split in the church.

Arius had touched a nerve: the understanding of the Trinity was embryonic and the appropriate terminology was still being honed. The ensuing discussion, in which the West was also involved, now seems arcane, but God's self-revelation was being explored by Greek thought, and this encounter would eventually shape the very idea of the person and have innumerable practical consequences. Although the fractures caused by this and other theological debates in that era were regrettable, they were not inexplicable because the

15

participants believed that if God was misunderstood, all else, from personal to social relations, would be affected.

The biblical belief in creation from nothing contrasted with the Greek and Roman conviction that the cosmos was a necessity to which humans had to conform. Rather than the cosmos as the ultimate term, the Bible proposed a Triune God who was not triune because of being three different Gods nor because of being three distinct pieces of God-substance but because of being an expression of God the Father in his only-begotten Son and in the Holy Spirit. As these concepts were deepened, the belief that human beings were made in the image and likeness of God became the basis for conceiving them as persons, lasting identities whose dignity did not lie solely in their social role. Ultimately this became the basis for their rights, but the discussion's immediate effect was a threatened split of the church of the East from that of the West. The expansion of Christianity was aided by its insertion in a culture using the Greek and Roman phonetic alphabets but, more than Christianity's original Semitic alphabets, these fostered the conviction that all truth could be conveyed in verbal formulas. Consequently if the disputes concerned formulations of the Christian message, bitter recriminations were inevitable and unity was endangered. Moreover communications became more difficult once Latin was introduced alongside Greek as a language of the church because terms that were considered equivalent sometimes had, instead, different connotations in the other language.

The controversy over Arianism was most virulent in Greek-speaking areas, where the language lent itself to fine distinctions, and the involvement of the emperors, whose aim was usually social unity rather than theological truth, complicated matters. Often the churchmen who prevailed were those who had the emperor's ear. It is only with hindsight that bishops can be readily assigned to one or the other camp in the controversy: there were many gradations within the "Arianizing" outlook.

In 325 Bishop Alexander brought to the council in Nicaea, as theological adviser, a young deacon, Athanasius, who was to be his successor and Arius's most implacable opponent. The 318 bishops who were Constantine's guests agreed on a creed that is still affirmed worldwide today: "...eternally begotten of the Father, God from God, Light from Light, true God from true God, begotten, not made, one in being with the Father." It hammered against an Arian interpretation of Christ as a creation of the Father. All the bishops signed it except for two friends of Arius, who, with him, were excommunicated. Although it seemed that the problem had been solved, the creed meant different things to different bishops.

Pope Sylvester was informed of the controversy but, on the grounds that he was too old, merely sent two priests as his representatives to the council. Constantine had not consulted him about convoking the council. Nor had Sylvester attended the Council of Arles convoked by Constantine in 314 to decide on the worthiness of a bishop of Carthage among other matters. This was the beginning of an enduring split in North African Christianity known as the Donatist controversy.

Constantine had enabled Sylvester to live in style by giving him as residence the Lateran Palace. The church in Rome had benefited spectacularly from Constantine, who endowed it with still other buildings and land, but there is no contemporary account of Christians' reactions. In fact, they had not fared too badly under Maxentius, who had been ousted by Constantine. It could be said that Constantine merely extended Maxentius's tolerant policy from Italy and Africa to the whole empire. But certainly the contrast with Diocletian's persecution, which had ended in the capital only in 306, was sharp, and, moreover, Constantine personally favored the church.

Several emperors before him had shown sympathy for, or at least a willingness to come to terms with, the Christians who, by the third century, were a conspicuous group in the empire not only because of their numbers but also because of their cohesion. From the time of Clement at the end of the first century, Rome had spoken confidently to the whole church on doctrinal and disciplinary issues. By the mid-third century Christians constituted the largest voluntary association in the capital and were giving financial aid to churches elsewhere. The Christian community, whose forebears had greeted Paul on his arrival in Rome, were proud that it was the burial place of Paul and Peter. The community boasted martyrs such as Lawrence and Agnes but also philosophers such as Justin, who in the mid-second century had begun a dialogue with pagan culture. Some Christians were thoroughly Roman, as shown by the writings of the lawyer Minucius Felix in the first half of the third century, and Christianity had been accepted by members of all social classes from slaves and the poor to rich matrons and senators.

It would have survived and grown without Constantine, but his encouragement abruptly changed its status, even if Sylvester himself seems to have been a lackluster figure. Or was he simply being discreet, not quite able to believe his luck and wary of Constantine, the so-called "Thirteenth Apostle," who had killed his wife and one of his sons?

The period immediately after Constantine was brought closer in 1993 when the Pontifical Commission for Christian Archaeology began excavating what was believed to be the basilica and mausoleum of Sylvester's successor, Mark. Before Constantine, Christians held their rites and meetings in each other's houses and occasionally in the catacombs. Some houses became house-churches or community centers: this was the case with Mark's house close by the Capitoline Hill. It then became a church on the site of the present St. Mark's, tucked into the short side of Palazzo Venezia.

On land donated by Constantine in what is now the St. Callixtus complex on the Appian Way, Mark built a horseshoe-shaped basilica, one of six of the same design. There are records of pilgrims visiting it until the eighth century, when it was destroyed, presumably by Saracen marauders. Giovanni Battista de Rossi, who in the mid-nineteenth century located the catacombs of the extensive St. Callixtus complex, formed a fairly accurate idea of the whereabouts of what remained of St. Mark's. But later archeologists sought it in a different zone and found the present site only when a workman noticed that shorter grass formed a tell-tale horseshoe pattern, beneath which were discovered the remains of the basilica's foundation.

It indicated that Constantine's influence was still felt strongly in Rome decades after he left for Constantinople, where he died in 337. It may be more than coincidence that Julius, the bishop of Rome elected in that year, was more forceful than Sylvester or Mark. He founded two important churches: the Julian basilica, on the site where the Holy Apostles Church now stands, and Santa Maria in Trastevere in the district near Tiber port, where there were many pagan temples to serve sailors and Eastern merchants. Previously house-churches had been established by Christians, whose names they bore, or basilica-churches by the emperor. Julius broke new ground by acting on his own initiative: he was the first bishop of Rome to build a church and on a scale almost comparable to those of Constantine; he could hardly have known what a precedent he was setting.

Julius's role in the Arian controversy was even more important. Constantine's attempt to heal the breach over Arianism at the Council of Nicaea was only a temporary success. After Constantine's death the Arians, who seemed likely to prevail with the support of his third son and successor Constantius II, exiled Athanasius from the see of Alexandria and Marcellus from that of Ancyra (Ankara). Pro-Arian bishops appealed to Julius to prevent the expelled bishops' return, but he affirmed that they had every right to appeal to Rome (as had Athanasius) and in 340 summoned a synod there that backed them.

Julius wrote to the pro-Arians, reproving them for taking the initiative instead of referring the matter to Rome:

> All of you should have written to us so that the justice of it might be seen emanating from all.... Are you ignorant that the custom has been to write first to us, and then for a just decision to be passed from this place?
>
> The church in Rome should have been informed about any suspicion regarding the bishop [of Alexandria]. But now, after doing as you please, you want our endorsement, although we have never condemned him [Athanasius]. Not thus the constitutions of Paul, not thus the traditions of the Fathers. This is another form of procedure, and a novel practice. I beseech you, bear with me willingly: what I write is for the common good. I mention these things because of the responsibility received from the blessed Apostle Peter.

Although Constantinople was the empire's political capital, Julius was asserting in effect that the ecclesiastical capital remained Rome. And he reaffirmed the strong links between the apostolic sees of Rome and Alexandria (apostolic because founded by the evangelist Mark). But the pro-Arian bishops would not accept Julius's ruling. At his request, the emperor proposed a council of the Eastern and Western church for Sardica (Sofia) but the Easterners, who would not agree to the participation of Athanasius and Marcellus, excommunicated Julius and other Western bishops. In 345, however, Athanasius was allowed to return to Alexandria and on his way there called on Julius to thank him for his support. Julius also had the satisfaction, two years later, of receiving the recantations of some pro-Arian Western bishops. When what seemed the majority of the empire's Christians were Arian ("The world groaned" wrote Jerome, "and was amazed that it had become Arian"), Julius had affirmed that without Rome it was impossible to decide such questions: doctrinal orthodoxy, not numbers or social cohesion, was to be the criterion.

Julius's firm rejection of Arianism was not maintained by all his successors up to 380, when Emperor Theodosius convoked a council that banned the heresy while reaffirming and enlarging the Nicene Creed. Some bishops of Rome made concessions to Arianizing emperors, although on the whole they adhered to the Nicene tradition, which affirmed that Christ was divine and of one substance with the Father. They did not recognize the need to respond to new queries. John Henry Newman was to write that, during the Arian crisis, the divine tradition committed to the infallible church was maintained more by the faithful than by the episcopate, and it is true that laity in Alexandria objected to the repeated expulsions of Athanasius. But there were many faithful bishops apart from Athanasius, such as Julius, Hilary of Poitiers, and Basil of Caesarea, while monks in Egypt also maintained the Nicene faith.

In Rome itself, by the mid-fourth century, Christians were living more comfortably than ever before, but this did not necessarily mean better Christians. Involvement in the catechumenate enabled a person to be identified as a Christian but did not oblige one to accept baptism, with all its demands. Usually the catechumenate involved three years instruction before baptism which was a grave commitment. Some postponed baptism, out of shrewdness rather than scruples, for with Christianity gaining strength, participation in the catechumenate could be a social advantage.

However, there were authentic conversions, sometimes of outstanding people such as the preeminent Latin Platonist Marius Victorinus. This was recounted later by a priest-friend, Simplicianus, to Augustine of Hippo who wrote of it as follows:

> Here was an old man deeply learned, . . . the teacher of so many distinguished senators, a man who on account of the brilliance of his teaching had earned and been granted a statue in the Roman Forum—an honor the citizens of this world think so great. He had grown old in the worship of

idols, had taken part in their sacrilegious rites, for almost all
the Roman nobility at that time was enthusiastic for them and
ever talking of "prodigies and the monster gods of every kind,
and of the jackal-headed Anubis—who all had once fought
against the Roman deities Neptune and Venus and Minerva"
and had been beaten: yet Rome was on its knees before these
gods it had conquered. All this Victorinus with his thunder of
eloquence had gone on championing for so many years even
into old age: yet he thought it no shame to be the child of
Your Christ.

Victorinus read his way to conversion through the Scriptures
and other Christian writings. He said to Simplicianus,

"I would have you know that I am now a Christian." Simplicianus answered: "I shall not believe it nor count you among
Christians unless I see you in the church of Christ." Victorinus asked with some faint mockery: "Then is it the walls
that make Christians?" ... The fact was that he feared to offend his friends, important people and worshipers of these
demons...but when by reading in all earnestness he had
drawn strength, he grew afraid that Christ might deny him
before His angels if he were ashamed to confess Christ before
men...so he grew proud toward vanity and humble toward
truth. Quite suddenly and without warning he said to Simplicianus, as Simplicianus told me, "Let us go to the church.
I wish to be made a Christian."

Simplicianus, unable to control his joy, went with him.
He was instructed in the first mysteries of the faith, and not
long after gave in his name that he might be regenerated by
baptism, to the astonishment of Rome and the joy of the
church....

Finally when the hour had come for the profession of faith,
which at Rome was usually made by those who were about
to enter into Your grace in a set form of words learned and
memorized and spoken from a platform in the sight of the
faithful—Simplicianus told me that the priests offered Victorinus to let him make the profession in private, as the custom
was with those likely to find the ordeal embarrassing. But he
preferred to make the profession of salvation in church. For
there had been no salvation in the Rhetoric he had taught, yet

he had professed it publicly.... From the lips of the rejoicing congregation sounded the whisper "Victorinus, Victorinus." They were quick to utter their exultation in seeing him and as quickly fell silent to hear him. He uttered the true faith with glorious confidence.

(During the Arian controversy, Marius Victorinus was to provide some of the most stringent pro-Nicene arguments).

Julius's successor, Liberius, was elected in 352, when the pro-Arian bishops had the ear of Constantine's third son, the emperor Constantius II. Liberius resisted Constantius's pressure to confirm the condemnation of Athanasius, but the emperor cowed other Western bishops. Realizing that not just Athanasius but the Nicene faith was being questioned, Liberius convoked a council in Milan. There the Nicene Creed was not discussed, but the emperor extracted a condemnation of Athanasius. As Liberius continued to resist bribery and threats, he was brought by force to Milan; then, as he still did not cede, he was exiled to Thrace.

While the bishop of Rome was in exile, the emperor made a triumphant entry to the city. The pagan historian Ammianus Marcellinus has left a tart account of this visit, which was to celebrate, without a title, a triumph over Roman blood.

> For neither in person did he vanquish any nation which made war upon him, nor learn of any conquered by the valor of his generals; nor did he add anything to his empire; nor at critical moments was he ever seen to be foremost, or among the foremost; but he desired to display an inordinately long procession, banners stiff with goldwork, and the splendor of his retinue, to a populace living in perfect peace and neither expecting nor desiring to see this or anything like it.

When, escorted by his troops in battle array, Constantius found the Senate, patricians, and populace gathered to greet him, he felt that "the sanctuary of the whole world was present before him." Constantius showed both "affectation" and "no slight endurance"; he did not respond to acclaim but, instead, remained "calm and imperturbable." He "both stooped when passing through lofty gates (although he was very short), and as if his neck were in a vise, gazed straight ahead, and turned his face neither to right nor to left, but (as if he were a mannequin) neither did he nod when the wheel jolted nor was he ever seen to spit, or to wipe or rub his nose, or move his hands."

His whole behavior as emperor, Ammianus Marcellinus maintained, reflected "his pride of lofty conceit." He was amazed by Rome, by the Forum, the sanctuaries of the Tarpeian Jove, the Pantheon, the Theater of Pompey, the Stadium and other monuments, but most of all by the Forum of Trajan, which Ammianus Marcellinus described as "a construction unique under the heavens and admirable even in the unanimous opinion of the gods." Constantius decided to add to the city's adornments by building an obelisk in the Circus Maximus. The city's pagan remains could still entrance an ambitious Most Christian Emperor. Christianity and paganism cohabited: a calendar of 354 juxtaposed their festivals and listed consuls with martyrs and bishops.

During the visit of Constantius, the Christians made their presence felt. When Pope Liberius was exiled, his principal assistant, Felix, had the clergy swear that they would elect no one else during Liberius's lifetime. However, they succumbed to the emperor's pressure and elected Felix himself.

Liberius was pining away in Thrace, where the local bishops tried to persuade him of the pro-Arian case. Finally he acquiesced in Athanasius's excommunication, endorsed an ambiguous creed that omitted the Nicene affirmation that Jesus was "one in being with the Father," and submitted to the unbending emperor.

It was no wonder then that Constantius, whose triumph was over a mild bishop rather than enemy armies, found Rome's Christians hostile. Even matrons of the better families demanded Liberius's return. In 358, to restore public order, the emperor allowed the broken bishop to return on the understanding that he would share power with Felix.

But Roman Christians, indignant at the idea of Felix sharing Liberius's ministry, welcomed the returning bishop enthusiastically with "One God, one Christ, one bishop" and drove out of the city the emperor's man, Felix. When he returned and attempted to celebrate Mass in the Julian basilica, they threw him out again. In the midsummer of the year he returned, Liberius dreamed that the Virgin Mary asked him to build a church in her honor where he found snow on the Esquiline Hill. Snow is unlikely in Rome's torrid summer, but hail sometimes gives the impression of it. On the site, identical with or close to that of St. Mary Major, he had a large basilica built.

After Constantius's death in 361 imperial support for Arianism ceased. His cousin Julian became emperor. Of course he had been brought up as a Christian but preferred paganism in the form of worship of the sun god, although he made this known only after assuming power. Brave, ascetic, humorless, stubborn Julian revived pagan cults but buttressed them by something similar to Christian organization and practices, such as help for the poor and sick. He discriminated against Christians in education, administration, and public life. Apostasy ensured preferment. In Rome, the venerable convert Marius Victorinus was excluded from teaching, which caused a public outcry. Julian planned to reconstruct the Temple of Jerusalem to show a mere man could disprove Jesus' prediction that it would not be rebuilt. In John Chrysostom's words, Julian aimed to "put the power of Christ on trial." But within months of launching the project, at the age of thirty-five and after a reign of only two years, he was killed by a Persian soldier's arrow. According to Jerome, some pagans commented: "How can Christians claim that their God is long suffering?"

Liberius tried to reconcile those true to the Nicene Council with those tempted by Arianism: he knew both sides himself. However, Felix retained the support of some rigorist Roman clergy and laity. He returned once more to Rome and bought a property on the Via Aurelia, where he built a church and resided. Julian the Apostate had done less damage to the church in Rome than the Most Christian Emperor Constantius, who fostered rivalry between the two bishops.

— IV —

TRUE ROMANS ALL

THE DIVISIVE CONSEQUENCES of the policies of Constantius emerged during the choice of a successor to Liberius, who died in September 366. In the Julian basilica a deacon Ursinus was chosen as his successor and consecrated bishop. It seems Ursinus was a rigorist who did not want to continue Liberius's irenic policy. The followers of Felix, who had died eight months before Liberius, preferred another deacon, Damasus, a Spaniard, who in 355 had accompanied Liberius into exile but then returned to Rome and took service with Felix, which made him vulnerable to the charge of being a turncoat. Damasus's supporters seem to have been more numerous than Ursinus's group; he was ordained bishop in the Lateran on October 1. Rome had two bishops instead of one.

War broke out between their supporters. During three days in late October, a gang of thugs slaughtered more than a hundred of Ursinus's supporters gathered in the Julian basilica. Damasus then convinced the city prefect, who was none other than the Saturnalia party host, the senator Praetextatus, to expel Ursinus and his followers. It was the first time in Rome that a bishop had resorted to the secular arm. However, mob violence continued. Ursinus's followers sought refuge in the Liberian basilica on the Esquiline Hill. The pro-Damasus thugs trapped them there and, according to the pagan historian Ammianus Marcellinus, killed 137.

At last Damasus was secure, but at what a cost. Bishops in the Italian peninsula were shocked that he had waded through blood to reach Peter's chair. In about 371 Ursinus's followers brought a "disgraceful charge" against him, perhaps of homicide, but his friends obtained an intervention by Emperor Gratian and the case was dropped. Damasus always kept on good terms with civil authorities, which makes it appropriate that an internal Vatican courtyard, where state visitors are received before taking an elevator to the papal apartments, is named after him.

Ammianus Marcellinus claimed that Damasus and Ursinus "burned above human measure" to become bishop of Rome because of the rich spoils: "Once made bishop there are no worries for the future: wealthy from rich matrons' donations, one travels in a carriage wearing expensive clothes; the bishop's banquets are more sumptuous than the emperor's."

Noting Damasus's lifestyle, Praetextatus reportedly said, perhaps nudging whoever was listening, "If they made me bishop of Rome, I too would become a Christian."

Damasus was on such good terms with wealthy matrons that a critic called him "the matrons' ear tickler," but at the same time he encouraged asceticism, which may be less of a contradiction than it sounds. As Christians became more comfortable and as expectations of an imminent Second Coming faded, there was a reaction by those seeking a sharper group identity. Admiring the martyrs, they wanted another way to die to the world and to the flesh and found it in the example of the hermit monks of Egypt and the Middle Eastern deserts. An ascetic movement, which ignored distinctions of class or gender, gained adherents in Rome: Damasus's own sister Irene was a consecrated virgin living at home. Many wealthy Roman matrons were attracted to the ascetic ideal, which may account for Damasus's relations with them. They lived austerely, studied Scripture, and helped the poor.

During the reign of Liberius a senator's daughter, Marcellina, had taken the veil as a consecrated virgin and seems to have established a kind of convent in her family house, which is now the Subiaco Benedictines' Rome headquarters near the Jewish quarter. Her father had been prefect of Gaul. Her brother, trained as a lawyer, was governor of the Italian provinces of Emilia and Liguria with his residence in Milan. The thirty-five-year-old governor went to a Milan church where a bishop was to be elected and there was press-ganged into the job himself. He was Aurelius Ambrosius, known as Ambrose, who was in the front line of the battle against Arianism in Milan and advised Damasus on the problem.

After Emperor Julian's death in 363, an interlude followed in which a Christian general, Jovian, had ruled; then the army brought yet another general, Valentinian, to power. He divided the empire again, giving the East to his brother Valens. Valentinian's successors in the West were his sons Gratian (375–83) and Valentinian II (375–92). When Valens died without heirs, Gratian nominated a Spanish general, Theodosius, as ruler of the East. Both Gratian and Theodosius were fervent Catholics. Theodosius abandoned the tolerance Constantine had shown even while favoring Christians: he issued an edict addressed to the inhabitants of Constantinople but of interest to the whole empire. It said that the emperors wished that all ruled by them should live in the religion that Peter had handed down to the Romans and that Damasus, as well as Bishop Peter of Alexandria, professed: "we believe in the one divinity of the Father and the Son and the Holy Spirit in equal majesty and Holy Trinity." Only those who adhered to this profession of faith were to bear the name of Catholic Christians: the rest were branded with the infamy of heresy, they were not to call their sects churches, and they had to expect not only divine but also imperial punishment. There was one empire and there was to be only one form of Christianity. This marriage of church and empire is often attributed to Constantine but, in fact, took place seven decades later.

It was a blow to the Arians but the staunchly Nicene Bishop Basil of Caesarea realized that, although Arianism was dissolving, there was need for more precise terms than those used at Nicaea and greater clarity about the Holy Spirit. Trinitarianism was the distinctive feature of Christianity as a monotheistic religion and now the Holy Spirit, who some claimed was similar to the angels rather than a person of the Trinity, was coming into sharper focus. Basil communicated his insights to Damasus, but they were ignored, and he denounced Westerners as arrogant.

In 381 a council in Constantinople responded to the insights of Basil, who died before it was convened, of his brother Gregory of Nyassa, and of Gregory Nazianzus, a brilliant trio of bishop-theologians. Whereas the Nicene Council had said simply "we believe in the Holy Spirit," the council approved the following formula still in use: "we believe in the Holy Spirit, the Lord and Giver of Life, who is to be adored and glorified, who spoke through the prophets."

Moreover, in answer to the affirmation of a Syrian theologian, Apollinarius, that Christ did not have a human soul but that his body was inhabited instead by divinity, the council asserted that he had been fully human, body and soul. Against Arius, the Nicene

Council had affirmed that Christ was divine; against Apollinarius Constantinople affirmed that he was fully human. The relationship between these two natures was a problem for the future.

Rome approved the council's declaration on Christ's humanity and on the life of the Trinity but took exception to a further deliberation of the same meeting; "the bishop of Constantinople should have the primacy of honor after the bishop of Rome, for this city is the new Rome." Previously the see of Byzantium, as it was called from the name of the city that had preceded Constantinople, had been under the metropolitan of Heraclea. Now it was being elevated above the apostolic sees of Alexandria and Antioch. If political importance rather than apostolic origin was to be the criterion, Old Rome could soon be taking second place to the New.

The following year the principal metropolitan bishops of the West met in Rome, including Ambrose from Milan. The meeting anathematized Arianism in a series of brief propositions, including:

> We anathematize Arius and Eunomius who, with equal impiety, although in different words, declare that the Son and the Holy Spirit are creatures;

> If anyone does not say the Holy Spirit is truly and properly of the Father, just as the Son, of the divine substance and true God—he is a heretic;

> If anyone does not say of the Father, Son, and Holy Spirit, that there is one godhead, strength, majesty and power, glory and dominion, one reign, and one will and truth—he is a heretic;

> If anyone does not say that the Holy Spirit, just as the Son and the Father, is to be adored by every creature—he is a heretic.

These anathemas did not cancel Arianism, particularly as it was accepted by the Goths. But their proclamation was a success for Damasus, who wanted to spell out for Easterners that matters of faith could not be decided without Rome, whose authority derived, not from the empire or councils, but from Peter and Paul. "The Holy Roman Church," according to what is known as the Decree of Damasus, has been placed at the forefront (of all the Catholic churches spread through the world) not by conciliar decisions of other churches, but has received the primacy by the evangelic voice of our Lord and Savior, who says: "You are Peter, and upon this rock I will build my church, and the gates of hell will not prevail against it; and I will give to you the keys of the kingdom of heaven, and whatever you shall have bound on earth will be bound in heaven and whatever you shall have loosed on earth shall be loosed in heaven."

In addition to this, there is also the companionship of the vessel of election, the most blessed Apostle Paul, who contended and was crowned with a glorious death along with Peter in the City of Rome at the time of the Caesar Nero— not at a different time, as the heretics prattle, but on one and the same day and at one and at the same hour: and they equally consecrated the above mentioned holy Roman Church to Christ the Lord; and by their presence and by their venerable triumph they set it at the forefront over the others of all the cities.

The first see, therefore, is that of Peter the Apostle, that of the Roman Church, which has neither stain nor blemish. The second see, however, is that at Alexandria, consecrated on behalf of blessed Peter by Mark, his disciple, and an evangelist who was sent to Egypt by the Apostle Peter, where he preached the word of truth and underwent his glorious martyrdom. The third honorable see, indeed, is at Antioch, which belonged to the most blessed apostle Peter, where first he dwelt before he came to Rome, and where the name Christians was first applied, as to a new people.

There was no mention of the minor see of Byzantium. That left Constantinople nowhere.

The council had exalted Rome against competitive Constantinople. Damasus's cultural policy likewise aimed to increase Romans' pride in the city's Christian character rather than in its persisting pagan prestige. Until the reign of Julian the Apostate (361–63), paganism and Christianity had been juxtaposed culturally, but Julian had briefly restored pagan predominance. Rome was still a cynosure for its pagan monuments. In the preceding century, the population had decreased perhaps a quarter from the

estimated peak of a million or more inhabitants, but it continued
to attract visitors who arrived on the impressive consular roads
used by Rome's all-conquering legions. Pagan monuments continued to be remodeled and redecorated. Below the Capitoline Hill,
a structure sacred to the twelve deities protecting Rome was rebuilt by the city prefect in 367, the year after Damasus became
bishop of the city. The influence of pagan senators ensured that
other monuments near the Senate in the various forums were kept
in good repair.

The pagan elite made a point of maintaining not only traditions
but also good taste, in contrast to the Christians, whose buildings
and sarcophagi tended to be rough and eclectic in style. Ivory dip-
tychs produced for the family of Symmachus in 380, four years
before the end of Damasus's reign, have a refinement that implied
superiority.

In this competitive atmosphere, Damasus took initiatives that
revitalized Rome's Christian past. He blended Christianity with
Roman civic awareness while encouraging Latinization of the
church in the West to counteract any cultural cringe toward the
East. Replacement of liturgical Greek with Latin had begun in the
mid-third century, but he completed the process.

To draw attention to the martyrs, Damasus had rubble cleared
from the catacombs, authorized liturgical ceremonies there, and
labeled the tombs with marble slabs whose handsome lettering
was invented for the purpose by his friend Dionysus Philocalus.
One of the fifty-nine surviving slabs, before Sixtus II's tomb in
the St. Callixtus complex, begins: "Here lie together a shoal of
saints" and ends "I, Damasus, confess that I would like to have
been buried here, but I did not want to disturb the saints' ashes."
With his mother and sister, he was buried in a nearby basilica.

In keeping with Damasus's claims for Paul, he built a large
church in his honor. Previously only a small structure sheltered
what was believed to be Paul's grave outside the city walls on the
way to the seaside. In 384 the ruling emperors Theodosius and
Arcadius agreed to finance the huge construction, which was completed in eight years. The basilica was almost as big as St. Peter's
but its proportions and decoration showed a more classical approach, as if it were to rival pagan monuments. Unfortunately,
little survived a fire in 1823; the rebuilt St. Paul's is like the first
St. Peter's. Damasus also built the church of St. Lawrence, now

incorporated in the Cancelleria building in central Rome, and rehoused the papal archives.

Instead of expecting now a dramatic Second Coming, the Christian community was faced with a long vista and needed a past to face the journey. It found a past both in refusing to separate the New Testament from the Old, as some of its members desired, and in Rome it replaced Romulus and Remus, whom the pagans considered the city's founders, with Peter and Paul. Martyrs took the place of pagan heroes. In fostering this awareness, Damasus helped the church forge a history to shape the future.

Important help in this cultural enterprise was provided by a brilliant, abrasive scholar, Jerome, whom he employed to elucidate Scripture. Damasus also encouraged Jerome to revise the inconsistent and faulty Latin translations of Scripture, which were a major reason why pagans considered Christianity culturally inferior. Damasus may have overestimated his own talent as a versifier but he spotted Jerome's as a translator; the result of his labors, the Latin Vulgate, was to be a major influence on Western culture.

It is not easy to reconcile Damasus's achievements as bishop with what pagans claimed was his bloodstained path to the office. He seems to prefigure bishops in Rome at the end of the first millennium who often fought for Peter's chair but also their Renaissance successors who were patrons of the arts. Damasus, who dedicated his pontificate to proving that Rome's glory was Christian and not pagan, died in the same year, 384, as Praetextatus, who was convinced that the opposite was the case.

– V –

DEFEAT OVER VICTORY

THE CHRISTIAN POET PRUDENTIUS wrote that paganism was voted out by the Senate presided over by Emperor Theodosius: Christ won hands down against Jupiter. This was fanciful, but the Senate did witness from a distance a memorable clash between the pagan Aurelius Symmachus and Bishop Ambrose. It was over the Altar of Victory surmounted by a winged statue that Pyrrhus (whose name is preserved in the phrase "Pyrrhic victory") brought from Epirus in the third century B.C. and that Augustus had installed in the Senate antechamber. As senators entered the hall they threw incense on the fire, which always burnt before the altar, and also took their oaths there. When Emperor Constantius visited Rome in 357, the altar had been removed, but Emperor Julian had replaced it during his revival of paganism. Possibly influenced by Ambrose, the young Christian emperor of the West, Gratian, renounced the traditional title of Pontifex Maximus, head of the pagan priesthood. Among the consequences were that bequests for pagan priests were prohibited, and the Altar of Victory was once again removed from the Senate.

In 382 the Senate sent Symmachus to Milan to ask the emperor to return the altar. Although respected as an upright administrator, Symmachus could also be callous: for instance, he acquired Saxon prisoners to use as gladiators in a performance in honor of his son. But on the eve of the exhibition, to avoid facing the wild beasts, they strangled one another. Symmachus said he would need recourse to philosophy to digest the financial loss. For a vestal virgin who broke her vow of chastity, he proposed revival of the old punishment: that she be buried alive with a little bread and water.

Damasus forwarded a message to Milan, when Symmachus went there, that many Christian senators would resign if he were heeded. But Symmachus was not even received. The situation seemed more favorable when Symmachus returned in 384. The previous year Gratian had been killed in an ambush near Lyons. His brother Valentinian II was little more than a child and the empress-regent Justina was Arian with pagan advisers. To counter the influence of Ambrose, she favored pagan senators: she ensured nomination of Praetextatus as prefect of Italy, Africa, and Illyria and of Symmachus as prefect of Rome.

Symmachus and Ambrose were relatives, had been school companions, and shared a pride in Rome's achievements. An almost contemporary mosaic in a Milanese church shows Ambrose as short with close-cropped hair, a sparse beard, and drooping moustache. He wears a long, white tunic beneath a reddish-brown bell-shaped garment whose right sleeve is folded back to the elbows as those of priests and bishops in sixth-century mosaics in Ravenna. Symmachus probably considered Ambrose a traitor to his religion and his class. Symmachus's petition seemed to needle Ambrose because it said more than once that Gratian's decisions, which "made the ruler unpopular," were inspired by others, although it did not attack Ambrose or Christianity directly.

Symmachus pointed out that earlier emperors had venerated the altar. "If the religious attitudes of the earlier emperors do not set a precedent," he argued, "let the policy of the blind eye adopted by more recent emperors be one. We are not on such good terms with the barbarians that we can do without the Altar of Victory." In other words, it was needed to restore Rome's military prowess. Where else, he asked, would senators take their oath of allegiance and what other sanctions could deter the treacherous from giving false evidence?

He averred that all paths to truth, described as "so tremendous a mystery," should be respected and then protested against the ruling that pagan priests could not benefit from private bequests: "Are we to take it that Roman religious institutions are outside Roman law?" Flouting Rome's religious traditions, he warned, had led to the recent droughts and famines: "it was blasphemy which wrecked the crops."

Ambrose obtained Symmachus's petition from the emperor and then, using his legal training, replied point by point. He agreed that imperial negligence of religious duty was dangerous, but he knew Valentinian II believed in Jesus Christ, not the pagan gods. "Without the true God who is the God of the Christians," Ambrose wrote, "there is no salvation or security."

The petition, he argued, did not represent the Senate but only its pagan members. Moreover, continued this heir of one of Rome's most eminent families, compared to the perils of excommunication of what importance were the complaints of a few old conservatives of a city that had lost its importance?

It was nonsense, Ambrose argued, to assert that pagan gods ensured victory because in a battle both sides claimed their protection but one always lost. Now a proud Roman once more, Ambrose argued that Rome's victories were not due to augurs reading animals' entrails but to its soldiers' valor.

A plurality of paths to the truth was unnecessary, Ambrose announced, for revelation had replaced research: "What you do not know we learned for certain from God's own voice; what you seek though hypothesis we learned for certain through Divine Wisdom."

Symmachus had praised the Vestal Virgins but Ambrose contrasted the luxurious lifestyle of these temporary virgins to the lifelong commitment and poverty of consecrated Christian virgins. (He had the example of his sister Marcellina, whom he once called "the light of my eyes, dearer to me than life itself").

Ambrose mentioned Emperor Julian's discrimination against Christians only twenty years before. Symmachus had evoked Rome's ancient glories; Ambrose cited Christianity's more recent ones and disparaged pagan religion:

> The pagans are worried about finances [because of Gratian's decree!]; we glory in the blood Christians have spilled.... Through persecution, misery, torture we grow, but they are convinced that their religion will not last if government financing is cut.... The church possesses only the faith; all its material possessions are for the poor. Let them [the pagans] tell us how many hostages they have ransomed, how many hungry they have fed, for how many exiles they have provided.

In contrast to Symmachus, who had warned against the dangers of change, Ambrose, sure that the future would be Christian, presented a dynamic vision. Ambrose and other early Christians described the church as a "moon waxing." What was called the "mystery of the moon" had many connotations, as recalled by John Paul II in *Novo Millennio Ineunte*, including that the church reflected the light of Christ and grew thanks to him. It also conveyed the fact that in the most obvious ways such as buildings, adherents, and influence, the church was burgeoning with the empire. Ambrose was confident that Christianity was winning out.

Symmachus returned to Rome, but not the Altar of Victory, with its statue, to the Senate. Today what some believe to be the Statue of Victory which surmounted the altar stands in the Centrale Montecatini Museum in Rome. It is reconstructed from 119 pieces of gray basalt found in the grounds of Symmachus's villa on the Coelian Hill.

Several times again Symmachus presented the Senate's request that Gratian's ordinances be abrogated. He did so in 389, when Emperor Theodosius came to Rome. Overawed by the city still replete with classic monuments, Theodosius gave important posts to prominent pagans such as Symmachus, whom he made consul. But, after some hesitation, he heeded Ambrose, who advised him to ignore the senatorial request to cancel Gratian's ordinances.

However, in 392 the request was granted by the usurper Eugenius, who, although a Christian, needed the Senate's support to maintain power. Jerome had written that paganism was finally dead: "Those who once were gods of the nation dwell now with the owls and bats under their lonely roofs," but when Eugenius took measures favorable to paganism, it revived rapidly: once more pagan priesthoods were financed and priests of Oriental cults held ecstatic processions while, as inscriptions on marble fragments from near St. Peter's show, people renewed the bulls' blood rites. Many Christians apostasized, which indicated that conversions had been superficial. Pagans, anticipating that Theodosius would march on Italy against the usurper Eugenius, formed an army in which pagan banners replaced those bearing the cross introduced by Constantine.

The pagan army gathered in northeast Italy, where Emperor Theodosius's forces arrived in September 399. Perhaps Rome awaited the results of the clash as it had the outcome of the battle between Maxentius and Constantine at the Milvian Bridge. The apostates may have been the most apprehensive of all. Even though they would have frantically revived old rites for obtaining victory, they were in for a disappointment. Their gods had lost the knack of winning battles because when the two armies clashed near the river Frigidus, today called Vipacco, a freezing wind, which funnels up the Adriatic, blew directly into the faces of the outnumbered pagans. It was a sure sign of divine displeasure. The pagans were routed and their leaders, like Brutus and Cato whom they considered models, took their own lives. They had wanted to turn back to the time before both Christianity and the empire, but the wind of history was blowing against them.

Some prominent pagans had been discreet and survived even this setback. One was Nicomachus Flavianus, who participated in the Saturnalia gathering at Praetextatus's residence; another was Symmachus. In 402, for the last time, the latter went to Milan as the Senate's envoy seeking, unsuccessfully once more, the return of the Altar of Victory. The state's symbols were to remain Christian, but surely Symmachus deserved a prize for sheer persistence.

About this time in Rome a poet and civil servant, Aurelius Prudentius Clemens, began a long poem on the clash between Ambrose and Symmachus. Born in Saragossa, Spain, in 348, Prudentius was interesting for his outlook as much as for his poetry. He was a pioneer of Christian literature, composing literary hymns, moral allegories, and ballads. At a time when many Christians rejected classical literature, he appreciated it but considered Christian writers had something special to contribute.

Although some Christians distanced themselves from society to preserve the distinctiveness of their faith, Prudentius accepted Roman claims while setting them in a new perspective. Virgil claimed that Rome had a mission, but, according to the Spanish poet, it was not only to ensure peace and good government but to be the center of a spiritual realm. For Prudentius the Tiber was sacred not as a river god but because it flowed past martyrs' tombs. In other words, Christianity was the culmination of Rome's history. The Spanish Catholic was a Roman patriot who wanted to show that Christianity was a decisive advance over "witless superstitions."

In a long poem he countered point by point Symmachus's arguments for the return of the Altar of Victory, even though he admitted the orator's eloquence. The poem concluded by contrasting the Vestal Virgins, admired by Symmachus, with Christian consecrated virgins who, in the preceding decades, had established house-convents in Rome. Ambrose had made the same comparison.

Vesta was the goddess of the hearth. The virgins performed

sacrifices and rites but also kept alight the sacred flame that symbolized Rome in their still extant house, or "convent," in the Forum. (The statues of the virgins there have their names inscribed, but one has been erased. It may be that of Claudia, who converted to Christianity in 364).

Initially the six Vestal Virgins were chosen by lot among girls between the age of six and ten, but by Prudentius's time fathers offered their daughters for this thirty years' service, which could be renewed by choice. Prudentius said the Vestals had no right to be considered the standard of purity as they did not make a free choice:

> Their purity is taken prisoner and made over to thankless altars. In the poor girls the gratification of the body disappears not because it is scorned but because it is taken from them; the body is kept immaculate, but not the mind, and there is no rest on a bed in which the unwedded woman sighs over a secret wound and a lost chance of marriage.... Hope survives and so the fire is not wholly killed, for one day it will be lawful to...throw the glad bridal veil over aged, gray-haired figures.... Vesta demands an immaculate body for an appointed time but in the end disdains a virgin old age.

The dismissed virgin, Prudentius writes, "learns to grow warm in a cold bed."

He describes a virgin in a "cushioned carriage and with face uncovered" riding to the Colosseum to take an honored place at the gladiatorial contests:

> The figure of life-giving purity and bloodless piety goes to see bloody battles, to see people killed, and to look with holy eyes at wounds men suffer for the price of their keep. There she sits conspicuous with the awe-inspiring trappings of her headbands and enjoys what the trainers have produced. What a soft, gentle heart! She rises at the blows, and every time a victor stabs his victim's throat she calls him her pet; the modest virgin, with a turn of her thumb, bids him pierce the breast of his fallen foe so that no trace of life shall lurk deep in his vitals under a deeper thrust of the sword.

Prudentius concludes with a query:

Does their great service lie in this, that they are said to keep
constant watch on behalf of the greatness of Latium's Palatine city, that they undertake to preserve her people and the
well-being of her nobles. . . . Or is it that they sit in the better
seats in the balcony [at the Colosseum] and watch how often
the shaft batters the bronze-helmeted figure with blows of its
three-pronged head, from what gaping gashes the wounded
gladiator bespatters his side of the arena when he flees, and
with how much blood he marks his traces?

The Vestal Virgins survived until 394; gladiatorial games were
abolished a decade later after enraged spectators in the Colosseum
stoned to death a monk who tried to separate fighting gladiators.
The extinction of the flame at the temple of the Vestals did not
mean, as feared, extinction of Rome. As it had acquired a new
spiritual sustenance, this was a victory as well as a defeat.

– VI –

A TREMOR
FROM THE STEPPES

URSINUS, LIKE SYMMACHUS, provided an example of fruitless doggedness. Elected pope as Liberius's successor in 366 but ousted by Damasus and exiled to Cologne, Ursinus put himself forward as a candidate on Damasus's death in 384. But a Roman, Siricius, who had been deacon to both Liberius and Damasus, was elected unanimously. A bishop of Tarragona had submitted fifteen queries on church discipline to Damasus shortly before his death. In 385 Siricius replied in a style similar to imperial rescripts: he did not make recommendations but issued commands and threatened sanctions if they were not obeyed. He claimed they were as binding as synodal canons and should be communicated to the bishops of Spain, Africa, and Gaul. Such decretals having the force of law became the Roman instrument of government. In this case they concerned issues such as the readmission of repentant heretics, the proper seasons (Easter and Pentecost) for baptism, age and qualifications for ordinations, clerical continence and celibacy, and penitential discipline. Another of Siricius's decretals stated that no bishop should be consecrated without the cognizance of the apostolic see.

Siricius was angered by the punishment inflicted on Priscillian, the well-to-do leader of an ascetic movement that began in the Iberian peninsula. A synod had condemned Priscillianism for its disciplinary excesses rather than for doctrinal errors; it was suspected of Manichean tendencies. Both sides in the dispute later had recourse to civil authorities and eventually Priscillian, condemned for witchcraft, was beheaded; it was the first time a church dissident had been beheaded. Siricius excommunicated Priscillian's accusers.

Innocent, whose sixteen-year reign began in 401, was even more imperious than Siricius and has been called "the first pope." He had the papacy in his blood: he was the son of his predecessor, Anastasius I (399–401), who had sired him before undertaking a clerical career. At this time, clerical celibacy and continence for married priests were being encouraged. Married men could still be admitted to the higher ranks of the clergy, but before ordination they had to promise they would no longer live in the conjugal state. Damasus had told the Gallic episcopate that a bishop or priest who asked continence of others had to practice it himself. Siricius had warned Spanish bishops there would be no clemency for married bishops, priests, or deacons who were not totally continent after ordination. Furthermore, Innocent decreed that monks who joined the secular clergy were to continue to observe celibacy.

He insisted on the universal jurisdiction of the bishop of Rome. Not only did he tell the Spanish bishops that Roman custom should be their norm and Rome their court of appeal, not only did he establish the papal vicariate of Thessalonica to avoid Greek-speakers there allying with Constantinople, but he also intervened in John Chrysostom's favor when the court of Constantinople expelled him because his sermons were too challenging. However, these and other interventions in the East were not always well received.

The feast of the Epiphany was celebrated in Rome for the first time during Innocent's pontificate. Christmas had been first celebrated there during the fourth century. Although some scholars maintain there is proof that December 25 is the birthday of Christ, many argue the date was chosen in contrast to the feast of the Sol Invictus, the Unconquered Sun, introduced by Emperor Aurelian (270–75). Christians contrasted Sol Iustitiae, the Sun of Justice or the Savior, to the pagan god. In Jerusalem, however, Christmas was not celebrated until about 430. In the East, the Epiphany celebrations had diverse meanings: sometimes Christ's birth, sometimes the homage of the Magi or the miracle at the marriage in Cana. The date January 6 may have been chosen to compete with a pagan feast although this is disputed. As the Epiphany celebration gained acceptance in the West, Christmas moved eastward. The conjunction of the dates enabled development of a liturgical cycle to rival that of Easter, which was already followed throughout the church.

During Innocent's reign Rome had first-hand experience of the barbarians (the name derived from the Greek *barbaroi,* which conveyed that the despised foreigners' speech sounded like sheep bleating) who had been troubling the empire for well over a century. For instance, after Germanic tribes reached the Po River in Lombardy, Aurelian built twelve miles of walls around Rome, which are still extant. Jerome, who came from the Pannonian-Dalmatian passageway used by the barbarians to enter Italy, left a graphic account of the impressions the barbarians made: "They arrived unexpected, swifter than news, and did not respect either age or religion, nor had compassion even for children in swaddling clothes." And again:

> Every day Roman blood runs from Constantinople to the Julian Alps.... All these provinces have been sacked, devastated, raided, raped by Goths, Sarmatians, Quads, Alemans, Huns, Vandals, and Marcomans. How many consecrated virgins and matrons, free-born and noble, have been prey of these beasts! Bishops captured, priests and clerics massacred, churches destroyed, horses hitched to Christ's altars, martyrs' relics thrown to the wind. Everywhere tears and mourning and multiple images of death.

The barbarians brought violence, fear, and plunder to the empire, but also trade. Most of the tribes were trying, not to destroy the empire, but to settle there. At times they crashed through the frontiers, but they also infiltrated the empire gradually. Roman expansion had put pressure on those at its advancing perimeter, and when it ceased, with the withdrawal from Dacia (Romania) after A.D. 270, their pressure was felt in turn, particularly when other tribes crowded on them from the north and east. In the third century the empire was attacked by the Goths and Sarmatians along the Danube and by the Franks and the Alemans along the Rhine. Marcus Aurelius managed to keep the German tribes on the far side of the Danube, but gradually the Romans came to terms with the barbarians, making treaties and alliances to obtain peace and even allowing some of them to settle within the empire as farmers with a duty to serve in its army. (The distinctive uniforms of the barbarians fighting for Rome are visible in Trajan's column in his Forum). It has been said that for the barbarians "the empire was not an enemy but a career opportunity."

The Chinese Han emperors' establishment of effective frontier defense from Eastern Turkestan to North China had saved their realm from the Huns, who, from 49 B.C., began instead to move westward. By the fourth century they reached Europe, applying pressure on the people from the steppes who had preceded them and the Germanic peoples who had moved southward seeking warm lands, perhaps because of demographic pressure. To avoid the Huns, in 375 the Visigoths requested imperial permission to settle south of the Danube. This was granted. However the Visigoths rebelled against imperial officials and, together with the Ostrogoths and Sarmatians, entered the Balkans. In 378, at Hadrianopoli (Edirne), the barbarian cavalry inflicted a crushing defeat on the Roman infantry in a battle in which Emperor Valens was killed. It was a key episode in the transformation of the empire because it destroyed the Roman legions' reputation for invincibility. As barbarian contingents became increasingly important within the Roman army, barbarians were defending Rome against other barbarians. Pagans and conservatives in the West considered Gratian and Theodosius too favorable to barbarians. On the death of Theodosius, the Visigoths revolted, ravaged the Balkans, and marched into Italy.

Ambrose in Milan, threatened by barbarians and Arians, said: "The only true Roman is a Christian" (meaning those in communion with Rome). The corollary was that Roman unity and order should be preserved and those who undermined it threatened the church as well as the state. One can hear a Roman senator in the words of the bishop of Milan who influenced imperial policy.

The West Goths, known as Visigoths, originated in the steppe between the Dneister River and the Don, the East Goths, or Ostrogoths, between the Dneister and the Danube. They were Germanic tribes who were mainly Arian, as they had been evangelized by an Arian bishop, but Ambrose's outlook enabled him to disqualify them as traitors as well as heretics. Seven years after Ambrose's death in 397, the capital of the empire in the West was transferred from threatened Milan to Ravenna on the Adriatic coast because its marshy surroundings provided a natural defense, and Constantinople could be reached by sea.

On the last day of 406, the Rhine froze, and, despite heavy losses, the Vandals, Sueves, and Alemans swept into Gaul. No sooner was one gap in the empire's long frontier closed than another opened. By 408 the Visigoths led by Alaric laid siege to Rome

demanding gold and other concessions. The Goths were not unknown invaders from beyond the border but a people who had
lived within the empire for decades and were simply seeking improved conditions when they moved westward into Italy. They had
proved their military prowess by victory over the Roman forces at
Hadrianople, which had shifted the strategic balance of power.
But the Goths did not aim to destroy the empire or even imagine
it could fall; they sought a better place in it.

Unlike conquered tribes who had to abandon their laws and
customs in a process of assimilation, the Goths maintained them.
In dealing with the Goths, the Romans discovered that, if you
don't beat 'em, they join you. The Goths were rebels rather than
invaders, allies but discontented allies, who felt the empire had not
honored pacts.

The Senate refused to buy them off with gold in 408 even
though, shortly before his death in 402, Senator Symmachus had
spent half the requested amount to obtain a praetor magistrature
for his son. The Senate objected on principle to buying off the
Goths. It was eight hundred years since Rome had been invaded.
Some inhabitants, famished and desperate because of the siege,
demanded sacrifices to the pagan gods on the grounds that they
would never have allowed such a calamity. Although such sacrifices were prohibited, it seems that some pagan rites were indeed
celebrated. Putting principles aside, the Senate eventually paid
more than had been requested originally, and the Goths withdrew.

Two years later they were back again because Alaric wanted to
force Emperor Honorius into negotiations. Pope Innocent went to
the emperor in Ravenna in a vain attempt to arrange a truce.

Rome's imposing walls were undefended when at the height of
summer, August 24, the Goths entered the city. Over three days
they burned mansions on the Aventine and Coelian Hills and went
on a rampage in the Forum. The Julian basilica was badly damaged. But it could have been worse. There had been negotiations;
there were no massacres or planned arson. Warnings were given
and asylum provided in St. Paul's and St. Peter's, where some
treasure from other churches was stored. The Goths, as Arian
Christians, respected Peter and Paul. Loaded with loot, and taking with him Gallia Placida, Emperor Honorius's sister who later
married Alaric's successor, Athaulf, the Goth led his forces south
as he intended to invade Sicily. He died, probably of malaria, near

Cosenza in Calabria, where some still seek his treasure, rumored to include 25 tons of gold and 150 of silver, near the Bisento River.

A poem by Claudius Rutilius Namatianus describes the havoc wrought by the barbarians seen as he returned from Rome to his native Toulouse region in the autumn of a year variously dated as 415–16 or 417. The son of a governor of Tuscia and Umbria, Rutilius probably studied in Rome before entering the imperial administration. In 413 he was prefect of Rome, which meant also that he was president of the Senate. His poem suggests that he was one of the Pagan Party and would have shared their exalted idea of civic duties but also their banquets, hunting, and holidays in luxurious villas.

To put his family estates in order after the barbarians' incursions, Rutilius sailed with a retinue of small ships up the coast from Rome. It was not so much a return home as exile from his adopted home, which he claimed had "as many monuments as there are stars in the sky" and had made "this divided world one city." The Rome of Rutilius is a timeless city, where even people seem to become statues. But after the barbarians' devastation he wrote:

> The monuments of past eras are unrecognizable,
> Voracious Time has consumed huge terraces
> Only traces survive amid collapsed, ruined walls,
> Roofs lie buried under huge remains.
> Let's not be indignant that mortal bodies disintegrate:
> Here's evidence that cities also meet that fate.

Even Rutilius's description of devastation is in the measured tones of the dignified Roman convinced that everything conforms to a tried and true pattern. But his decorum is abandoned when he deals with those who defy social conventions. At Falisca, near the island of Elba, he describes a Jewish innkeeper as a "beast who eats separately from other men." He calls Jews filthy people who shamelessly cut off the tip of their penises and rest every seventh day in imitation of their weary God.

Rutilius's scorn erupts: who would ever believe, he asks, the Jews' delirious claims, rubbish typical of slaves? He expresses regret for the Roman conquest of Judaea because it enabled the "contagious plague to spread wider and the defeated to oppress the victors."

He likewise scorns the Christian monks he saw on the island

of Capraia, described as self-imprisoned madmen who flee the world and live in filth. His vehemence might reflect a hatred of Christians as a whole. The cultured administrator's composure is disturbed again by monks on the island of Gorgona, near Corsica, particularly as a rich young aristocrat has joined them because the "unhappy man believes that the things of heaven want to be nourished" and "oppresses himself with more violence than a vendetta by angry gods." He concludes, with one of his frequent Homeric references, that "in this case hearts, rather than bodies, have been turned into swine."

The barbarian incursion in Rome made a huge impression. In Jerusalem Jerome wrote that it was the end of the world: "Words fail me, my sobs break in...the city to which the whole world once fell has fallen." But according to the Byzantine historian Procopius, the first Roman emperor of the West, Honorius (394–423), was unconcerned. In his capital, Ravenna, he bred birds and one of his favorite fowls was named Roma (Rome). When the eunuch responsible for the aviary told him that Roma had perished, the shocked emperor said that, only minutes before, it had been eating from his hand. The eunuch explained it was the city that had perished. Honorius was much relieved.

When the following year Honorius came to the city he had left undefended, it too ate from his hand: he was welcomed as a victor, another Trajan. The Romans' capacity for putting on a show was considerable but, after Alaric, some Christians concluded that for defense they could rely only on the city's bishop.

In 418 the church in Rome was divided again when rival factions each elected a bishop: a Greek Eulalius and a Roman Boniface. The city prefect was a relative of Ambrose's opponent, Symmachus. He dispatched a report favoring Eulalius to Honorius, who accepted him. However Boniface, who was a friend of Honorius's powerful half-sister Gallia Placidia, had the majority of Roman clergy on his side. Eulalius wrecked his case by forcefully occupying the Lateran to preside at the Easter ceremonies. Honorius expelled the Greek and confirmed Boniface. Although elderly and frail, Boniface was a true Roman, affirming that "it has never been lawful for what has once been decided by the apostolic see to be reconsidered." The papacy's confident assertion of authority was unaffected by the growing tremor from the steppes.

– VII –

OUT OF DESERTS
PROPHETS COME

E VEN THOUGH he lived only a few years in Rome, Jerome
regarded himself as its representative and was an influential
upholder of Roman primacy. During five pontificates, he
made his presence felt in controversies, through translations of
the Bible and commentaries on it, and by inspiring ascetics.

Born probably in 347 at Studion in the Roman province of
Dalmatia, the eldest of five children of a Christian landowner,
Jerome completed his education in Rome. As there were no separate Christian schools, Jerome studied the pagan classics, receiving
a thorough grounding in grammar, rhetoric, and classical literature; he would have studied also mathematics, science, and music.
Later he frequently reproved opponents for sloppy grammar and
clumsy prose. While suffering a fever, he saw himself at the judgment seat of Christ. When Jerome described himself as a Christian,
Christ replied: "You lie. You're a Ciceronian, for where your heart
is, there your treasure lies."

Some Romans had accepted Christianity without it making
them uneasy about their culture. Although Christianity became
their religion, their culture remained classical: the two cohabited.
In the first decades after Constantine, it was easy for Christians,
no longer liable to the charge that they were subversives because
they would not swear allegiance to the emperor, to get along with
pagans. But Emperor Julian's choice of paganism had been an un-
pleasant surprise for Christians. And the Pagan Party considered
burgeoning Christianity a threat to all that had made Rome great.
By Jerome's time, more Christians and more pagans felt that they
had to take sides; as a young man, Jerome himself found it difficult
to reconcile his religion with his culture.

Although there were Christian emperors and a Christian ma-

jority, education was still based on the study of the past, which
meant pagan history and mythology. Emperor Theodosius I, who
made the Roman form of Christianity the empire's official religion, entrusted his son's education to a pagan. Rules of conduct
were derived from pagan sources, although efforts were made to
provide Christian substitutes. Rhetoric, the cornerstone of higher
education and the key to professional careers, was studied from
pagan texts, and Christians were despised partly because of the in-
elegant Latin of the Bible. Jerome, who was to do much to remedy
this, found its style "rude and repellent."

Interested in a legal career, Jerome attended Roman courts to
observe barristers in action; in later polemics, he relentlessly used
their point-scoring style. In his youth, Jerome was a gourmet: he
said that he found it easier to cut himself off from home, parents, sister, and relatives for the kingdom of heaven than from
dainty food. He enjoyed Rome's sensual pleasures: although he
exalted virginity he told a friend it was because he admired what
he had lost.

On Sundays, with fellow students, he visited the catacombs:

Often we would enter those crypts which have been hollowed
out of the depths and which, along the passageway's walls,
contain corpses. Everything was so dark that the prophet's
saying "let them go down living to hell" [a quote from Virgil's
Aeneid] seemed almost to have been fulfilled. Here and there
a ray of light from above relieved the horror of blackness, yet
it seemed not so much a window as a funnel pierced by the
light itself as it descended. Then we would walk back gingerly,
wrapped in unseeing night, with Virgil's line recurring to us
"Everywhere dread fills the heart, the very silence dismays."

Jerome's use of the pagan Virgil to express his reactions to the
catacombs and his description of him as a "prophet" show he was
imbued with the classics.

Many at that time delayed baptism because penance was so
harsh. Jerome was baptized in Rome and attributed great importance to receiving from the see of Peter "the vesture of Christ"—a
reference to the white garment donned immediately after baptism.

After his studies, Jerome left Rome for Trier on the Moselle
River and then Aquileia on the Adriatic coast, where he may have
worked in the civil administration, and finally the Middle East. For

a period he was a hermit in the Syrian desert, where, he was to recount later, "I would imagine myself taking part in the Roman social whirl. Although my only companions were scorpions and wild beasts, time and again I was mingling with girls dancing. My face was pallid with fasting and my body chill, but my mind was throbbing with desire, my flesh was as good as dead, but the flames of lust raged in me." He had gone to the desert believing that the hermits had made it a paradise, but he left it swearing that "the company of wild beasts was preferable to that of the monks."

Jerome was an ardent spirit capable of wild enthusiasm and warm friendships, which could turn rapidly into disillusionment and recriminations. He was quick to anger and slow to forget, capable of pursuing opponents even beyond the grave.

He often called their arguments "vomit" or "drivel" and employed a bestiary of epithets for them: dogs, asses, pigs, tortoises, and serpents. His own emblem surely was the wasp. He was catholic in his antipathies: not only did he hammer heretics but he also pilloried future saints such as John Chrysostom, bishop of Constantinople, and Ambrose of Milan, whom he called a plagiarist, "an ugly crow with someone else's feathers." He omitted Ambrose from his book *Famous Men* with the comment, "I shall refrain from giving my opinion of Ambrose lest I should be accused either of toadying or of speaking the truth."

Perhaps the most erudite man of his age, Jerome had a graphic style that attests to his vitality. An incessant worker, he was always doing what he called "rush jobs." Everything was hot copy. He claimed to toss off complex, lengthy polemical pamphlets in a few days. His hastiness is often revealed by a decline in standards as a work progressed. However, he was also tenacious, as shown by his twenty-two-year commitment to a complete revision of the Latin translation of the Bible, the Vulgate, which helped shape Christianity. He recognized it was a "perilous and presumptuous task" that would expose him to much criticism, but he went back to the original Greek when translating the New Testament to "correct the mistakes introduced by inaccurate translators, and the blundering alterations introduced by confident but ignorant critics, and all that has been inserted or changed by copyists more asleep than awake."

Jerome left the Syrian desert for Antioch (where he was ordained) and Constantinople. Not unexpectedly he became involved in ecclesiastical controversies but also made the acquaintance of leading theologians. He had already written to Pope Damasus when living among hermits at Chalcis, east of Antioch, to request a ruling on local discussions about the Trinity. His letter pointed to the growing semantic gap between Latin- and Greek-speakers. Jerome straddled the gap: he knew that while *hypostasis* meant substance for Latins, it was also used by some Greeks to mean acting subject or "person" (to use the language of a later day). Jerome saw the possibility of confusion this entailed in discussion of the Trinity: it could be taken to mean three divine substances or gods, which would be a reversion to polytheism. And he feared that many outsiders would interpret it in this way. He realized that even when he and others with whom he argued shared the same belief, they could become enemies because of insistence on the use of certain terms.

It is not known if there was any response to his plea for a clarifying ruling. Certainly there was none when he had written from Antioch to Damasus about three claimants to the see. He was not ignored, however, when he returned to Rome as an adviser and interpreter for one of the claimants, Paulinus. Just fifty, and already suffering severe eye trouble, Jerome had a growing reputation as a scholar, an exegete or commentator on the Bible, and a translator. He was in the right place at the right time. Damasus appreciated Jerome's abilities and peppered him with exegetical queries, either his own or from synods. For instance, Damasus asked the meaning of this passage in Genesis "Whosoever slayeth Cain, vengeance shall be taken on him sevenfold."

Jerome's answer was that "the slayer of Cain shall complete the sevenfold vengeance which is to be directed upon him." Again Damasus asked why Abraham received circumcision as the seal of his faith as stated in Romans. Jerome referred him to the explanations given by Tertullian, Novatian, and Origen. Why, asked Damasus, was Isaac, a righteous man and dear to God, allowed to became a dupe of Jacob as recounted in Genesis? The day after receiving the query Jerome responded that Paul, Daniel, David, and Elisha all made mistakes, which showed they had a limited view of reality. He added, as if in warning, "holy men only know what God reveals to them."

Jerome's apartment may have been in a building where Damasus placed the archives of the church and which is now the Palazzo della Cancelleria, site of the ecclesiastical marriage court, the Sacred Rota. In one of his notes to Damasus, Jerome explained that he was late in answering because a Jewish friend had arrived with a book that the Jew, pretending he wanted to read it himself, had borrowed from the synagogue. Jerome had stopped working on Damasus's query to transcribe the Hebrew immediately. He had close relations with Jews and, most unusually for the time, had learned Hebrew. Encouraged by Damasus, he began to revise or replace the existing Latin translation of the Bible, but some criticized his improved version of the Gospels as tampering with the Lord's words. "Two-legged asses," Jerome called them.

Jerome of the Desert, the monk and ascetic who had the bishop of Rome's ear, was welcomed as a spiritual guide by those interested in the ascetic life, such as a rich matron Marcella. Not all concerned were rich, but, in a society where Christians had become comfortable, many of the rich gave crucial testimony by renouncing their wealth.

After her husband's death twenty-five years before, Marcella had devoted herself to a life of chaste widowhood, fasting, and Bible study. Her house on the Aventine Hill had become a meeting place for women who shared the ascetic ideal that had been popularized by Bishop Athanasius's *Life of Antony,* a hermit of the Egyptian desert. Acute and scholarly, Marcella frequently asked Jerome for explanation of difficult biblical passages. He complained about her as a "taskmistress," recounting that on one occasion he had been kept up to the small hours preparing a reply until atrocious stomach pains had made him desist.

He could also be harsh, as when he consoled Marcella on the death of a consecrated virgin called Lea by contrasting her after-life with that of the pagan Praetextatus. Praetextatus's wife, Paolina, had written a moving epitaph in which she asserted that he had gone to glory and that she looked forward to joining him. Jerome told Marcella that Praetextatus had been regarded as an exemplar of old-fashioned integrity and that, on his death, out of respect and grief people had even stopped going to the theater. However, Praetextatus was no longer in his triumphal robes, Jerome wrote, but "clothed in mourning and asking for a drop of water":

A few days ago the highest dignitaries of the city walked before him as he ascended the Capitoline Hill like a general celebrating a triumph, Romans leapt up to welcome and applaud him, and at the news of his death the whole city was moved. Now he is desolate and naked, a prisoner in the foulest darkness and not, as his unhappy wife falsely asserts, set in the royal abode of the Milky Way. On the other hand Lea, who was always shut up in her closet-like room, who seemed poor and of little consequence, and whose life was accounted madness, now follows Christ and sings "as we heard, so have we seen in the city of our God."

Pagans were uncertain about life after death, considering it a realm of shadows, but Christians were convinced that the afterlife of the saved would be more vivid and satisfying than this world. Martyrs had testified to this but, when persecution ceased and Christians became comfortable, some considered asceticism and virginity ways to continue their testimony. Pagans were shocked by the ascetics' behavior and drab dress, but they were challenging society just as martyrs had by insisting on public executions. Death in an arena dramatically concentrated attention on martyrs whereas the ascetics gave testimony day-in, day-out. As it was claimed to be the path of perfection, some Christians asked where that left married couples.

Jerome illustrated the distractions inevitable in marriage by describing a wife running a busy household where she has to handle children, cook, and manage domestics and accounts: "Then a message comes that her husband has brought his friends home. She circles the rooms like a swallow: Is the couch smooth? Is the floor swept? Are the cups properly set? Is dinner ready? Tell me, where in all this is the thought of God?"

Lifelong voluntary virginity was a startling new possibility for women. Christian esteem for virgins showed that women's value no longer depended simply on the male with whom they were associated. Only males were trained in rhetorical skills, which were the key to success in public life, but consecrated virgins were encouraged to study Scripture and learned commentaries on it. In other words, consecrated virginity enabled them to develop intellectual, as well as spiritual, interests. (Praetextatus did not have any women at his party).

Jerome, the most forceful advocate of this new style of life practiced in homes, which could become house monasteries, said that bishops and clergy should "look up to" Asella, a consecrated virgin. Of another, he wrote admiringly that she "stored her money in the stomachs of the poor rather than keeping it in her purse."

Paula, who had been influenced by Marcella, was a thirty-five-year-old widow when Jerome met her, probably because she offered hospitality to Paulinus, whom he had accompanied from Antioch. After she had finally given her husband a male heir as their fifth child, for religious reasons she refrained from sexual intercourse. Paula and her third daughter, Eustochium, were among those Roman women whose life centered on Jesus Christ and the Bible in contrast to peers whom Jerome berated as "those who paint their cheeks with rouge and antimony; whose made-up faces, inhumanly white, look like idols, and if, in a moment of forgetfulness, they shed a tear, it furrows the painted cheek; they to whom years do not bring the gravity of age, who load their heads with other people's hair and enamel a lost youth upon the wrinkles of age." In contrast, ascetics eliminated sexuality, neglected their appearance, wore plain clothes, and bathed infrequently. They also helped the needy. Some became destitute by giving all away; others established hostels and hospitals.

For the rest of his long life, Jerome was to be close to Paula and her family. Blesilla, Paula's beautiful elder daughter, enjoyed the smart set's social life, married at twenty-six, and was widowed seven months later. She continued to enjoy a hectic social life, for which Jerome admonished her. After a fever, she undertook penance and studied Scripture and Hebrew; and then, within four months, she died. Some Romans blamed Jerome. Paula was inconsolable; Jerome reproved her for "disgraceful, excessive, unchristian" grief.

On June 29, 384, probably the feast day of Peter and Paul then as now, Eustochium sent Jerome a present of bracelets, doves, and a basket of cherries. In his letter of thanks Jerome said the cherries recalled a virgin's blushes. He extolled virginity and recommended suppression of lustful thoughts but perhaps unwittingly provided material for them: in a passage perhaps influenced by the Song of Songs, he told Eustochium to remain alone in her room and let her lover sport with her: "when sleep overcomes you, he will come behind the wall, will thrust his hand though the aperture, and will caress your belly and you will start up, all trembling and will cry 'I am wounded with love.' "

As was the practice, the letter was copied and circulated by those who argued that, as sexual intercourse occurred only after Adam and Eve's expulsion from the Garden of Eden, virginity was superior to marriage. Although Jerome claimed that he did not disdain marriage, he implied that intercourse was intrinsically defiling. He believed it should serve only to produce children who, if all went well, would choose virginity.

In 383 a Roman layman, Helvidius, published a pamphlet using the New Testament references to Jesus' brothers and sisters to argue that, although Mary had been a virgin at the time of Jesus' conception, after his birth she lived a normal married life, bearing several other children. Helvidius aimed to prove that marriage had equal dignity with celibacy in contrast to the views of Damasus, Ambrose, and others. He may have been influenced by Roman Christians seeking to draw out the implications of the fact that, unlike some forms of paganism, Christianity taught that God created the body.

After pointing out that in Hebrew usage "brothers and sisters" could mean a relative, a member of the same tribe or merely a fellow Jew, Jerome tore into Helvidius, maintaining Mary's perpetual virginity and the superiority of the celibate life. He ignored Helvidius's point that generation of children was an extension of the divine creation.

Jerome crushed Helvidius, but opposition to Jerome grew in Rome as the health of his patron, Damasus, declined. Jerome did not suffer fools gladly and found them everywhere. He flayed worldly clerics whose "hair is curled and still shows traces of the tongs, their fingers glisten with rings, and if there is water on the road they cross it on tiptoe so as not to splash their shoes." He complained that "purple dye is used in pergamen, gold is used for lettering, manuscripts are adorned with gems but Christ dies naked at their [the clerics'] doors." He denounced matrons who helped the poor for vainglory and mercenary priests who could not wait until the rich they helped died, leaving them money. He also criticized unworthy monks: "we hold out our hands for alms while we have gold hidden under our rags." He would probably have agreed with Ammianus Marcellinus's comment that Constantine "first opened his supporters' greedy jaws," after which Constantinus had "rammed the wealth of the provinces down their throats." Jerome promised to write a history of Christianity showing that, under the Christian emperors, it had gained power and wealth, but lost virtue.

There was no way to silence him: "With Christ's help, my mouth will never be shut," he wrote, probably worrying his friends as much as his enemies. "Cut off my tongue and it will still manage to stammer something." He could be rude: he told an opponent "show no nose upon your face and keep your mouth shut. You will then stand some chance of being counted both handsome and eloquent." Yet he was surprised when people took offense, asking, "Have I ever written a word in bitterness?"

Jerome claimed the privileges of a satirist but suffered the satirist's fate: if his accusations were inacccurate people were indignant but if they were justified people were resentful. He accused clerics of careerism, but almost immediately on his return to Rome he had become its bishop's confidant, exchanging notes and badinage with him. He warned against the dangers of sex but was lionized by beautiful and rich widows. Between jealous clerics bruised by his polemics and those who deplored that they provided ammunition for pagan polemicists, an ominous anti-Jerome front must have formed.

His lampoons of conformist Christians had to be accepted as long as Damasus lived, but when his successor, Siricius, was elected in 384, Jerome was accused, as he wrote, of being

> an infamous rascal, a slippery turncoat, a liar who used Satanic arts to deceive. Some kissed my hands, yet attacked me with tongues of vipers, sympathy was on their lips but malignant joy in their hearts. One would attack my gait or my way of laughing, another would find something amiss in my looks, another would suspect the simplicity of my manner. Such is the company with which I have lived for about three years.

Jerome said he has mistakenly thought he had left scorpions behind when he left the desert, and then added:

> Before I became acquainted with the family of the saintly Paula, all Rome resounded with my praise. Almost everyone concurred in judging me worthy of the episcopate. Damasus, of blessed memory, spoke only of me. Men called me holy, humble, and eloquent.

About Jerome's eloquence, there was no doubt. But how many called humble this firebrand, who advocated holy arrogance, is not known.

Church authorities held an enquiry into his activities. He probably had this in mind when he wrote later of a "Senate of Pharisees." It may have been because Siricius authorized the enquiry that Jerome considered him guileless. The charges against Jerome, which are not known, were retracted, apparently in exchange for leaving the city, which he now compared to Babylon, the great harlot whose abominations the Book of Revelations described.

In August 385 he packed up his library and, escorted by many disciples, went to Rome's port to take a ship for the Holy Land. After travels in the Middle East, Jerome established a monastery in Bethlehem, where at times he "could hear Christ crying in the manger." It was a Roman enclave, an outpost of Latin Christianity in the East. Paula, who financed him, established a twin convent there and soon pilgrims were coming from as far away as Britain:

> The illustrious Gauls congregate here, and no sooner has the Briton, so remote from our world, made some progress in religion than he leaves his early-setting sun to seek a land which he knows only from reputation and the Scriptures. And what of the Armenians, the Persians, the peoples of India and Ethiopia, of Egypt, of Pontus, Cappadocia, Syria, and Mesopotamia? ... They throng here and set us the example of every virtue. The languages differ but the religion is the same; there are as many choirs singing the Psalms as there are nations. Here bread and vegetables grown with our own hands, and milk, country fare, are our plain and healthy food. ... Let Rome keep its crowds, let its arenas run with blood, its chariot racecourses go mad, its theaters wallow in sensuality, and, not to forget our friends, let the senate of ladies receive their daily visits.

Jerome's example, and his translation of works by the Egyptian monk Pachomius, fostered a growing monastic movement in the West. If Jerome was willing to forget Rome, Rome had not forgotten him. In 393 Roman friends asked him to refute a pamphlet by a monk named Jovinian. Once Jovinian had gone barefoot and was unkempt and pale from a sparse diet, but, deciding all this was irrelevant for Christians, he decided to dress well, take baths, and, while remaining celibate, mix freely with women. In his pamphlet Jovinian maintained that, in bearing Jesus, Mary had lost her virginity. He downgraded celibacy, arguing that no distinctions should be made between single, married, and widowed Christians, between those who ate and drank freely and those who fasted. In other words, in a people transformed by baptism, considerations of different states of life were inappropriate.

Jerome refuted Jovinian's assertion that those who abstained from sex were not automatically superior to married couples with normal sexual relations. A keystone of Jerome's argument was that Adam and Eve embarked on marriage only after the Fall and that while "marriage replenished the earth, virginity replenished paradise."

The stimulating effect of food and drink worried Jerome: "eating meat, drinking wine, having a well-fed belly—there you have the seedbed of lust." He quoted the observation of the medical authority Galen that men and women "glow with innate warmth"; adding to it by food and drink could make nature "burn to force its way to carnal intercourse." He seemed to fear a conflagration; if only he had believed in baths, he could have recommended frequent cold ones. In lieu of that, he counseled cold food and drinks but in moderation, for undigested food, he warned, likewise stimulated the genitals.

He ridiculed Jovinian's suggestion that baptism made distinctions irrelevant in the Christian community and closed his response with a slur on Jovinian's name: "derived from that of an idol (Jove). The Capitol is in ruins, the temples of Jove with their ceremonies have perished. Why should his name and vices flourish now . . . when your ancestors gave a heartier welcome to the self-restraint of Pythagoras than they did to Epicurus's counsels of debauchery?"

Even before Jerome's response reached Rome, a synod there condemned Jovinian's teachings. In Milan, Ambrose endorsed the judgment and Jovinian's subsequent excommunication. The battle had been won, but those who had requested Jerome's help realized that, with such friends, they had no need of enemies. He had gone overboard again, making an unwarranted assumption that Jovinian was a debauchee, using a bludgeoning tone, and describing marital intercourse as an obstacle to prayer, tolerable only because fornication was worse. Jerome had mistaken the tone needed when laity in Rome seemed to be seeking a reassessment of the significance of their marital life.

Jerome's friends asked him to try again. Jerome complained that there was no decent obscurity for him: lesser scribes had time to reconsider what they wrote but he was always responding to urgent requests from people who then immediately circulated his work. He admitted that these were the perils of pamphleteering, adding that, as certain swine had attacked even Virgil, a minor figure such as himself could not expect anything better. He wrote a more temperate tract in which he said that he had nothing against marriage—for those who could not aspire to anything better.

Jerome was still influencing certain Roman women. Furia, a recently widowed aristocrat, sought his guidance on the ascetic life, and he supplied it in detail. Another Roman Christian aristocrat who sought his guidance was Fabiola; she had married a debauchee, divorced him, and, before his death, had remarried. After her second husband's death, she presented herself as a penitent, in sackcloth and ashes, before the bishop and the congregation in St. John Lateran. Restored to communion, she devoted her wealth to the needy, founding a pauper's hospital, where she herself worked. In 394, with a friend of Jerome, she went on pilgrimage to the Holy Land. She studied the Bible with Jerome and even fled with him, Paula, and others to ships when Huns devastated Syria and threatened Bethlehem. Eventually she returned to Rome and established a travelers' hospice at its port. Jerome remained in correspondence until her death and wrote understandingly of her second marriage: "a wretched marriage is better than fornication without marriage."

Controversies continued throughout Jerome's declining years as did an endless stream of biblical commentaries, polemical pamphlets, propagandist history, hagiography, and lengthy letters. He had admired the third-century scholar Origen but came to feel that, although he was a great exegete, he was a dubious theologian with, for instance, too ethereal an idea of the resurrection. Jerome had a literal concept of it involving genitals, teeth, and intestines. Moreover he did not believe in an afterlife where prostitutes would be equal to virgins.

A close friend from school days, Rufinus, translated Origen and cited Jerome as his admirer without acknowledging his changed opinion. This angered Jerome and created a storm in Rome, where Jerome's friends brought pressure on the bishop to condemn both Origen and Rufinus. Siricius refrained from doing so, but his successor, Innocent, came down on Jerome's side. Jerome continued to attack Rufinus even after his death in Sicily in 410. He referred to him as the "Scorpion" and the "Grunting Pig" who "turned good Greek into wretched Latin."

A youngish, relatively unknown North African bishop wrote to him confessing his distress at this "disastrous bitterness" between two mature men who had abandoned the world. Jerome was swamped with respectful letters from far and wide, usually requesting instruction, and did not give much attention to the pesky provincial who signed himself Augustine of Hippo. But Augustine persisted.

An American scholar, James J. O'Donnell, has pointed out that Augustine never saw a Bible. He did not know the Greek-language Bible, and the earliest Latin Bible in a single volume dates from the mid-sixth century. He referred always to Scripture, various texts that together correspond roughly to the Bible as we know it. Of course he brought his acute mind to all he read; his writings are steeped in Scripture, but he was not a scholar or linguist in the way Jerome was. Through correspondence, Augustine sought his guidance.

The imperial post carried official correspondence but private letters were entrusted to bearers. One of Augustine's letters to Jerome went astray in Italy, where a version of it appeared that sent Jerome's blood pressure soaring. He responded, "if by any chance you write more letters, see that they are delivered to me before Italy and Rome get them."

Jerome considered Augustine's questions to be criticisms. This was not surprising as Augustine dared suggest that there were holes in the scholarship of the prickly older man and even that "what you think does not correspond to the truth." Jerome warned Augustine against trying to make a reputation by disputing with him but was cautious enough to adopt a humble tone: "It does not become me, who have spent my life since youth sharing the arduous labors of pious brethren in a monastery in the depths of the countryside, to presume to write anything against a bishop." He also suggested, however, that "the tired ox walks with a firmer step" and was prepared to put Augustine in his lowly place: "So huge a stretch of land and sea lie between us that the sound of your voice, sir, hardly reaches me."

Eventually Jerome was to suggest that they disarm and "play together in the fields of Scripture." Jerome and Augustine gamboling together on scriptural sward is an attractive image, but Augustine rejected it: "As for me, I prefer to do things in earnest, not to play." For him, it was not a matter of level playing fields but scaling mountains. "If you choose the word 'play' to imply that what we do is an easy exercise, then let me tell you, frankly, that I expected more of you—as if studying Scripture were a matter of romping on level grass, not puffing and panting up a steep mountain face." It seems that Jerome was dealing with someone as edgy as himself.

Jerome's decision to translate the Old Testament into Latin from the Hebrew worried Augustine who feared it would upset the faithful accustomed to Latin based on a Greek version. Jerome's interpretation of Paul's account of his clash with Peter, "I opposed him [Peter] to his face, since he was manifestly wrong" (Gal. 2:11–14), as a feigned clash seemed to Augustine to undermine the historicity of the Gospels. For him, Peter had erred and was corrected.

As Jerome's scholarship was questioned by the North African, who also reproved his attitude to Rufinus, inevitably their relationship was strained. But, after a break of some years, their correspondence resumed with a new tone. Augustine acknowledged the value of Jerome's translation, and Jerome accepted the younger man's interpretation of the Paul-Peter clash. Even more importantly, they had identified a mutual enemy in Pelagius.

By 410 Jerome, who was sixty-three, in his own words had "furrowed brow and oxen-like dewlaps." Perhaps by now his emblem should have been a bulldog. Gray-haired, nearly blind, and with money worries since the death of Paula six years earlier (she had given away her wealth and died in debt), he had to employ secretaries to take dictation as he pushed ahead with his biblical commentaries. He abandoned them temporarily, however, to "translate the words of Scripture into deeds and, instead of speaking saintly words, act on them." He devoted himself generously to caring for refugees from various parts, including Rome, which had been invaded again by Alaric. But he did not care at all for one of them, Pelagius, who may have clashed with Jerome earlier in Rome. He had certainly criticized Jerome at the time of his controversy with Jovinian and won adherents for asceticism in the same Roman circles as the older man.

Although Pelagius's ideas had already been censured by the African bishops, this was not known in the Holy Land. Enjoying the support of the powerful Anicii family in Rome and prominent churchmen both in and out of the city, Pelagius was a moral reformer who taught that human nature, not corrupted by original sin, was free to do good.

Jerome smelled a rat or, rather, a "big, bloated Alpine dog," which was one of the epithets he applied to Pelagius, whom he considered a purveyor of "nonsensical puerilities." He described heavy-shouldered Pelagius, who was "slow as a tortoise," as a "dolt laden down with Scots porridge" (he was a Briton). He accused the newcomer, who was on excellent terms with Jerome's enemy, the bishop of Jerusalem, of deviousness ("yours is the only heresy which is afraid to speak in public"), of flattering women to gain influence with them, and of being smug because allegedly passionless, immune from temptation and sin. He rebutted Pelagius's teaching in detail, but a local synod came out in his favor.

In a letter of 414 to a friend Ctesiphon, who had been influenced by Pelagius in Rome, Jerome claimed Pelagianism was a compendium of heretical poisons. He saw it as propounding that virtue could be acquired by the mind and will while ignoring the body. For Jerome, the body was valuable as it was where salvation happened. Although he knew its dangers, he did not want to deny its existence but rather to discipline it. "I do not despise the flesh in which Christ was born and resurrected," he wrote, "I love that flesh which knows it is going to be judged, that which is, for Christ at the hour of martyrdom, broken, torn to pieces and burned." Jerome denied that he had Manichean tendencies to split the body from the soul but added that, all the same, one could not ignore scriptural passages such as the Pauline "I do not the good I desire, but the evil that I do not want" and "the Spirit is willing, but the flesh is weak" of the Passion narratives.

In 416 Rome was shocked to hear that thugs had attacked the twin monasteries in Bethlehem: they burned the buildings, assaulted the nuns and monks, and killed a deacon. Jerome had saved himself by fleeing to a fortified tower built against possible

Bedouin attacks. Pope Innocent was informed by Eustochium and Paula (Granddaughter of her namesake who had established the monasteries with Jerome, Paula had joined the monk in Jerusalem shortly before the raid.) Innocent wrote to Jerome that he wanted to punish the assailants.

It was not discovered who were responsible, but Augustine was convinced they were Pelagians. Shortly afterward, Pope Innocent excommunicated Pelagius and his followers. His successor, Zosimus, was initially favorable to Pelagius. "People who ought to be the world's champion," wrote Jerome at this disappointing news, "are backing the cause of perdition." In 418, however, Zosimus condemned Pelagianism. Augustine and Jerome had won out against their mutual enemy, but the sick old scholar remained vigilant. In 419 a new pope, Boniface, wrote to Jerome announcing his election. Nearing seventy-two and his death, Jerome advised Boniface to pursue the Pelagians: "Let the heretics know you are a foe to their perfidy and let them hate you." True to his idea of himself as a warrior, he recommended that they be "wiped out and spiritually slaughtered. They must be cut to pieces with Christ's sword, for neither plasters nor soothing medicaments can enable them to recover sound health." He was true to what he had written earlier: "I have always done my utmost that the enemies of the church should also be my enemies."

In his later years in Bethlehem, Jerome became a one-man-Rome-across-the-sea. Not only was he a tenacious, and often vehement, defender of Rome's teaching but was also reconciled with classical culture. He achieved a synthesis of the two Romes that earlier, even to himself, had seemed in conflict.

– VIII –

OUT OF AFRICA

JEROME BEGAN THE CONTROVERSY against Pelagius, but Augustine concluded it. Opposition to Pelagius fostered agreement between them and also strengthened their ties with Rome, where the two provincials had crucial influence. They had both been in Rome in 383–84 but had not met. Jerome stayed longer and achieved prominence there; when distant he maintained contact with Roman friends. Augustine, who was twice in Rome but not for long, was not nearly as well known personally there as Jerome. But he recorded his admiration for ascetic groups in Rome, and, more importantly, made the most significant response to the sack of Rome.

By that time Augustine had been for fifteen years bishop of Hippo Regius, which today is Annaba in Algeria. He lived in a complex consisting of a church, a separate baptistry, a chapel, a residence, and a monastery that overlooked his garden. Abutting the church was a mansion owned by a Roman Christian lady who rarely came to Hippo. The complex was a mile from the central city monumental zone with its large forum, a theater that could seat six thousand, public baths, and a temple. Pagan inscriptions were everywhere. Augustine's cathedral was a stone's throw from the villas of the rich overlooking the harbor.

After Alaric's sack of Rome, many fled to "Rome-across-the-sea," North Africa, which seemed the most secure territory. It had had outstanding Christian apologists such as Tertullian, bishops such as Cyprian, and many martyrs. Some of the refugees were wealthy Christians who had embraced the ascetic life but had not necessarily dispensed with a retinue. Melania, a wealthy matron influenced by Jerome, established a huge estate outside Thagaste, which was Augustine's birthplace. Some of the newcomers had participated in the revival of paganism inspired by the misfortunes of Christian Rome. One was Volusianus, the son of Albinus, a personage of Macrobius's *Saturnalia*. Volusianus wrote to Augustine posing questions about the Virgin Mary, which he said had been raised by a friend at a dinner party. His tone was respectful although he may have had his tongue in his cheek. In a way the presence of these pagans rekindled the conversation begun in *Saturnalia*.

Augustine, like Hilary of Poitiers before him, was a rare Westerner who could match the subtlety and penetration of the major Eastern theologians. He relished knotty problems. His prose reveals the sinews of his thought but also the secrets of his soul with surprising candor. Moreover, he seems to have been genuinely humble both personally and intellectually: he wanted to be considered an asker of questions rather than a source of definitive answers. Even though he had a strong constitution, his health was delicate, probably because he was highly strung: he complained frequently of debility but lived until seventy-six and died with all his faculties intact. Although he disliked travel, when he was sixty-five, at the request of Pope Zosimus, he undertook a journey to the province of Mauretania.

Aurelius Augustinus was born in 354, one of three children of Patricius, a hot-tempered farmer, and a redoubtable mother, Monica. As a young woman, she had occasionally drunk too much. Monica was intensely Catholic but Patricius, who was unfaithful to his wife, did not become a Christian until shortly before his death in 372. The domestic culture was Latin. The family lived in Thagaste (today Souk-Ahras in Algeria), a town on an inland plateau where wheat and olives were cultivated. Augustine's parents, who were not well off, made sacrifices to prepare their most brilliant child for a career in the imperial bureaucracy; a distant relative, Romanianus, who was a local landowner, helped pay for the boy's education, which was mainly in Latin literature and oratory.

Reading Cicero's praise of Wisdom while a student in Carthage set Augustine "on fire to fly away from earthly things." But when he turned to Scripture he found the translation crude, Old Testament morality deplorable, and the genealogies of Jesus inconsistent. Some well-spoken missionaries won his trust. They were followers of Mani, "the apostle of Jesus Christ," who had been executed by the Persians in 276. Mani came from a Christianized Jewish family, and his followers considered themselves the true Christians, but Manicheeism also seems to have been an attempt to form a world religion combining elements of Christianity, the Zoroastrianism of Persia, and Buddhism. The basis of its complex beliefs was that God and Satan each had his own kingdom; in this dualistic system, the Satanic principle invades the Kingdom of Light. It appealed to Augustine as a clear-cut response to his abiding concern: how to account for evil. Moreover, it did so without him having to admit any responsibility for it. When Monica learned that her son had become a Manichee, she temporarily shut him out of her house.

In his late teens Augustine, by his own admission, "boiled with both love and lust." Although Monica warned him against sexual passions, "she did not consider that if they could not be pared to the quick, they had better be brought under control within the bounds of married love." She did not want Augustine to marry because she feared a wife would hinder his studies: his prospects of a career in the imperial service, perhaps culminating in a governorship, would be ruined if he had to settle in a provincial town. "Both my parents were unduly set upon the success of my studies," Augustine charged. "I was left to do pretty well as I liked and go after pleasure not only beyond the bounds of reasonable discipline but to sheer dissolution in many kinds of evil."

At eighteen he took a partner whom "wandering lust and no particular judgment had brought my way," and he was faithful to her. He learned "what a gulf there is between the restraint of the marriage covenant entered into for the sake of children and the mere bargain of lustful love, where if children come they come unwanted—though when they are born, they compel our love."

In fact, a son, Adeodatus ("God-given"), was born the following year. Subsequently Augustine became a Manichee: they discouraged procreation and advocated contraception. There were no other children during the following fourteen years of Augustine's relationship. Some historians suggest that Augustine did not marry her because it would have been socially unacceptable.

Augustine taught rhetoric first in Thagaste and later in Carthage, until in 383, giving his mother the slip, he sailed with his de facto wife and son for Rome. It was a magnet for ambitious provincials, additionally attractive to Augustine because its students were reputedly less boisterous than those of Carthage.

The twenty-nine-year-old Manichee-on-the-make, who had already written his first book, lodged in Rome with a senior member of their proscribed religion but was unimpressed by the fellow religionists he met. Doubts about Manicheeism had arisen before leaving Carthage when he had found that one of their most esteemed theologians, although pleasant and eloquent, was an intellectual lightweight. In Rome he realized that the Manichees' astronomical calculations, crucial to their beliefs, were mistaken. He was also becoming doubtful whether it was possible to know the truth at all.

But adherence to Manicheeism proved useful to Augustine. In Rome he fell seriously ill and on recovery found that, although the students were less boisterous than those of Carthage, they did not pay for their lessons: once the time came to do so, they changed teachers. When the city prefect Symmachus (an interlocutor in Macrobius's *Saturnalia,* which was completed about this time) received a request from Milan for a public orator, his fellow religionists helped Augustine, despite his quaint African accent, obtain the post. It meant teaching rhetoric to some of the high-ranking court officials and delivering public orations.

In Milan Augustine encountered Ambrose, who likewise had been born in the provinces but as son of the governor of Trier in the Moselle. "All unknowing I was brought by God to him," Augustine wrote, "that knowing him I should be brought to God." Although they had little direct contact, Augustine said that Ambrose "planted and watered him." Augustine aspired to an important imperial post but Ambrose had already had that experience as a provincial governor before being coopted as a bishop. Moreover Ambrose's culture was impressive: unlike Augustine he read Greek fluently. His sermons were in polished Latin, he knew the Neo-Platonists, and his understanding of the Scripture was more profound and subtle than anything Augustine had encountered. Finally Augustine's sensitive ear would have been responsive to the beautiful psalm chants Ambrose had composed. But Augustine's reconciliation with Catholicism was not immediate. "Soon, in a little while, I shall make up my mind," he wrote later to describe his hesitation. Among other things, he had to struggle to conceive of God as incorporeal substance, uncreated being.

Monica joined Augustine in Milan and convinced him to repatriate his de facto wife so that he could eventually marry a more suitable local heiress after she reached the marriageable age of twelve. His de facto wife swore that she "would never know another man" and, as a voluntary widow, may have been sustained by a Christian community in North Africa. Augustine, who "held her very dear," was "broken and wounded and his heart bled." Obviously there was more than lust between them, but he let her go. Surely his later words apply to this relationship:

> If a man and a woman live together without being legitimately joined, not to have children, but because they could not observe continence, and if they have agreed between themselves to have relations with no one else, can this be called a marriage? Perhaps but only if they had resolved to maintain until death the good faith which they had promised themselves.... But if a man takes a woman only for a time, until he has found another who better suits his rank and fortune; and if he marries the woman, as being of the same class, this man would commit adultery in his heart, not toward the woman he wished to marry, but toward the woman with whom he had once lived.

Augustine's prospective wife was ten and he was thirty, a substantial difference even at a time when men chose younger wives who would not only have many child-bearing years ahead of them but also be able to nurse their husband in his old age. Her family's wealth was important because, although Augustine was in contact with influential courtiers, an important public office would have to be purchased. While awaiting his marriage, Augustine took another mistress, but this did not heal "the wound from cutting off my former partner."

He was aided by the Neo-Platonists to conceive of evil as the result of free choice and of God as wholly spiritual, while reading St. Paul enabled him to accept that, in Jesus Christ, God had become incarnate. However, he was still "hot for honors, money, and marriage" and felt "a slave of lust" until he learned of Egyptian hermits such as Antony who had mastered such desires. In a Milanese garden he heard a voice telling him to open the New Testament. The passage he hit upon, Romans 13:13–14, convinced him that he could change his life: "...no drunken orgies, no promiscuity or licentiousness and no wrangling or jealousy. Let your armor be the Lord Jesus Christ, forget about satisfying your bodies with their cravings." As he reached the end of the sentence, Augustine recounted, "it was as though a light of utter confidence shone in all my heart, and all the darkness of uncertainty vanished."

At this point, Augustine no longer wanted to teach. It was partly because he was weakened by a lung infection and partly because his discovery of Christ and the New Testament confirmed his suspicion that rhetoricians were mere "hucksters of hot air" who coached people to tell lies convincingly. This perception was to affect his assessment of the empire because rhetoric helped form a favorable consensus by supplying the *exempla* through which men were taught to live and rule. However, recommending patience to himself, he did not abandon his post before the imminent end of the school term. Then with his brother Navigius, Adeodatus, Monica, and a group of friends he went to a country house lent to him during the grape harvest. Here, at Cassiciacum near Lake Como, he wrote a series of books justifying Catholic doctrine without renouncing any of the rights of reason or research. "Love reason very highly," he later advised a correspondent who had emphasized the need to submit to church teaching.

He resigned his teaching post and prepared for baptism, for which Ambrose advised him to read Isaiah. Perhaps Ambrose himself prepared Augustine, who was thirty-three, for baptism in the spring of 387, warning him against idolatry and polytheism and introducing him to the mysteries of the faith such as retribution after death. It was standard practice for the Lord's Prayer to be made known only at this stage. A biographer of Augustine, Peter Brown, has imagined the baptism as follows:

> On the eve of the Resurrection, Augustine and the throng of other *competentes* (as those qualified for baptism were called), of all ages and both sexes, would troop to the baptistry beside the main basilica of Ambrose. Passing behind curtains, Augustine would descend, alone, stark naked, into a deep pool of water. Three times, Ambrose would hold his shoulders beneath the gushing fountain. Later, dressed in a pure white robe, he would enter the main basilica ablaze with candles; and, amid the acclamations of the congregation, he and his fellow neophytes would take their place on a slightly raised floor by the altar, for a first participation in the mysteries of the Risen Christ. The theme of "putting off the old," of "putting on the new," of rebirth and rising again from death,

of the consequent ascent of the soul to heaven made possible by the descent of Christ to earth, reverberated in Augustine's imagination.

After his baptism, Augustine left with his entourage for his homeland, where he intended to establish a religious community, but for a year a naval blockade due to a civil war marooned them in Rome. Augustine described himself and his mother looking from a window of their house, at Rome's seaport Ostia, into an internal garden and speculating about eternal life. Monica said that she had lived only to see Augustine become a Catholic, and she no longer knew what she was doing on earth. Within five days she was feverish and died shortly afterward. In 1945 boys digging in Ostia found a marble fragment of the inscription above her tomb.

Augustine stayed in Rome until late summer 388. Since he had left the city five years earlier, he had become a full-fledged Christian, and Siricius had succeeded Damasus as bishop. Possibly Augustine saw the construction work, funded by Emperor Valentinian II for whom he had delivered a panegyric, to enlarge St. Paul's, which would have been evidence for Ambrose's affirmation that the church was waxing. The Manichees, however, boasted that their morals were superior to those of Catholics. To call their bluff, Augustine drew on his personal experience of both religions to write *On the Morals of the Catholic Church and of the Manichees*. Indeed he was to conduct lifelong anti-Manichee polemic, which may have been intended also to counter recurring charges that Manichees still influenced him.

Looking back on his writings in *Reconsiderations*, he explained that he had been moved to write because he "could not hear in silence the vaunting of the Manichees about their pretended and misleading continence and abstinence." He scorned their "amazingly fatuous" ideas and "silly, impious, mischievous" precepts that contributed to a "circus of superstition." He recounted a story he had heard of a rich, zealous Manichee in Rome who gathered together adepts in his house to follow the religion's precepts, but they quarreled and accused each other of crimes: "the revelations were vile beyond description." In short, a nest of vipers.

Augustine contrasted the Manichee's fanaticism about avoiding wine, meat, and certain other food with the attitude of Christian groups:

There is charity in their choice of diet (the same people who abstain from meat when in health take it when ill without any fears if it is required as a cure. Many drink no wine, but they do not think that wine defiles them, for they give it to those who need it for medical reasons), charity in their speech, charity in their dress, charity in their looks. Charity unites them, and inspires their acts.

He added that in Rome he had known several Christian groups "living in charity, sanctity, and liberty," each presided over by "one eminent for character, prudence, and divine knowledge":

They sustain themselves by their own hands. I was told that many practiced fasts of quite amazing severity, not merely taking one meal daily toward night, which is everywhere quite common, but very often continuing for three days or more in succession without food or drink. And this among not only men but also women, who live together in great numbers as widows or virgins, gaining a livelihood by spinning and weaving, presided over in each case by a woman of the greatest judgment and experience, skilled and accomplished not only in directing and forming moral conduct, but also in instructing and understanding.

With all this, no one is pressed to endure hardships for which they are unfit; nothing is imposed on anyone against their will; nor is anyone condemned by the others because too feeble to do as they do, for they bear in mind how strongly Scripture enjoins charity on all.

(By this time Jerome had left for Bethlehem and Pelagius had become a guide for Rome's ascetics, but it is not known if Augustine spoke of the groups influenced by Pelagius.)

Augustine wrote yet another book in Rome and began one on free will, which he completed only seven years after his return to Africa. He did not leave again. Shortly after his homecoming, his son Adeodatus died. In Thagaste, with friends, Augustine founded a community for religious studies. In 391 he traveled the forty-five miles to the coastal town Hippo Regius to advise a friend in the imperial service who was thinking of becoming a monk but decided against it. Augustine recounted that he avoided all places without a bishop as he feared being forced, like Ambrose and others, into the office by acclaim. Hippo had a bishop but, as he preached on the needs of the church, the congregation turned to Augustine, acclaiming him, and reluctantly he agreed to become a priest, even though he felt his vocation was monastic rather than ministerial.

In 397, at the age of forty-two, he was appointed bishop of Hippo. He found his episcopal duties a "packload," which sometimes left him no time to study Scripture or even to eat. He complained constantly that "free time becomes busy time." In response to a request for a favor, he wrote that he spent much of his day in unnecessary matters: "You would be astonished at the number of things which I cannot put off, which pluck my sleeve and prevent me from doing what you are asking."

He cared for the needy but was also much in demand as a preacher: he delivered substantial, lively ex tempore homilies, hundreds of which have survived thanks to stenographers. He also found time to write, or rather dictate, most of his 212 books, and conduct a voluminous correspondence. In 1981, an Austrian researcher published twenty-six new letters of Augustine, which he had discovered in France, bringing the number preserved to 245. The bulk of his writing, which amounts to over five million words, arose out of his pastoral experience. In his writings Augustine, who had made detours outside Christianity, showed his delight in its perspectives and alerted other Christians to its distinctiveness.

One of his most onerous tasks was arbitrating, even in civil cases, between consenting parties, a faculty and obligation of Catholic bishops. Augustine's clients were by no means confined to Catholics. He arbitrated in his office by the church with the Sacred Scriptures always close at hand.

In the precincts of his residence, Augustine established a religious community in which all was shared. His first experience of communal living had been with friends near Lake Como, in conformity with the Roman-Greek tradition of philosophical study in a comfortable rural setting. Augustine carried something of this convivial tradition into his monastic community, which differed from those influenced by Egyptian and Middle Eastern desert monks, who stressed drastic mortification. Augustine valued renunciation and virginity but did not consider the monastic life as the only path to perfection. Perhaps he was reacting against Jerome's exaltation of the ascetic life over marriage.

Influenced by figures such as the Cappadocian monk Basil, he saw monastic life as creation of a community, a voluntary association liberated from social constraints, in which relations with others and God became paramount as in heaven. It was an urbane goal compared to the harsh and heroic ideals of desert monasticism.

This type of community, and Augustine's writings about it, were to influence subsequent developments of monasticism but Augustine's own community had some black sheep. In 404 he was troubled when Boniface, a priest, and a seminarian called Spes accused each other of sexual advances. In a letter to the faithful, Augustine explained that the case had tormented him and that he had decided to send both men on pilgrimage to the shrine of St. Felix near Naples, where "divine intervention can more readily expose the guilty conscience, and through threat of punishment, draw one to confess." Toward the end of his letter, he exclaimed that, just as it was hard to find better men than the best in monasteries, "I have not found worse than those in monasteries who have fallen into sin." He also commented that "there are crooks in every profession."

As bishop, Augustine, who applied to himself the biblical expression "servant of the servants of the Lord," wore a simple robe. Priests who worked with Augustine, elderly and retired priests, plus lay brothers lived in the community; some of the lay brothers had jobs as clerks for waterfront merchants. All followed a strict regime, wore a habit and, in public, distinctive headgear. They kept to a vegetarian diet, but Augustine, who discouraged excessive mortification, allowed consumption of wine. To discourage gossip, a verse was inscribed on his dining room wall:

> Whoever thinks that he is able
> To nibble at the life of absent friends
> Must know that he's unworthy of this table.

Near the community a convent of nuns was established, headed by Augustine's widowed sister. Some Christians, who considered pagan festivals and spectacles to remain tributes to gods as they had been in origin, condemned any Christian attending them. At the beginning of his episcopate Augustine merely advised Christians to avoid them as frivolous rather than diabolical. Later, when Christian-pagan relations became tenser and people felt they had to take sides, he called on Christians to avoid attending them because, even if they considered them mere entertainment, their presence could be seen as a tribute to idols. But he advised Christians to avoid entering pagan private property to destroy cult statues: "Let us act rather to break the idols in their hearts: when they convert to Christianity, they will either invite us to help them with the good work or even carry it out themselves.... but now we must pray for them, not burn with anger against them."

There were tensions not only with pagans but also with the Donatists, who were the largest group of Christians in Hippo, and throughout North Africa vied with Catholics to be the major denomination. One of Augustine's first initiatives as priest had been to write an anti-Donatist jingle that could be remembered easily by people unlearned in Latin. Probably from Ambrose he had learned to use music in church to instruct as well as delight. He became the Donatists' most redoubtable opponent. The Donatist schism had lasted almost a century, splitting the church and society and dividing families: Augustine himself had Donatist relatives. The movement, named after a bishop Donatus, had arisen out of a refusal to recognize a bishop of Carthage (Cecilian) because one of those who consecrated him had allegedly compromised his faith during Diocletian's persecution by offering homage to the emperor. Eighty bishops had appealed to Emperor Constantine, who referred the matter to the church of Rome. It rejected the appeal on the grounds that a sacrament's validity did not depend on the celebrant's worthiness. But the Donatists retained a strong following for mixed religious and social motives: they claimed to be a continuation of the church of the martyrs uncompromised with the empire. The Donatists were particularly strong among the rural underprivileged, and the Berbers who did not welcome Roman suzerainty.

They considered themselves the Church of the Perfect and the Pure, who had preserved ritual purity and the Law in its entirety. Arrogantly they asked whether Catholics wanted to become Christians. One of their bishops claimed that the Donatist Church was the Ark of Noah "well tarred inside and out to keep within itself the good water of baptism and repel the world-defiling waters."

They brought water imagery to Augustine's mind also but it was that of a marsh: "The clouds roll thunderously, that the House of the Lord shall be built throughout the world; and these frogs sit in their marsh and croak—we are the only true Christians!"

For Augustine, the fact that the Donatists had not been in communion with Rome since 313 disproved their claim to be considered the true church. He believed that the Donatists had a static, limited, even nationalistic, notion of their alliance with God when the church, instead, had become coextensive with the world. For Augustine, Donatists' anxiety about preserving identity seemed at odds with trust in God's aid, and he needled the self-proclaimed Church of the Perfect about its members' imperfections.

In Rome and Milan Augustine had seen the catholicity of the church, which contrasted with the Donatists' provincialism: they were limited to North Africa with some adherents in Rome, where, at one point, they had a series of six bishops until Damasus convinced civil authorities to expel Claudian, the last of them. As Augustine shared Ambrose's confidence that the church was waxing, the Donatists' preoccupations seemed petty.

One of his sermons discovered by a French scholar in the municipal library of Mainz, Germany, in 1990 showed Augustine's confidence:

> Kings come to Rome. There are the temples of the emperors who, in their pride, demanded divine honors from men and, since they had power, extorted them rather than meriting them. The Fisherman could demand nothing similar. There is the Fisherman's burial place, there the emperor's temple. Peter is in his sepulcher, Hadrian in his temple [presumably a reference to Hadrian's mausoleum, now transformed into Castel Sant'Angelo, which is within sight of St. Peter's]. Let us see where the king goes when he wants to kneel: the emperor's temple or St. Peter's tomb? Here, taking off his crown, he beats his breast on the Fisherman's tomb; by means of him [Peter] the king wants to reach God; praying he realizes that he is helped. This is what He who is scorned and dies on the cross has done; here is He who has won over the nations, not by the ferocity of arms but with the spurned wood of the cross.

Indeed the church itself was a miracle that was not damaged by its members' shortcomings:

After all the Christian bloodshed, after all the burnings and crucifixions of martyrs, fertilized by these things churches have sprung up as far afield as the barbarian nations. Multitudes enter upon this [Christian] way of life from every race, forsaking the riches and honors of the present world, desirous of dedicating their whole life to the one most high God.

North African ecclesiastical struggles were fierce: during the Donatist crisis, there was physical violence on both sides. Donatists not only whitewashed Catholic churches to purify them but killed some Catholic priests and blinded many more, using quicklime and vinegar. By chance Augustine himself evaded an ambush. Squads of Donatist thugs aimed to kill a Catholic for Christ and then be killed in turn to attain martyrdom. For religious motives, they did not use swords, but had no compunction about wielding clubs or other weapons.

In 398 the most influential Donatist bishop made the fatal mistake of aligning himself with a usurper who was defeated. The religious rebels could now be considered also as traitors. From Ravenna in 405, the Catholic emperor, Honorius, issued a decree against Donatists as heretics, but was probably concerned principally about the social disorder they fomented.

As elsewhere the church, initially subject to intermittent persecution, was now faced with the problem of how to react to violence used in its defense. Subsequent anti-Donatist rulings were extremely strict. Initially, the law decreed that the Donatist Church be disbanded: it was deprived of its bishops, its churches, and its funds while its members' civic rights were restricted. Outside the cities the law was not applied immediately, but laity who did not become Catholic were liable to fines. Like other North African Catholic bishops, Augustine, who hated violence, was uneasy about these measures at first but when he found coercion brought genuine conversions he justified it, adducing the biblical wedding parallel in which people were compelled to come to the banquet. He claimed that "correction" could aid the will to make a choice. He recommended leniency to civil authorities, requesting that even a Donatist who had murdered a Catholic priest not be put to death. He ruled out torture but, using the model of a father of a family and mindful that his hated schooldays had produced benefits later, argued that "the rod has its own kind of charity."

His arguments for coercion were used in the Middle Ages by those advocating much harsher measures against heretics.

Augustine was endorsing coercion of those at least as numerous as Catholics who had set altar against altar, claiming to be the authentic church. They were rebellious and supercilious co-religionists, not followers of other religions such as Judaism, Manicheeism, or the different varieties of paganism.

Donatists and others objected that it was contrary to Christianity to impose conversion. Augustine reminded them of their violence and that they themselves had appealed to civil authorities first as well as coercing those who had broken away from Donatism.

Between 397 and 401, Augustine wrote his *Confessions* addressed to God, in which he confesses above all his love for the Creator but also his faith and his sins. Overhearing Augustine's conversation with God enables readers to come closer to him than any other figure of late antiquity. He admits distractions: "As I sit at home, I cannot turn my eyes from the sight of a lizard catching flies or a spider entangling them in her web," which brings readers an idle Augustine on a hot, drowsy North African day watching buzzing flies being silenced for ever. Convinced that acknowledgment of failings fostered the humility necessary for conversion, he wanted to recover his past and his failings as the way to know himself, and hence God, which made him a fearless autobiographer. He admitted not only youthful oat-sowing but the persistence of troubling sexual dreams. He saw a continuity between his sexual yearnings and those that brought him eventually to Christ.

He recalled himself as a young man "in love with loving....I set about finding the occasion to fall in love, so much in love was I with the idea of love." He did not believe that the only sins "were those in which you used your genitals." Rather he examined his youthful participation in a theft of pears. He was intrigued by the pull to do wrong, by the force of bad habit and, fifteen hundred years before Freud, recognized that a lapsus could be revealing. He was aware of the influence of language on behavior; both Ludwig Wittgenstein and Jean Piaget were to profit from his reflections on learning to talk. He studied nonverbal communication and the relationship of words, meaning, and reality. For him the human soul was of labyrinthine complexity, a cockpit of good and evil where "which side will win, I do not know....I just do not know."

His acceptance of Christianity a decade earlier had come to mean acceptance of responsibility for his sins, a recognition of a divided self. In his own words, he had become a question to himself and his questioning was to continue lifelong.

He was more complex than when, living near lake Como immediately before his baptism, he had provided unassailable proofs of Catholic doctrine. A reading of St. Paul had made Augustine less confident that people reasoned their way to God but more convinced of God's initiative toward people. Moreover, perhaps because of his years as a priest, he was acutely aware of the difficulty of breaking ingrained habits, the ambiguities of motivation, the limits of conscious control. As perfection was unattainable, the important thing was to aspire. "It is yearning that makes the heart deep": a dynamics of the soul and a grammar of desire underlie his autobiography, which probably benefited from his interest in Plotinus, who saw the human mind as a correlate of God.

In the *Confessions* Augustine had plunged into his own past; in *The City of God* he plunged into the past of Rome. He explained why he wrote its twenty-two books:

> Rome had been swept by the invasion of the Goths under the leadership of King Alaric and the impact of a great disaster; and the worshipers of the many false gods, to whom we commonly give the name of pagans, attempting to attribute this visitation to the Christian religion, began more sharply and more bitterly than usual to blaspheme the true God. Burning with the zeal of God's house, I decided to write against their blasphemy and errors the books of *The City of God*.

Pagans claimed the gods' empire had been undermined by a religion which emphasized debilitating virtues such as meekness. They felt the empire had become vulnerable since auguries and bloody animal sacrifices, which placated the gods, had been suppressed. Constantine had abandoned the old gods because he was convinced the Christian God was a winner, but defeat undercut this assumption. Pagan objections to the new religion, which flared up again after the Goths' incursions, probably troubled some Christians as well.

To rebut the argument that Rome had been undermined by Christianity, as well as being devastated by Christian (Arian) barbarians, Augustine made a compilation of learned references, quotes, and apposite examples to supersede all pagan compilations. Augustine was showing that he could beat the pagans at their own game because, in a sense, Roman traditions and literature were the cultured pagans' religion.

He began by arguing that the Goths' sack of Rome was only to be expected in a war but that at least their faith in Christ made them respect churches as sanctuaries. Augustine maintained that the persistent vices of Roman society had only been fostered by Greco-Roman religion, which had not avoided disasters such as the Punic wars. Christianity provided a much more exalted religious motivation: "Has anyone ever chosen death rather than deny, when commanded to do so, that Romulus and Hercules and the rest were gods?"

Augustine criticized traditional pagan religion but also Plato and the Neo-Platonists such as Plotinus, Porphyry, and Apuleius, whom, in some respects, he admired. He demythologized Roman life and history, pointing out that the protagonists were simply human: "What, after all, are human beings but human beings?" He scoffed at the reverent hush that accompanied accounts of Rome's rise, which he attributed, instead, to "lust for domination." He found the empire better than its predecessors but not, as pagans claimed, worthy to last forever. By relativizing Rome's history he helped Christians regard with greater equanimity the empire's eventual collapse, which was closer than he realized, at least in North Africa.

Other Christians had criticized the content of Roman religion, culture, history, and education, but Augustine went deeper, for he saw that they were all sustained by rhetoric, which he attacked for telling lies elegantly to manipulate consensus. "Let us refuse," he wrote, "to be fooled by empty rhetoric" and "to let the edge of our critical faculties be blunted by high-sounding words." For instance, he spotted the question-begging involved in using a term like "province" to legitimate Rome's territorial acquisitions. He criticized Cicero, whom in many ways he admired, for hiding his awareness that Roman religion was a hoax in order to promote a political consensus. Roman ideals, Augustine believed, were inadequate to achieve justice, which was a requisite for peace. He compared states without justice to robber bands "that are little kingdoms."

He regarded the Roman heroic ideal as inferior to the Christian teaching that even leaders should practice virtues such as humility. Augustine's prime example of a Christian ruler behaving differently from pagan counterparts was Theodosius I. His military background had helped him appreciate the valor and fidelity of barbarian warriors. As there was a shortage of recruits from among the longer-settled inhabitants of the empire, making a virtue of necessity Theodosius incorporated many barbarians into the Roman army, which irritated conservatives. In Thessalonica, a Gothic commander of auxiliaries to the Roman army arrested a popular homosexual chariot race driver because of laws against homosexuality. There was a riot in which the Gothic officer was killed. Possibly because he feared that, unless the killing was avenged, the Goths might revolt, Theodosius had allowed them to overrun a stadium during a sporting event and, in about three hours, slaughter an estimated seven thousand people.

Ambrose, the bishop of Milan, had the courage to write to the authoritarian, irascible emperor pointing out that he should do public penance: "Listen, venerable emperor: I cannot deny that you have faith, and also fear God. But you are impetuous; if someone calms you, you become merciful, but if someone incites you, you become excitable and cannot control yourself."

As Ambrose tells the story, after a meeting with him, the emperor publicly recognized his error in a church on Christmas night. "What was more marvelous," Augustine later observed, "than the pious humility of Theodosius...who humbly did penance?" He claimed that Theodosius won more credit for his penance than from "fear of his majesty."

Augustine's strictures on the pagan Roman empire went beyond the claim that the Roman heroic ideal induced vainglory whereas the Christian invitation to humility led to conversion. He saw that the rhetorical medium shaped the message: it was not that the emperor had no clothes but that the rhetorical clothing of all public discourse was a cover-up for the empire. He was the first Christian author to recognize that a just society is impossible where information is manipulated, as happened consistently in pagan Rome, for political purposes.

This insight persuaded Augustine that true glory was not to be found in Rome's past. For him glory would be found only in the heavenly Jerusalem, the city of God: "most glorious is and will be the city of God both in this fleeting age of ours, wherever she lives by faith a stranger among infidels, and in the days when she will be established in her eternal home."

For Augustine, what he termed "the City of God" and the earthly city, the sacred and the secular, the heavenly Jerusalem and Babylon are intertwined both in individuals and society until the end of time: "Cain founded a city: Abel, however, did not found anything, as if he were always a foreigner." In fact, for Augustine the city of God is the heavens, even though it shapes citizens on earth, where it is present in a transitory way until the time of the Kingdom comes. In "city" he found a strong image, but he often used the word as a synonym for "community."

Augustine had avoided the temptation to identify the church with the state when the emperor was Christian. The Goths' sack of Rome in 410 helped him look beyond the empire and assert that Goths had the same claim as Romans to citizenship in the City of God. His massive study was influenced also by the arrival in Hippo, in the winter of 424–25, of the recently discovered relics of the first martyr Stephen. They shaped Augustine's conception of the resurrection because these bone fragments persuaded him that Stephen's powers were intact in every particle. Consequently no sliver could possibly be missing at the resurrection.

He was ever more convinced of the miracles wrought by the grace the church conveyed. It would be impossible to believe in Christianity, Augustine came to think, but for the fact that it is true:

It is incredible that Christ should have risen in his flesh, have ascended to heaven; it is incredible that the world should have believed a thing so incredible; it is incredible that men so rough and lowly, so few and unaccomplished, should have convinced the world, including men of learning, of something so incredible and have convinced men so conclusively.

It was also incredible that the synagogue continued after the advent of the Messiah. For Augustine it had to be part of God's plan, which made him disapprove the slaughter of Jews in Alexandria in 425. He argued that Jews should be free to practice their religion until their conversion, as Scripture predicted, just before the Second Coming of Christ. Until then they were a reminder for pagans and heretics of the continuity between the Old and New

Testaments, evidence of their error in rejecting the Messiah and a sign to the church that the kingdom of God was not yet fully realized.

Augustine was confident the church could survive even the fall of the empire but feared it was threatened by a refugee from Rome, Pelagius. Initially, he had respected Pelagius as an ascetic and a thinker. He had been absent from Hippo when Pelagius called on him but later sent a cordial note to the Briton. Jerome, Pelagius, and Augustine were considered the outstanding ascetics of the West to judge by the request of a Roman matron to each to write an essay on the ascetic life on the occasion of her daughter becoming a consecrated virgin.

Gradually, however, Augustine's suspicions were aroused, partly because Pelagius's zealous disciple, a Roman aristocrat called Celestius, tried to convince North Africans to abandon infant baptism on the grounds that children were innocent. This ran deeply against the grain for in third-century Carthage St. Cyprian had been a champion of infant baptism and his sermons in favor of it were in the Carthage archives. Celestius also argued that, by willing it, Christians could and should be perfect, which probably seemed to Augustine an echo of the Donatists' irritating claim to be the Church of the Perfect. The North African bishops censured Pelagianism, but Pelagius himself had moved to the Holy Land.

The more closely Augustine read Pelagius, the more pernicious he seemed. He accused Pelagius of disingenuousness, of trimming his views to the tastes of the bishops who questioned him. For the rest of his life, Augustine was to combat Pelagius and his follower Julian of Eclanum.

In a sense, Augustine and Jerome invented Pelagianism (Jerome was the first to use the term) by criticizing a renewal movement as if it were a doctrine. For their admirers, they were drawing out its implications, but for others they were willfully distorting it.

Pelagius was certainly a layman, and perhaps a monk, who professedly aimed to "think in and with the Catholic Church." Some members of the movement, such as Celestius, were more extreme than Pelagius himself, to judge from extant fragments of their writings cited by those refuting them. As often happens, the debate gave importance to issues, such as infant baptism, which to those who were criticized seemed of minor weight.

Augustine called Pelagians enemies of the grace of God because they "believe that man can fulfill all the commandments of God without it [grace]." Pelagius thought that baptism alone washed away sins (although he did not believe in inherited original sin) and enlightened the mind. He claimed that it was not difficult, certainly not impossible, for Christians to live a sinless life. He wanted to empower humans.

For Augustine, grace meant more, much more, indeed everything. Grace was necessary for faith itself and to enable humankind to love what it should do. According to Augustine, redemption is not elevation to a higher life, as Pelagius suggested, but rather the giving of Christ's life to the soul. It was not earned by humans but, instead, was absolutely gratuitous. This was to lead a long way and perhaps too far, in fact to Augustine's affirmation of predestination, for, if grace is gratuitous, those who receive it must be the elect. Augustine claimed that this was not in contradiction with free will or with the concept of a just God.

Pelagius was making a worthy attempt to shake Christians from complacency, which was perhaps inevitable as they became the majority, and also perhaps from the influence of the determinism preached by the Manichees. He told Christians that they could pull themselves up by their own bootstraps and reject sin: what they should not do was to "behave no differently from when they were good pagans." He deplored the sadism of judges who, although Christians, prescribed torture and other brutal punishments. In Rome in 405 he had heard a bishop quote Augustine: "You command continence; give what You command and command what You will." "I can't stand it!" Pelagius had exclaimed, because it seemed to him that Augustine's words justified the slothful who wanted an excuse for avoiding commitment, that they excused sexual licentiousness because total dependence on God's grace made humans irresponsible.

For Pelagius, Augustine was spreading error. After all, God had created human nature and provided the commandments: it was only a matter of obeying them and imitating the virtues exemplified in Scripture. His motto could have been: Just Do It. Augustine, however, considered virtuous living a matter of approaching a mystery and not simply a question of knowledge and will, which, by themselves, spawn stultifying pride. For him, charity and humility are needed also to receive the grace that enables moral growth.

Temperamentally, Augustine and Pelagius seem to have been opposites. Pelagius believed in the optimism of the will; he fostered a kind of moral rearmament. His message that Christians could be perfect was a short step from saying that they must be perfect. It was an attempt to define Christians more convincingly in a society where many were only nominally Christian, but Augustine was conscious that perfection is not of this world. He distrusted elite notions that could split Christians into authentic and inauthentic.

Pelagius's insistence on the freedom of human nature meant that social defects were due to the faults of individuals or, more specifically, to residual paganism and had to be removed. He was a visionary moralist, whereas Augustine was more aware of human complexity that foils sweeping claims. So confident was Pelagius about the will's capabilities that Augustine suspected he had no need for a Redeemer or grace. For Augustine, who in the *Confessions* had described the drama of the divided will, Pelagius was recounting fables. Augustine, instead, preserved a bracing tension between body and spirit. Whereas Pelagius saw human beings as wholly responsible for their actions and hence their sins, Augustine subtly pointed out that "many sins are committed through pride, but not all happen proudly;...they happen so often by ignorance, by human weakness." He was capable of acknowledging the "sheer sweetness of sinning." Augustine's awareness of human limitations made him tender with the fumbling, average Christian. He responded to Pelagius:

> A man...who indulges his incontinence within the decent bounds of marriage, who both exacts and pays the debt of the flesh and sleeps with his wife—though only with his wife!—and does so not only for the sake of bringing forth offspring, but even for sheer pleasure,...who will put up with wrongs done to him with less than complete patience, but burn with angry desire for revenge,...who guards what he possesses and gives alms, though not very generously, who does not take another's goods but defends his own in a court of law...acknowledging his own ignominy and giving glory to God would be received among the saints destined to reign with Christ.

So patient was Augustine about inner healing that he could seem to recommend a golden mediocrity.

Augustine considered Pelagius doctrinaire. While Pelagius spoke only of an ideal human being, Augustine said he was not concerned "with planning human nature but healing it." And for him freedom, another Pelagian banner, was not an absolute value but always a freedom to do something.

Whereas Pelagius was convinced that human beings could free themselves from sin, Augustine warned that suppression of one sin could lead to another that might be less obvious.

Pelagius was a hero of the straightened will, but Augustine knew the deeper issue was the orthodoxy of the heart, not what people choose but why they do so. For Augustine, the ideal was not that people force themselves to do good but that they do good for the love of it.

After a thirteen-year battle, Augustine won out, perhaps partly because of violence against Jerome's monastery attributed to the Pelagians. Pelagianism was condemned by the papacy as well as by Eastern and North African bishops. Eighteen Italian bishops refused to accept Rome's condemnation; the most talented of them, Julian of Eclanum near Benevento, took refuge in the East after he was deposed. The son of a bishop, Julian had married the daughter of another bishop. During a famine Julian had sold his aristocratic family's estates to feed the starving. He considered North African "pessimism about human beings" unsuitable for Italy and complained of Augustine's influence: Julian could have accepted his removal as a bishop but not expulsion and an attempt to end all discussion.

In response to the claim that infant baptism was necessary to avoid children going to hell, Julian said that only an unjust God would punish babies because of Adam's sin. "What kind of God" he asked, "sends tiny babies to eternal flames?" Julian considered that would offend any true Roman's sense of just government.

But for Augustine God's justice was inscrutable. And his omniscience could not be questioned. Therefore, original sin was the only explanation for the mysteries of suffering, for the "blatant misery of the human race." Sin and the Devil were powerful forces to which grace was the only adequate response. Certainly suffering was not at all proportionate to guilt, but it provided an opportunity for spiritual growth. (True to his experience in the olive-growing Thagaste region, Augustine in a sermon compared suffering to pressing olives, which produced pure golden oil).

Unlike many predecessors and contemporaries such as Jerome, Augustine, revising his earlier view, came to believe that there was sexual intercourse before the Fall. In other words, it was the result of human nature rather than of sin, although sin, by altering human beings' will, had changed the connotations of the sexual act. His affirmation that there "was no reason why there should not have been honorable marriage in paradise" made Augustine comparatively moderate on sexual matters: he called it pardonable if married couples enjoyed conjugal union without intention to procreate. Alone among the early Church Fathers, he wrote a defense of Christian marriage arguing that it was good in itself and not merely a lesser evil. This seemed an implicit response to Jerome, who tended to exalt virginity by downplaying marriage. Augustine considered consecrated virginity the superior lifestyle but insisted that no virgin could claim to be superior, a priori, to a married Christian. He wrote that every sexual act is, to a degree, self-serving, but he measured the sexual act against the wholly disinterested acceptance of martyrdom. He added that the gratification entailed was justified within marriage because it fostered the fidelity of the couple. In the *Confessions* he had suggested that the tone of sexual intercourse itself might be altered by Christian marriage. But needled by Julian, he stressed that the sexual act transmitted the post-Fall flawed human nature.

When Julian spoke of sexuality as an energy that might be used well, Augustine blustered,

> You would not have married couples restrain that evil? I refer, of course, to your favorite good. So you would have them jump into bed whenever they like, whenever they feel tickled by desire? Far be it from them to postpone this itch until bedtime: let's have your "legitimate union of bodies" whenever your "natural good" is excited. If this is the sort of married life you led [it is thought that Julian's wife was dead or in a convent], don't drag up your experience in debate.

Julian was the bane of Augustine's declining years; the nastiest controversialist had been reserved for last. Augustine was less prickly than Jerome. Sometimes from the pulpit he repeated criticism of himself without even attempting a rebuttal. But Julian made him crotchety, possibly because he had such a sharp pen or because Augustine had been a friend of his father and, indeed, had once sent him his writing on music as a gift for young Julian. When Julian wrote that Augustine's mother had been a drunkard in her youth, Augustine responded, "What has my mother done to you, you foul-mouthed fellow? Yet small wonder that you cannot bear her since you cannot bear the grace of God which enabled her to free herself from the weakness of her youth. I knew your parents as honorable Catholics. I call them fortunate in having died before they could see you as a heretic."

Julian piled on abuse after abuse. He called Augustine a Manichee, a detestable Punic Aristotle, a quarrel seeker and babbler, a slanderer and even one who used the poor's money to feed horses and then sell them to bribe officials. It inspired a poet to write:

> Against the great Augustine see him crawl
> This wretched scribbler with his pen of gall.

Julian felt Augustine's maneuvers had caused his condemnation as a heretic without a proper debate, but his polemical distortion of Augustine's arguments did not encourage a fruitful exchange. Indeed the slanging match between them has been called a dialogue of the deaf. Julian seems to have been in the tradition of those who thought sexuality could produce progeny and then be set aside, if necessary, by laity and clergy, whereas Augustine had the more dramatic view that it could affect both laity and clergy at all ages and at any moment.

There were other preoccupations in Augustine's last years: the Vandals were at the walls of Hippo, although they did not enter the city until after Augustine's death on August 28, 430. Not only had the end of the Roman empire in North Africa come more quickly than Augustine had anticipated but the conquerors were adherents of Arianism, a heresy he had combated in many ways, including his study *On the Trinity*. Emperor Valentinian II's invitation to the ecumenical council at Ephesus in 431 to discuss the dispute over the two natures of Christ between Cyril of Alexandria and Patriarch Nestorius of Constantinople arrived after Augustine's death. But that same year Pope Celestine acknowledged the church in Rome's debt to the provincial bishop: "a man of such great wisdom that he was always reckoned by our predecessors among the greatest teachers." Posthumously, Augustine had found a Roman pupil who at least paid tribute.

– IX –

AN ARIAN ALLY

THE VICTORY OVER PELAGIANISM, which had denied the need for infant baptism, was reflected in Roman churches. The baptistry of the Lateran, where formerly all baptisms were celebrated once or twice yearly by the bishop, was remodeled internally, and new baptistries began to function both inside and outside the city walls. Baptismal facilities were installed in fifth-century churches such as St. Sabina, St. Marcello al Corso, St. Vitale, St. Lorenzo in Lucina, and St. Mary Major. Baptistries were also installed in older churches such as St. Crisogono. Not only bishops but also parish priests now administered baptism.

In stone, frescoes, and mosaics, these churches reflected recent theology. The largest, St. Mary Major, completed in the 430s, celebrated the Council of Ephesus's proclamation that Mary was the Mother of God. Pope Celestine had backed Bishop Cyril of Alexandria, who wanted recognition of the popular belief that Mary was "Godbearer," even though Bishop Nestorius of Constantinople and others insisted that she was only the mother of the man Jesus Christ. One can hardly overestimate the importance of the affirmation that the personal union between the human and the divine took place in a woman's body. The murals reflected the conciliar exaltation of Mary by the prominence given to her as a prototype of redeemed humanity.

The apse mosaic of St. Pudenziana, the earliest extant figural representation in a Roman church, completed by the beginning of the fifth century, shows the apostles dressed in senatorial togas, reflecting the Christianization of Rome but also the Romanization of Christianity. Many senators were Christian, with at least one who attended Senate assemblies in his monk's habit. But the mosaic also hinted at a senatorial takeover of the church. What in its early days was considered a slave's religion had been adopted by many of the aristocracy.

86

Christianity had arrived culturally as well as socially. It had been difficult enough for pagans when opposed by Christians, such as Ambrose, who had a classical culture. But it became almost impossible for them when Christians accepted classical culture, although intentionally paring it of pagan religious significance. The Christian and classical melded.

Jerome was a case in point, and it was true also of Rome's fifth-century churches that adopted the ripest classical style, as in St. Mary Major with its double order of columns, the stucco tendrils originally in the arcade, and the airy landscapes of its murals preserved in reproductions. Classical antiquity was revived as a vehicle for the Christian message of its mosaics—the first large-scale biblical cycle extant in Rome.

From St. Costanza, with its second-century columns and capitals, to the Lateran basilica, Rome was a collage of entablatures and revetments, of marble and granite from gutted pagan buildings that were somehow transubstantiated into the body and blood of a new city. The miracle was that most of it fell into place to create a unique palimpsest.

With its golden proportions, its twenty-four sturdy Corinthian columns, its large windows, and the lettering of the dedicatory inscription, Santa Sabina was luminously serene. Yet work had begun on it about 425, only fifteen years after Alaric's invasion. It suggested that the invasion was considered a mere episode, the sort of thing that happened once every eight hundred years. And it reflected the fact that the church had emerged from the invasion better than the Senate: many aristocrats had fled but churchmen remained.

Mansions on the Coelian Hill near the Lateran began to be abandoned as people moved into the imperial monumental area in the Campus Martius and the Tiber bend, encroaching on the temples, theaters, and colonnades, some of which were quarried for new churches. In a green, spacious zone with good aqueducts nearby, St. John's was not only far from the city's civic center (the Forum) but also from St. Peter's, which was beyond the Tiber and outside the walls. As an apostolic site, St. Peter's attracted pilgrims whereas St. John's, like Constantinople, was only an imperial foundation.

An ambitious building program undertaken in the Lateran zone could have been an attempt to balance St. Peter's appeal. Or it may have been because the demands on St. John's were too great now that the majority of the population was Christian. This could explain the use of what came to be known as "stational" churches for papal ceremonies that previously had taken place solely in the Lateran. To celebrate the liturgy on certain feast days, the pope and his retinue would go in procession to other churches, such as Holy Cross in Jerusalem on Good Friday, St. Mary Major for midnight Mass at Christmas, and St. Stefano Rotondo for St. Stephen's feast day. The Lateran was the hub. These churches did not have their own clergy but were staffed from the Lateran. They probably reflected the papacy's new importance as the effective ruler of the city.

Independently of Theodosius's coercive legislation of the 390s, which may have been a disadvantage, the Catholic community in Rome rapidly gained importance in the late fourth and early fifth centuries. The laity participated in lively debates, and there was a radical ascetic movement as if there had been sufficient time since Constantine for intellectual and spiritual maturation.

Election of Leo in 440 meant a new level of leadership for what he called

> a holy people, an elect nation, a priestly and royal city, become, through the see of Peter established here, the head of the world; ruling more widely now through divine religion than it ever did by worldly dominion. Though enlarged by many victories, you have spread the authority of your rule over land and sea. What your warlike labors have obtained for you is less than what Christian peace has brought you.

Probably born in Rome of Tuscan parents, Leo had a rare combination of talents: Roman to the core in his legal understanding of his office, he also recognized the missionary potential of the empire:

> The empire grew to frontiers which made it everywhere the closest neighbor of all peoples. For this it was adapted by divine decree to the work of redemption: that through the unity of many lands with one Imperium, the universal proclamation had access to the peoples which stood under the direction of one city.

His sermons and letters show he was a skilled communicator. The sermons stressed the need for anonymous almsgiving in contrast to the self-promoting pagan philanthropy that benefited only citizens rather than going, as did Christian donations, to all the needy. He associated almsgiving with fasting and special collection days, which he contrasted with the days on which pagans had worshiped "their demons."

Some pagan festivals, such as that for the winter solstice, had been reinterpreted but others remained even if distant from their religious origins. The Christian liturgical calendar had consisted initially of Easter and Sundays, but then a cycle had been built around Christmas and days began to be assigned to martyrs whose cult increased rapidly when persecution ended to show the continuity of the church despite its more comfortable circumstances. Leo wanted to knit the faithful into a Time that was sacred, a salvation history that was all contemporary.

He called church paintings the Bible of the Poor (i.e., the illiterate) and is believed to have planned the magnificent mosaics of St. Mary Major and to have been responsible for biblical-cycle paintings in St. Peter's, St. Paul's-Outside-the-Walls, and St. John Lateran. He had influenced his predecessors Celestine (422–32) and Sixtus III (432–40). In 436 he dissuaded Sixtus from rehabilitating Augustine's opponent, the Pelagian Julian of Eclanum, to his bishopric unless there was full proof of his orthodoxy. He was an experienced negotiator.

Although Leo made greater claims than ever before for the papacy and gave them a new basis by asserting that the other apostles received their power through Peter, his tact won extensive collaboration. Damasus had stressed that the church in Rome was not simply an Eastern import but had local roots. He coined the term "Apostolic See," underlining that Peter and Paul were its foundation, and maintained its importance was due to divine will rather than to conciliar decisions. He called other bishops "sons." The full implications emerged only when his successor Siricius (384–99) began to use the title "pope" meaning "Father." Innocent (401–17) claimed all major disputes had to be decided by Rome, and Boniface (418–22) added that there could be no appeal against its judgment.

Siricius had spoken of the pope as Peter's heir, which Leo interpreted in Roman legal terms, deducing that each heir has all the rights and duties of Peter, his function, authority, and privileges. In Leo's view, he was not so much successor to Siricius as to Peter. He contrasted Peter and Paul to the founders of pagan Rome, Romulus and Remus, underlining that one of the twins, Romulus, had killed the other. Even after his death in 461 he kept close to Peter by being buried, the first pope to choose the site, in St. Peter's basilica.

As more power had been entrusted to Peter than to other apostles, Leo argued, the pope had more power than other bishops. He was the "primate of all the bishops." Leo felt he had a duty to preserve true doctrine throughout the whole church and ensure also its morals and discipline.

His claims were mitigated by his affirmation that although Peter was preeminent, all bishops shared in the church's pastoral care. In other words, all bishops were equal in dignity but not in rank. And he was so judicious that hierarchies in Western countries readily accepted his judgments, although he met opposition in the East. He settled disputes between bishops in northern Italy and ensured their practices were uniform; he advised Spanish bishops how to combat a revival of the Priscillianist heresy; even the North African episcopate, jealous of its autonomy, recognized his rulings on irregularities. By observing those who took the consecrated bread but refused the consecrated wine at Communion, he identified Manichees (who never drank wine) among his flock. Many had fled to Rome from the Vandals, who had crossed the Straits of Gibraltar in 429 and a decade later took Carthage. At Leo's behest, civil authorities revived penal sanctions against them. Leo attacked Pelagianism. When a bishop of Arles began acting as if independent of Rome, Leo obtained from Valentinian III, emperor of the West, a rescript recognizing papal jurisdiction over the entire West.

Of course, Rome was the only apostolic see in the West whereas there was more than one in the East. On the election of Dioscorus in Alexandria, Leo wrote congratulating him and suggested that their relationship should be like that between Peter and Mark, that is, teacher and pupil. But Dioscorus did not recognize any special position for Rome. And Emperor Theodosius II spoke simply of "Patriarch Leo." In 448 Leo received an appeal from a monk Eutyches, who had been deposed by Bishop Flavian of Constantinople for teaching that Christ's human nature had been absorbed by his divine nature. Leo wrote an important letter affirming that

Christ had two distinct and complete natures united in one person. However, a synod held at Ephesus in 449 spurned his letter, endorsed Eutyches' views, and condemned Flavian. One of Leo's legates, the Sardinian Hilary, who was to be his successor, escaped alive from the synod only because he hid in John the Evangelist's burial chamber outside the city walls.

Two years later the fourth general council was held at Chalcedon on the Bosphorus. This time Leo's letter, based partly on Augustine's writing on the personal union of Christ's two natures, was heard, and in it the delegates recognized "the voice of Peter." It was a decisive recognition of Rome's doctrinal authority and culminated a development begun 125 years earlier at the Council of Nicaea, which had affirmed that Christ was divine, and continued when in 381 the Council of Constantinople added that he was also fully human. For decades debate had raged about the relationship of Christ's natures. At Chalcedon, there was a decisive advance because it affirmed that in the one person of Christ the divine and human natures were neither confused nor separated.

Rome's satisfaction at the acknowledgment of its doctrinal prestige was offset by the council's declaration that Constantinople had patriarchal status like Rome as they were both imperial cities. The council wrote to Leo that the "devout and Christ-loving emperor" had ratified his judgment on the Christological question, implying that he should accept, in a sort of fair exchange, Constantinople's patriarchal status as second only to that of Rome. The letter added that, although Leo's delegates had "vehemently resisted" the proposal, his wisdom would ensure its acceptance. It was similar to the deal proposed after the Council of Constantinople in 381, and once more Rome rejected it; indeed Leo's reaction was the fifth-century equivalent of "Fiddlesticks!" He delayed endorsement of the council's decisions, and did so only after declaring invalid the canon regarding Constantinople's patriarchal status.

The Huns must have been the most fearsome of all barbarians to judge from the hostile descriptions of them. Ammianus Marcellinus said that the Huns, who exceeded "every degree of savagery," originated near Lake Azov, and their cheeks were incised with the result that, like eunuchs, they aged without beards. "They are squat, robust with thick necks, and something in their build inspires fear. . . . Their habits are almost bestial. They eat the roots of wild plants and the flesh of the first animal they find, which they cure while riding by keeping it under their thighs." Ammianus claimed also that they spurned houses as if they were tombs, stank so badly that it frightened animals, ate and slept in the saddle and attacked enemies without any order while emitting bloodcurdling screams.

Perhaps they inspired acute fear because, unlike other barbarian peoples who settled once they found good land, the Huns settled for a time but resumed marauding when Attila became their leader. Known as "the scourge of God," they were such fleet, hardy, ruthless warriors that they struck terror even into other barbarians, some of whom collaborated with the empire's forces against them. Yet Honoria, the sister of Emperor Valentinian III, sent her ring to Attila offering to become his wife. An envoy from Constantinople to Attila formed a different impression from that of Ammianus Marcellinus. He found a punctilious etiquette at meals, where each guest was attended by a waiter who poured his drink into a golden chalice. The guests' bedrooms had multicolored drapes.

Attila, swarthy, stocky, broad-shouldered, with a flattened nose and sparse beard, had informers even among Emperor Theodosius's collaborators. In 452 he conquered Aquileia, where even today some still search the river Natissa for treasure hidden at that time. The invaders then overran one town after another in the Po valley: Padua, Vicenza, Verona, Brescia, Bergamo, Milan, and Pavia. But near Mantua Pope Leo and a delegation from Rome convinced Attila to withdraw; his death the following year ended the Hun threat.

Leo was now Rome's sole protector but, four years later, he failed to stop Gaiseric, who had brought his Vandals from North Africa, outside the city walls. The Vandals blackened their faces and shields before their attacks made always at night, which contributed to their fearsome reputation. Leo obtained a promise, which was honored, that they would respect the major basilicas and refrain from arson, rape, and massacre. For two weeks they looted and, according to some accounts, took the golden treasure of Solomon's Temple, which Emperor Titus had brought from Jerusalem, and half the bronze, gold-plated roof from the Temple of Jupiter on the Capitoline hill.

Barbarian forces constituted a constant threat to Rome and, moreover, were promoting Arianism. The Suevian chieftain Ricimer, who backed an Arian bishop in Rome, established an Arian church, St. Agatha of the Goths, which still stands on the Viminal Hill. When Pope Hilary heard that Ricimer's successor might approve meeting places in Rome for Arians, he confronted the barbarian chieftain in St. Peter's and convinced him to desist.

In 476 the military commander Odoacer, chieftain of a Germanic tribe in imperial pay, deposed the last Roman emperor of the West, youthful Romulus, nicknamed Augustulus (the Little Emperor). Romulus, who had been put in power by Attila's former secretary, was pensioned off in a villa near Naples. The church of Rome had outlasted the Western empire and claimed the succession, but an Arian, Odoacer, was in control of Italy. Accepting that only a Roman could wear the purple, Odoacer returned the imperial insignia to Constantinople and contented himself with the mere title of Patrician but effective power. He preserved the imperial administration and established good relations with both the church in Rome and the Senate.

Indeed the popes of this period found it easier to reach an understanding with Arian barbarians than with co-religionists in the East. Felix II (483–92) was the first pope to announce his election to the emperor in Constantinople, but he was involved in a bitter dispute with him over renewed claims that, instead of being true man and true God, Christ had only one nature. Felix told the emperor to keep his nose out of church affairs. His intransigence, and excommunication of the patriarch of Constantinople in 484, caused a thirty-five-year-long schism between East and West.

His successor, Gelasius, of North African origin, was even more unyielding than Felix in his relations with the East, which caused concern in Rome. Although personally humble and generous, his pronouncements seemed arrogant. He was the first pope to be saluted as "vicar of Christ." He wrote to Emperor Anastasius that the two powers governing the world were the consecrated authority of bishops found in the pope and the emperor's royal power, but the greater was papal authority as it enabled the salvation of the temporal.

Theodosius I, who made Christianity the state religion in 394, had been sovereign of the whole Roman empire, but on his death it was divided between his sons Arcadius, seventeen, who commanded the East Roman Empire, and Honorius, ten, who was to rule the West. The empire was split administratively and there was a deepening linguistic gap between its two sectors. Rome itself was losing contact with its bilingual classical tradition, which had aided understanding between the Eastern and Western churches. Gelasius employed Dionysius, a monk from Dacia (corresponding roughly to present-day Romania) whom he had met in Constantinople, to translate from Greek into Latin doctrinal debates and hagiographic and philosophic works. Shortly before Emperor Justinian in Constantinople issued his new codification of Roman law, Dionysius published a collection of canons and decretals that became the basis of ecclesiastical law. Although Romans called Dionysius "Exiguus," the Small, he made a large contribution to the calculation of dates and, therefore, of Easter.

Gelasius successfully clamped down on the surviving pagan feast of Lupercalia in which half-naked youths ran through Roman streets striking women with strips of the skin of sacrificed dogs or goats to prevent barrenness. The participation of Christians had been tolerated by Gelasius's predecessors. But unlike those Christians who participated, Gelasius did not consider it an innocent tradition. He was denying there was a neutral ground of civic traditions between Christians and pagans where the faithful and non-Christians could frolic. Indeed, he blamed Rome's misfortunes on such surviving "vain superstitions." He was involved in a dispute with a senator who said Gelasius should discipline unworthy clerics: there were senators who aspired to speak for the emperor as supervisors of the church.

Emperor Zeno in Constantinople decided to kill two birds with one stone: the Ostrogoths who settled within the empire in the Balkans were a potential threat while the loyalty of Odoacer's regime was dubious. Zeno sent the Ostrogoths to fight Odoacer.

Being caught between the Roman empire and the advancing Huns forced the Goths to become more cohesive. Theodoric, who was recognized as leader by all the Ostrogoths, was born in the Danube province as son of the chieftain Thiudmir. As a hostage for his people, he had spent his youth in Constantinople. At Zeno's behest, he led an estimated hundred thousand Goths, of whom about a fifth were warriors, to Italy, where for three years he besieged Odoacer in Ravenna. Finally Odoacer agreed to share power. At a banquet held to celebrate the agreement, Theodoric sunk his knife into Odoacer, remarking that "it seems this pig's boneless." That murder removed any possibility of disagreement between them.

At the beginning of the fifth century Alaric, a Visigoth, had attempted something similar to the exploit of the Ostrogoth Theodoric: to lead his people from the east of the empire to Italy; but he had not managed to settle them there. Theodoric, combining military prowess with treachery and diplomacy, had more success. Because he was the leader of an army approved by the emperor, Theodoric was a *princeps romanus* and respected Roman traditions. Moreover, he was an Arian who respected Catholics (his wife was Catholic, the daughter—or sister—of the Frankish King Clovis). He had good relations with Pope Gelasius and did not interfere with the Catholic Church any more than with secular institutions. He was shaping a religiously and ethnically pluralistic state.

As Theodoric himself said, "A poor Roman plays the Goth and a rich Goth the Roman." Although Theodoric warned that the Germanic Ostrogoths might lose their warrior virtues if they fraternized with the locals, their leaders seem to have assimilated to the aristocracy while their rank and file became one with the peasantry. Theodoric recommended that Roman monuments, such as the palaces on the Palatine Hill, be preserved. He admired Roman law, learning, and ordered government and the quintessential Roman institution, the Senate, whose good will was important for land reform as it included many big landowners. The Goths were given a third of all farmland in return for their military services when required. Bishop Emmodius of Pavia, an aristocrat well-disposed toward the Gothic newcomers, praised Senator Symmachus, who had negotiated this settlement program for "having enriched the countless hordes of Goths with generous land grants yet Romans have hardly felt it." In effect, they had arranged for the Goths to do much of their farming and fighting. The Goths and the indigenous people got along famously in contrast to the nastiness between the Vandals and the inhabitants of North Africa.

Although it had become merely a municipal body, the Senate had great traditions, and its members still had great wealth and connections. The renowned Anicii family, for instance, had intermarried with the imperial family in Constantinople, had bishop relatives, and owned huge estates in Gaul, North Africa, and Spain as well as in the Italian peninsula. Theodoric forced the Senate to admit some new men, including Goths, from the administrative capital, Ravenna, but in return he embellished its meeting place, the Curia in the Forum, and restored after centuries its right to mint coins.

It is not surprising then that when in 500, the seventh year of his reign, Theodoric visited Rome, senators praised him in Ciceronian periods for military victories that they asserted were in the Roman tradition. Pope Symmachus, a Sardinian who had been born a pagan, and his clergy prayed with the Arian at St. Peter's tomb. The populace enjoyed the free food and circus games that marked such occasions and, indeed, they had reason to rejoice because Theodoric had brought a new period of peace and prosperity. Fulgentius, a monk from North Africa who was in Rome at this time, commented: "How wonderful must be the heavenly Jerusalem, if this earthly city can shine so."

A description in a history that appeared in the East about the same time listed statistics about Rome with awe: "[it] has 24 churches of the blessed apostles. It contains two great halls where the king sits and the senators are assembled before him every day. ... It contains 324 great and spacious streets, ... 80 golden gods, 64 ivory gods."

Rome could awe the East just as it dazzled a North African visitor: aqueducts still marched majestically across the countryside, bringing water for public baths. Although gladiatorial contests had been abolished, there were wrestling matches and wild beast shows in the Coliseum; chariots still raced in the Circus Maximus, and indeed Constantinople's leading charioteer, Thomas, had transferred recently to Rome. Literary meetings still took place in that wonder of the ancient world, Trajan's Forum; in the main Forum people still swapped gossip and bought slaves; there was a curator for the palaces on the Palatine, and the churches, which look huge even today, must have made a strong impact in a city that now had perhaps few more than a tenth of its former million inhabitants. Several churches were comparatively new. For instance, St. Peter-in-Chains, built with money given by Empress Eudoxia to house the chains that supposedly had bound Peter during imprisonment in Jerusalem and Rome, had been completed about 440.

Although Rome made Fulgentius think of paradise, it could also sadden those aware of its past glories. The abandoned mansions and the ruins standing amid fields and vineyards showed the city had shrunk. Many buildings were shabby and dilapidated. In 459 spoliation was approved for buildings "beyond repair," which encouraged relentless pilfering. Classical architectural elements were reused in this period as can be seen, for instance, in the columns with elaborate capitals of the east basilica of St. Lawrence-Outside-the-Walls.

Little money was available for maintenance. At a closer look, the aqueducts marching across the countryside proved to be limping: they needed repair as did the sewers. Public granaries collapsed; marble revetments fell from walls. Theodoric's chancellor Cassiodorus recorded attempts to repair some buildings but admitted that much had been abandoned to "spoliation and ruin" and that at night the eerie sound of looters tapping bronze statues could be heard (there were an estimated four thousand public statues in Rome).

Theodoric's rule extended beyond Italy to southern Gaul, part of what is now Austria, and into the Balkans while marriage alliances gave him influence also with the Vandals and Visigoths. The king of the Franks, Clovis, was on the verge of marrying Theodoric's sister (but did not do so) and one of his sisters (some historians say she was instead a daughter) married Theodoric. Theodoric was forging a Germanic-Latin realm that was also Arian-Catholic: the Danube was to flow with the Tiber. He was drawn into the feud between Pope Symmachus and the archpriest Lawrence over which had the right to be bishop of Rome but eventually referred the matter to a synod. He was not anxious to interfere in the church's doctrinal or disciplinary affairs and even approved a mission by Emmodius, later bishop of Pavia, to the emperor.

It was said that Theodoric could not spell and even had to stencil his signature, which may have been an exaggeration as he had grown up in Constantinople. But collaborators such as the cultured Catholic laymen Cassiodorus and Boethius were invaluable in countering prejudices against his regime as barbaric and ignorant.

Cassiodorus belonged to the fourth generation of a family of high public officials with the same name. They were Calabrian landowners who, among other things, supplied horses for the Gothic army. They continued the traditions of the great imperial families who had an ideal of public service. Late in his life Cassiodorus was known simply as The Senator. His father had been a high official under Odoacer but switched his allegiance to the victorious Theodoric. The future senator was raised at the court of

Theodoric in Ravenna and, at the age of twenty-one, delivered a fervent panegyric about "our Lord Theodoric." He never looked back. He became Theodoric's chancellor, wearing a knee-length woolen cloak dyed in purple, which prompted him to compare himself to Joseph at the court of the Pharaohs. As he aimed at harmony between the Goths and the indigenous people, he tirelessly presented Theodoric as heir to the Roman tradition.

The philosopher Manlius Anicius Boethius, a member of the prominent Anicii family, was a formidable scholar with perfect Greek whose translations of, and commentaries on, Aristotle influenced medieval philosophy. He has been called "the last of the Romans and the first of the scholastics" and "schoolmaster of the West." He wrote textbooks on arithmetic and music as well as commentaries on Cicero.

Because of the early death of his father, he was brought up in the household of the city prefect Symmachus, a descendant of the senator of the same name who had clashed with Ambrose over removal of the Statue of Victory from the Senate. The city prefect was a Catholic, and Boethius married his daughter Rusticana. He was versatile: Theodoric commissioned him to construct a water clock for Guidobad, king of the Burgundians, and invited him to become a lyre player for Clovis. Boethius said that he entered public life in accordance with Plato's dictum that states would be happy when philosophers ruled or their rulers turned philosophers.

Theodoric benefited from the protracted tension between Constantinople and Rome over the Chalcedonian declaration on Christ's nature. If Constantinople and Rome found an accord, Constantinople might then send an army against the Arian leader. In 517 Emperor Anastasius wrote resentfully to Pope Hormisdas, who was adamant about maintaining the Chalcedonian position: "It is absurd to show that courtesy of prayer to those [meaning Hormisdas] who, with arrogance in their mouth, refuse to be entreated. We can endure insults and contempt, but we cannot commit ourselves to be commanded." The stand-off between Rome and Constantinople continued.

The situation changed, however, the following year when Anastasius died and his successor, Justin, an illiterate, Latin-speaking guardsman from Illyria, described by a contemporary as "stupid as a donkey," endorsed the Chalcedonian conclusions, as did his influential nephew Justinian. Justin and the new patriarch wrote to the pope that they wanted peace and invited a papal delegation to Constantinople. The welcome papal legates received along the Via Egnatia from Durazzo to Constantinople made it the world's longest triumphal route. Justin not only accepted the church of Rome's teaching but gave it stacks of bullion. Rome had won all along the line: at least temporarily, its break with Constantinople was healed.

– X –

RECONQUEST

RESTORED HARMONY between Rome and Constantinople was bad news for the Arian Theodoric. Moreover his son-in-law King Sigismund of Burgundy had accepted the Catholic faith, while in North Africa Hunneric, the son of a Roman noblewoman and grandson of Emperor Valentinian III, on succession to the throne ended, if only temporarily, the Vandal persecution of Catholics.

Following the agreement between Constantinople and Rome, Arians began to be persecuted in the East while in Rome, Ravenna, and Verona synagogues were burnt. Theodoric had the perpetrators flogged and a Catholic church in Verona destroyed; non-Goths were disarmed and the martial heirlooms of great Roman families were confiscated. The understanding between the Goths and the locals, as well as the Goths' respectful relations with the church of Rome and the Roman Senate, were brusquely broken.

Informers told Theodoric that the Senate leader Albinus had been plotting against him with Constantinople "to maintain the integrity of the Senate and restore liberty to Rome." Albinus was arrested and the Senate president Boethius was summoned to Theodoric's capital, Ravenna. Echoing Seneca, Boethius told Theodoric, "Even if I had known of a conspiracy, you would not have known."

It was a proud but inopportune quotation. Now seventy and feeling threatened, Theodoric arrested Boethius and reverted to his earlier ruthlessness. In his prison cell Boethius wrote *The Consolation of Philosophy*, which grapples with problems of fate and free will, good and evil but does not mention Christ or Christianity nor refer explicitly to the Bible; he maintained that philosophical reflection is sufficient to lead to knowledge of God. Boethius's father-in-law, Symmachus, rushed to Ravenna to plead for him, but he too was arrested. In prison, "calm as Cato," he wrote a history of Rome. Boethius was bludgeoned to death and Symmachus was executed; it would be many centuries before philosophy revived in Rome. Moreover the Senate lost whatever prestige it retained because it cravenly approved the sentence. (In 1883 Leo XIII beatified Boethius.)

In 523 newly elected Pope John, a Tuscan, angered Theodoric by demanding for Catholic use the Arian churches in Rome. Two years later Theodoric summoned aged, frail John to Ravenna and gave him an impossible mission—to tell Emperor Justin in Constantinople to bring back to Arianism those who had undergone forced conversions. John promised only to promote peace between the emperor and Theodoric. He sailed to Corinth where he had to borrow a horse to reach Constantinople, the first pope to do so. At twelve miles from the city, he was welcomed by Emperor Justin and his officials. He celebrated Easter in full imperial splendor and then crowned Justin. It was not quite what Theodoric had in mind.

A month later, probably recalling the bludgeoning of his close friend Boethius, John arrived back in Ravenna. He was thrown into prison, where he died. As his body was transported to Rome, along the route he was hailed as a saint and martyr. During his burial, senators tore pieces from his vestments as relics. At a banquet three months later, Theodoric took fright when served a large fish. The historian Procopius explains that Theodoric saw it as Symmachus newly slain: "Indeed, with its teeth set in its lower lip and its eyes looking at him with a grim and insane stare, it greatly resembled a threatening fate." Shortly afterward, Theodoric collapsed from a stroke and died: Romans would not have been surprised.

His mausoleum on the outskirts of Ravenna, built before his death in 526, is a compact structure of Istrian limestone whose dome is a 240-ton single slab. Gently curved, it gives the impression both of a crown and a nomadic people's tent, which is appropriate for a barbarian king. Imposing without being pompous, it is nearly fifty feet high and thirty-three in diameter. It is decorated by medallions with the names of the evangelists and apostles and, at its base has a frieze of pliers that were used to shut the Goths' tents. Beneath a stucco cross on the interior of the cupola is a porphyry sarcophagus, but there is no trace of Theodoric. German sagas recount that a devil-mounted black horse took

Theodoric from Ravenna to dump him in the crater of Stromboli. It is more likely that the Goths took his remains with them when later they fled from the Byzantine victors.

Theodoric's daughter Amalasuntha, a Catholic and the most pro-Roman of the Goths, became regent. She gave Felix IV, whose pro-Gothic tendencies may have helped his election, permission to convert public buildings into churches. One in the Forum became the Church of Cosmas and Damian, two Arabian physicians martyred under Diocletian, which reflected the new popularity of Eastern saints. It also meant that, two centuries after Constantine and under Gothic patronage, a church finally stood on the pagan Sacred Way at the center of the city. Its apse mosaic has the earliest papal portrait (of Felix) by a contemporary, but it may have been altered during restoration. Felix's good relations with Amalasuntha and her charge, dissolute Athlaric, probably accounted for an edict that civil or criminal charges against the clergy should be tried by the pope. Many Roman clergy opposed Felix's pro-Gothic policy and that of his successor, Boniface. Born in Rome of a Germanic father, Boniface was the first pope of barbaric origin, which may have accounted for his strong Gothic sympathies.

In 533 Justinian, who had succeeded Justin as emperor and was to reign for forty-seven years, found a pretext to invade North Africa. The Thracian general in charge of the expedition, Belisarius, was a brilliant strategist. Defeats and lack of manpower had convinced the imperial army to avoid frontal clashes, except when it had superior numbers, and use instead flanking attacks by cavalry units in which every man was an archer. With less than twenty thousand men Belisarius overthrew the Vandals, acquiring a fleet and booty that may have included the treasure of the Temple of Solomon removed from Rome by Gaiseric.

After seeing in 1996 on the Arch of Titus in the Roman Forum a depiction of the menorah, a seven-branched candlestick, among other sacred objects pillaged by Romans from the Jerusalem Temple, the Israeli Minister for Religious Affairs, Shimon Shitrit, asked John Paul II to institute a search of Vatican storerooms for this symbol of Judaism and Israel, reputedly made of 150 pounds of pure hammered gold. Shitrit claimed there was evidence that the menorah was in the Vatican; if so, Belisarius may be credited with retrieving it from the Vandals.

The murder of Amalasuntha on an island in Lake Bolsena

in 555 gave Justinian a further pretext, this time to invade the Italian peninsula. It has been suggested that Empress Theodora, suspecting that Amalasuntha had designs on Justinian, persuaded Theobadat to kill her. Knowing that the Goths would never accept a queen, Amalasuntha had decided to rule together with her cousin Theobadat. As he was an avaricious misogynist whose only ambition seemed to be to extend his Tuscan estates, she gave him a large allowance and hoped to rule in his name. Among the Goths he was a sport, a pusillanimous scholar who justified all Theodoric's fears about enervating Italian influences. He devoted all his time to philosophy, particularly Plato.

Justinian was on the verge of reestablishing the authority of Constantinople in the West because Belisarius's advance was delayed only by a three-week siege of Naples. Once again, as at the time of Constantine some two hundred years before, an army was marching on Rome led by a dashing young commander. Constantine had descended from the north; Belisarius was coming from the south. Both had the cross as the portent of their success.

Theobadat sued for peace. "From my earliest years" he wrote, "I have been passionately addicted to scholarly discussions to which I have devoted all my time. Consequently until now I have been far removed from the confusion of war. It is therefore absurd for me to aspire to honors that royalty confers and to lead a life fraught with danger, when I can avoid both."

Pope Agapitus, an aged, infirm aristocrat who was summoned to Constantinople to negotiate a settlement, had to pawn church plate to pay for his trip. In Constantinople he was forced to confirm Theodora's appointment of a suspect patriarch, Anthemus, but there were no concessions in exchange from Justinian, who hinted that the pope might be spending his remaining years in exile. "Instead of the Most Christian Emperor Justinian," Agapitus complained, "I have found Diocletian." Agapitus summoned the courage to condemn Anthemus for Monophysitism. He returned to Rome in a lead coffin; he had died in Constantinople before Justinian could carry out his threats.

Once news of Agapitus's death reached Rome, Theobadat bullied the Roman clergy into electing Silverius although he was only a subdeacon; to elect a subdeacon as pope was unprecedented. He was the son of Pope Hormisdas, whose reign had ended only thirteen years before. The clergy resented Theobadat's pressure for a pro-Gothic pope but finally accepted Silverius for the sake of unity against yet another threat.

Empress Theodora, who did not accept the Council of Chalcedon's affirmation of the personal union between Christ's two natures, had promised the nuncio in Constantinople, Vigilius, that she would have him elected pope if he ensured the rehabilitation of Anthemus as patriarch of Constantinople. As a result, the Roman clergy wanted at all costs to foil Vigilius: in fact, by the time he reached Rome, Silverius had been consecrated pope and had no intention of stepping down.

This made for a tense situation in December 536, when Belisarius occupied Rome without opposition because the Goths had withdrawn to regroup further north. Before leaving, Theobadat had summoned the pope, clergy, and populace to harangue them on the gratitude they owed him. However, the Goths themselves were less than grateful, for as they retreated a General Vitges dragged Theobadat from his horse and slit his throat. Vitges then returned to besiege Rome. He cut all its aqueducts; it was to be just over a thousand years before they again brought water to the city, which in the meantime had to depend on the Tiber.

Silverius was summoned to Belisarius's headquarters on the Pincian Hill, where the commander produced forged letters to prove that the pope had planned to open the city gates to Vitges. Belisarius demanded that Silverius recognize Anthemus as patriarch of Constantinople, but he refused even though forecasting that it would cost him his life. Belisarius deposed Silverius on March 11, 537, and deported him to an Anatolian seaport. However the local bishop protested to Justinian that, although there were many rulers, there was only one pope, who ruled the whole world. Justinian sent Silverius back to Rome for a fair trial; if found innocent, he was to be reinstated.

But there was already another pope: Vigilius. Boniface had nominated him as his successor and then, after protests, had revoked the decision. Empress Theodora had promised to make him pope but Silverius had beaten him to the post. He had allied himself with the Goths and the Byzantines, with Arians and Monophysites, and now that, at long last, he was pope, Silverius reappeared. To Vigilius it must have seemed altogether too much that Silverius should want a fair trial. Vigilius had Belisarius arrest Silverius and then dispatched him to the island of Palmera in the Gulf of

Gaeta, where, on November 11, 537, probably under duress, he abdicated. The following month he died from his hardships.

Initially the Byzantine army had surprisingly swift success in Italy as it had in North Africa. This may have convinced Constantinople that the war would end rapidly, but the Goths rediscovered their warrior vocation and in Vitges had a fierce, energetic commander. As the war dragged on, the Byzantines had to fight on two fronts, as they were also pitted against the Persians. They switched troops between the two theaters of war according to need, and they brought some devastating plagues to Italy.

The resurgent Goths besieged and blockaded Rome, wakening atavistic instincts: some aged senators tried to open the doors of the temple of Janus, as had always been done during wars in Republican times. But the hinges would not turn. The Sibylline Books were consulted and mistakenly foretold that the siege would soon be raised. All able-bodied Romans were pressed into sentry duty, and the old were evacuated to the south. The Goths made several assaults in which they almost carried the day. In one of these, they came close to taking Hadrian's mausoleum, which was incorporated into the city wall. Under the cover of archers who rained crossfire on the defenders, infantry began climbing up scaling ladders. The Romans' arrows and darts bounced off the assailants' armor. In this desperate situation, a defender smashed a marble statue on the ramparts and hurled fragments at the Goths. As others joined in, the assailants were forced to retreat under a hail of marble feet, biceps, buttocks, and breasts.

After this setback, the Goths spent such a long time licking their wounds that Belisarius took the offensive. In response, Vitges arrested and executed all senators not in Rome; only Pope Vigilius's brother and another senator escaped to Milan.

Vigilius had retrieved some of his honor by refusing to recognize Anthemus as patriarch of Constantinople. "Although unworthy" he said, and it would have been hard to disagree, "I am the vicar of the blessed apostle Peter as were my predecessors Agapitus and Silverius, who condemned him [Anthemus]." He composed prayers expressing Romans' fear and suffering at a time when food was so scarce that baggage mules were being made into sausages. Then bubonic plague was added to starvation. But a Hun garrison stationed near St. Paul's downstream ensured a route to the sea, through which reinforcements arrived, enabling Belisarius to bring pressure on the Goth besiegers. After fourteen months, Vitges was forced to lift the siege and withdraw to Ravenna.

As it seemed that the Byzantine forces had the upper hand, Belisarius was sent to the Persian front, which remained Constantinople's major preoccupation. The Byzantine commanders who remained were disliked. The army's financial administrator, nicknamed "Clipper" from his practice of shaving the rim off coins, also saved on the troops' rations; they, in turn, looted wherever they could. The ministrations of the Most Catholic Emperor's agents inspired nostalgia for the Arian realm but also fostered an Italian consciousness, whereas previously the inhabitants of the peninsula tended to think of themselves as members of the Roman empire with its capital in Constantinople.

An anecdote illustrates this disquiet: before leaving Rome, Theobadat was supposed to have asked a Jewish sorcerer how the combat against the Byzantines would finish. The Jew put in pens three groups of ten pigs labeled respectively Greeks (Byzantines), Goths, and Romans. After ten days all the Goths were dead, half the Romans were dead and the remainder had lost their bristles, but few of the Greeks suffered.

An insight into the situation is provided by Belisarius's secretary and legal adviser, Procopius, who became the major historian of Justinian's reign. Procopius wrote the history of the wars of Justinian and Belisarius but also another, secret history which, as it was libelous, could only be published after their deaths. Procopius did not live to see its publication, however, for it seems that he died in the same year (565) as Belisarius and Justinian, who was eighty-two. The "Secret History" is a scurrilous account of the Byzantine quartet: Justinian and Theodora, Belisarius and his wife, Antonina. It has the venom of disappointment—Procopius became disillusioned with the cost of the Byzantine Reconquest and with his hero, Belisarius, perhaps because he did not displace Justinian despite the emperor's ingratitude. Procopius attributed Belisarius's shortcomings to his wife, Antonina, whom he berated as a prostitute before marriage and promiscuous after it. Her ally in abominations and iniquity, according to Procopius, was the Empress Theodora. For him they were both prostitutes on the make.

Procopius not only accused Theodora of abortions, infanticide, and other vices but also claimed she "destroyed the Roman empire root and branch." He admitted Justinian was accessible and affable but undercut this praise by claiming he dissembled. He condemned the couple as contemptible, greedy, arrogant, blood-thirsty, and concerned with their own aggrandizement rather than the empire's good. Because Justinian made exalted claims for himself as God's instrument, disillusioned Procopius saw him as possessed by the devil. His attack is so extreme and, at times, self-contradictory that it loses credibility even if there was a basis to it: Theodora, born in Cyprus, had been a promiscuous actress, but Byzantines liked to think of her as a Mary Magdalene. Procopius's comments on policy, however, deserve attention. He claimed that Justinian the lawgiver was a capricious law-breaker and that his ecclesiastical policy was bad for both church and empire: "They [Justinian and Theodora] began by creating a division between the Christians and, by pretending to take opposite sides in religious disputes, split the whole body in two. Then they kept the factions at loggerheads."

He mistakenly attributed this to duplicity and malice rather than conviction (in the 1960s a grateful Monophysite bishop wrote a play praising Theodora's defense of the faith), but it shows Procopius was sensitive to the disruptive effect of imperial religious policy. As a tolerant, commonsensical Christian, Procopius was aware of the dangers of Justinian's authoritarian approach, for he had an unprecedented inclination to decide doctrinal issues himself without reference to church authority.

"Under the pretext of piety," Procopius charged, "Justinian did not think that putting men to death counted as murder unless they were of his own persuasion." And further: "I will not even record the points of disagreement [between Constantinople and Rome] on doctrine, since I think it crazy folly to enquire what is the real nature of God. Humans cannot even understand human things fully, let alone what pertains to God's nature. I can say nothing about God except that He is totally good and has everything within his power."

Procopius claimed that Antonina was responsible for Belisarius deposing Silverius. As is attested by an exterior plaque, the small Church of Santa Maria in Trivia or dei Crocefissi in the square behind the Trevi fountain in Rome was originally a hospice founded by Belisarius as penance for exiling Silverius.

Procopius had direct experience of what was involved in the

Reconquest, which had begun so auspiciously. He was in Rome during the first Gothic siege, which lasted over a year, and described the Romans as reduced to eating nettles after boiling them to stop their pricking. When there were no more nettles, dogs, or mice to eat, some Romans took their own lives. Procopius describes a Roman surrounded by his five children all pulling at his clothes and begging for food. Calmly he asked them to follow him. On arrival at a bridge over the Tiber, he covered his eyes with part of his clothes and threw himself to death.

Roman suffering reached a new intensity once the Goths chose Totila as leader. In 542 he swept down the peninsula, winning battles in the open countryside and avoiding cities such as Rome. He wrote to the Senate saying it had misled inhabitants by propagating a false conception of the empire: he was reiterating the Theodoric-Cassiodorus argument that the Goths preserved Roman traditions. The Byzantines intercepted the letter, but Totila had copies of it stuck on the city walls. He had a point, but Roman disaffection with the Byzantines did not necessarily make them supporters of the Goths. They were more inclined to wish a plague on both the armies that were destroying their city and countryside.

Despite this nightmare atmosphere, in April 544 a literary-religious event suggested Rome was Arcadia. A subdeacon named Avator, imprisoned by the Goths, had vowed that, if they did not cut off his hands, he would versify the Acts of the Apostles. They did not, and he fulfilled his vow. He recited his composition in St. Peter's on April 6, 554, and repeated the performance some days later in St. Peter-in-Chains, but so many encores were demanded that he took three days to read it all. It was a reminder of happier days when the upper clergy, like some senators, had leisure to cultivate literary interests.

Totila captured Tivoli, in the hills behind Rome, murdering all the inhabitants including its bishop. On imperial orders Vigilius was arrested while celebrating Mass on November 22, 545. He was put on a ship bound for Sicily and, as it sailed down the Tiber, Romans who credited the rumor that he was a multiple murderer yelled, "Good riddance and take the plague with you." From Sicily, Vigilius sent to Rome a convoy of grain ships under Bishop Valentine of Silva Candida and a Roman priest who was to take charge of ecclesiastical affairs in his absence. The ships were captured, and Bishop Valentine was taken to Totila, who ordered that his hands be chopped off.

Although anything on four legs was being killed for food in Rome, the Byzantine commander Besas refused inhabitants permission to leave. "It was impossible to feed the inhabitants," said Besas, who had immense riches stored away, "unsafe to release them, and, as they were the emperor's subjects, unlawful to kill them." Nevertheless he sold exit permits to the rich.

Boethius's widow, Rusticana, used her fortune to help the needy as did a deacon Pelagius (not to be confused with the adversary of Jerome and Augustine), who was chosen by the Romans to lead a delegation to Totila. The Goth rejected the pleas to preserve the city walls and spare Sicily, which supplied much of Rome's food, but he was impressed by Pelagius.

Belisarius returned from the Persian front, but it was too late to break the blockade. A city gate was treacherously opened and Totila entered Rome, where few had survived. Some, such as Besas, the Byzantine commander, fled to churches; several senators sought refuge in St. Peter's, where soldiers slaughtered eighty people before Pelagius, who as vicar for the absent Vigilius, convinced Totila to make them desist. Totila threatened that Roman aristocrats would become beggars. In fact, Rusticana, who had helped the needy, was seen begging. Recent discoveries suggest that, at this time, some Romans withdrew into the Colosseum, making it a residential fortress. The ground floor became a stable, the arches above were closed-up to provide living space, there were internal vegetable gardens and even a cemetery.

Pelagius was sent to Constantinople with Totila's terms for peace and the threat that, if they were not accepted, Rome would be reduced to a cow pasture.

Late in 546 Totila had to leave for Apulia, and Belisarius, who had been confined to Rome's port, immediately occupied the virtually empty city. Totila wanted to marry a Frankish princess, who taunted him that he could not be king until acknowledged as such by the Romans. He rushed back to Rome, besieged it again and, when once more Belisarius was recalled for urgent tasks in the East, occupied it.

Totila slaughtered many of the remaining inhabitants and then brought the surviving senators back and told them to rebuild their precious city. He staged circus games, the last to be held.

Perhaps he heeded the words Belisarius had addressed to him: "[Rome] remains a monument to the virtues of the world. Destroying Rome, you will lose not the city of another but your own. Preserving her, you will enrich yourself with the world's most splendid possession."

In 551 the Byzantine forces returned to the attack under aged, squint-eyed, dwarfish Narses, an Armenian eunuch who had commanded the imperial city guard before fighting Vitges. Narses's troops marched through the Balkans into Italy. Totila, confident after a decade of victories against the Byzantines, went to face them but was routed by the cavalry of a huge army that included Hun and Persian units. Resistance dragged on for two years, largely because Franks came to the Goths' aid. But defeated by heat and plague, they succeeded only in destroying the countryside. The seventeen-year war had destroyed not only the Gothic kingdom, but much of the Italian peninsula.

– XI –

THE FOUR HORSEMEN
RIDE THROUGH ROME

THERE WAS MORE CAUSE for rejoicing in Constantinople than in Rome over the demise of the Goths. Emperor Justinian could pride himself on reestablishing the Roman empire in the West, for he had ousted the Vandals from North Africa, annexed part of Visigoth Spain, and crushed the Gothic kingdom. But it had taken unconscionably longer than had seemed likely when Belisarius swept through North Africa and then advanced on Rome. In the meantime, Rome had been devastated; the aristocracy had all but disappeared, while secular institutions and learning had collapsed.

The church in Rome was also in difficulty. The emperor had cowed Pope Vigilius, who had been brought from Sicily to Constantinople. Justinian had condemned writings known as *The Three Chapters,* which were extracts from the works of three theologians who, as a whole, were in line with the Chalcedonian position on Christology. Justinian probably believed that the condemnation would gain him the support of many Monophysites in the East, but this was not the case. It did, however, cause a protracted division between East and West. Justinian demanded that Pope Vigilius endorse his anathema, as he did after initial resistance and with a rider that Chalcedon remained valid.

Despite the rider, indignation in the West was so intense that he withdrew his verdict but gave a secret written assurance to Justinian that he would obtain condemnation of *The Three Chapters.* However, when Justinian again condemned *The Three Chapters* in an edict of 551, Vigilius, who was still in Constantinople, called for withdrawal of the edict and then sought sanctuary in a church. Justinian's police assailed him at the altar, and he was put under house arrest. He fled across the Bosphorus and, at Chalcedon

111

itself, found refuge appropriately in the church where the council had taken place. Justinian summoned a council on the issue, but Vigilius, who claimed Western representation was inadequate, refused to attend; Justinian scuttled him by revealing the pope's secret undertaking to ensure condemnation of *The Three Chapters.* Obediently the council condemned them.

Now Justinian wanted complete submission from Vigilius, who was obviously a weak man in a thorny situation. Pelagius, who had become nuncio, was thrown into prison while Vigilius was again put under house arrest. After six months' isolation, Vigilius succumbed and endorsed the council's anathema. "Do with me as you will," he said. "I'm receiving the reward for my deeds."

He was free to return to Rome but, as his behavior ensured a hostile reception, he stayed in Constantinople for a year until Justinian issued his *Pragmatic Sanction,* which, after seventy-eight years of barbarian dominion, officially reestablished imperial rule over Italy. It ensured rights and privileges to the church whose leader Justinian had crushed. The Arian Church was suppressed and the Catholic Church took its property. But Justinian obviously expected to influence church doctrine.

Justinian wanted Rome, which he had never visited, restored to its former glory. He had, one of his officials said, "given back to Rome all its privileges"—provided the Romans paid for them. But Rome was a shambles, and its inhabitants could not rebuild it. Despite Justinian's avowals, he left Rome weak, which was yet another pointer to his failure to reestablish the empire in anything but name. Soon it was to be invaded by the Lombards from the north and the Saracens from the south.

One aristocrat, a stubborn survivor, decided to start all over again in his native Calabria. He had been born twenty years after the death of Leo the Great, had begun to work for Theodoric at the age of twenty, and had served his successors, even Theobadat, who was suspected of having murdered Theodoric's daughter Amalasuntha, and Vitges, who had ordered the murder of Theobadat. Probably because some considered him a traitor for his collaboration with the Goths, Cassiodorus had spent years in Constantinople before returning to his native region.

After thirty years at the Gothic court he had seen his hopes of Romanizing the Goths, to form a durable Roman-Gothic realm, destroyed along with the remnants of senatorial Rome, and the emergence of what he called, the first writer to do so regularly, the "modern" age. But he had a still earlier project: establishment of the first academy for Christian theology in the West, where theological education lagged behind that of the East. In 538 Cassiodorus had urged Pope Agapitus to "collect subscriptions and have Christian rather than secular schools in Rome." Agapitus, an aristocrat who had a library of the Church Fathers in his family mansion on the Coelian Hill (the remains of which still stand), welcomed the suggestion and provided books and a reading room in what is now the nearby Church of Sts. John and Paul, but war halted the project. After the demise of the Goths, Cassiodorus had revived it by establishing a monastery called Vivarium (Fishpond) on his family estate in Calabria.

Its library, built up at great expense, gave an honored place to secular literature and not only to religious books: it was a center of Christian humanism. Cassiodorus collected patristic writings and prepared a reliable scriptural text of the first Latin Bible in one volume: "Satan receives many wounds," he wrote, "as the words of Christ are copied." The copying preserved some condemned texts, such as those of Pelagius. Cassiodorus insisted that his monks be skilled in bookbinding and that they study three linguistic disciplines as well as four mathematical sciences, arithmetic, geometry, music, and astronomy, which later became the basis for the study programs of cathedral schools and then universities.

Cassiodorus was one of the first Christian encyclopedists, with interests ranging from natural sciences to music, from producing fine wines to breeding fish to ensure a regular supply and writing a commentary on the Psalms. He instructed his monks in a sixth-century form of word processing and the last of his many books, written three years before his death at the age of ninety-six, was a kind of spell-check manual: it was aimed to ensure that copiers did not make mistakes such as confusing "m" with "n" or "f" with "h." His monastery was an intellectual powerhouse: later the Benedictines were to have a similar commitment to culture.

With indomitable spirit, Cassiodorus built for the future, but in Rome myriad problems threatened to narrow the church's horizon. Vigilius, who had died in Syracuse, was succeeded by the emperor's nominee, Pelagius. Because of his closeness to Vigilius, many Western bishops were suspicious of Pelagius, and much of northern Italy became schismatic over the *Three Chapters* issue.

On his election, Pelagius took the unusual step of affirming his loyalty to the first four general councils (those of Nicaea, Constantinople, Ephesus, and Chalcedon). Moreover, because he was suspected of complicity in Vigilius's death, in St. Peter's he swore to his innocence, holding aloft the Gospels and the cross.

The church's income had been drastically reduced by the prolonged war. For example, in the late fifth century its annual revenues from holdings in the central Italian province Picenum were 2,160 soldi, but by the time of Pope Pelagius this figure had fallen to 500 soldi. Immediately after his election, Pelagius had written to the bishop of Arles asking aid, "for Italian fields have been so ravaged no one can restore them." (People were reduced to competing with pigs for acorns, and there were reports of cannibalism). In 561, Pelagius requested food aid from Boethius, son of the philosopher, who was prefect of North Africa.

Pelagius refused to be "depressed by a failing world." With the help of a lay banker, he put papal finances on a sounder basis and increased the efficiency of papal farms in Italy, Gaul, North Africa, and Dalmatia. He recovered much of the church plate that had been dispersed. He ransomed prisoners of war, campaigned against simony, encouraged monasticism, and recruited clergy whose ranks had been depleted. In impoverished, dilapidated Rome he even built on the site of the Julian basilica a huge church, now known as the Holy Apostles, to honor Narses's victory over the Goths. It was modeled on Justinian's Apostoleion: Was Rome to be the second Constantinople?

At least it indicated that Rome was not to become, as Totila had threatened, a cow pasture. But then the dread news arrived that yet another horde of barbarians was on the march. In 558 Germanic Lombards overran much of north Italy. They took Milan, the main city of a region that was to take its name from them, overran the rich Po valley, and later established themselves in central-southern Italy in the duchies of Spoleto and Benevento. The tall, fair herdsmen had left northern Germany many years before but had arrived most recently from the plain between Italy and what is now Hungary. "They shaved their necks," wrote their historian Paul the Deacon, "and left them bare up to the back of their heads while their hair was parted from the forehead and hung down as far as the mouth. Their garments were loose and mainly linen, such as the Anglo-Saxons wear, decorated with broad borders woven in various colors. Their boots were open almost to the tip of the big toe and were tied by crossed laces. But later they began to wear trousers, over which they put waterproof woolen leggings when they rode."

A Roman delegation complained to Emperor Justin II, who had succeeded Justinian, that they preferred Gothic slavery to living under the extortionist eunuch Narses. Before going mad, Justin dismissed Narses, who retired to a villa near Naples. An enemy recommended that he return to spinning thread as eunuchs did in the women's quarters of the Constantinople palace.

But Pope John III pleaded with the eighty-year-old general to defend Rome from the Lombards. On his return to Rome, Narses lived in the imperial palace close to the church (the Holy Apostles) built to honor his victories. The pope's initiative was so unpopular that he himself had to take up residence in a church on the Appian Way outside the city walls.

As Rome was being besieged by the Lombards when Pelagius II, the son of a Goth named Unigold, was elected in 579 he was consecrated without awaiting the emperor's ratification and immediately dispatched a deacon, Gregory, to Constantinople to request aid, although with scarce results. Next he vainly sought help from the Franks, but in 586 the Byzantine emperor's representative (exarch) in Ravenna reached an armistice with the Lombards.

Pelagius II energetically restored Roman churches. He placed the high altar of St. Peter's directly over the Apostle's shrine and tomb with an inscription asking him to defend the city. He even reconstructed St. Lawrence-Outside-the-Walls, where on the triumphal arch the pope is portrayed in a contemporary mosaic. The reconstruction, which enabled St. Lawrence's grave to be more readily seen, could have induced pilgrims to return to Rome, but this hope was crushed by terrible events. The Lombards broke the armistice, and in Rome one calamity followed another as an eyewitness recounted in a letter to Bishop Gregory of Tours:

Last November [588] the Tiber flooded and destroyed ancient buildings and the church's granaries. Thousands of bushels of wheat were lost. Then followed an epidemic called *inguinaria* [bubonic plague]: it broke out in the middle of January and first of all attacked Pope Pelagius, who quickly died of it, and many followed him.

Rome was prostrate. It seemed the Four Horsemen of the Apocalypse, war, famine, plague, and flood, were riding roughshod over it. "With our own eyes," one Roman recounted, "we saw arrows shoot from heaven and fell people one by one." He described dead cattle and dragons, probably water snakes, being swept along by the tumultuous Tiber. This witness was to work so effectively in restoring the fortunes of the city that "the Great" was added to his name Gregory.

– XII –

CAPTAIN OF A
SHATTERED SHIP

O N GREGORY'S ELECTION Rome was shaken by the effects
of war, flood, plague, and famine. On his death it was afflicted by famine, plague, flood, and war. He had wanted
only to be a secluded monk, but his fourteen-year pontificate had
to face one calamity after another. He reorganized the church's
agricultural holdings to feed Romans but died with them cursing
him as responsible for their starvation. He believed that the end of
the world was nigh but worked as if laying the foundations of a new
Rome. To the best ancient Roman qualities of just administration
and prudent management he added the art of the guidance of souls.
Because he combined firmness and fairness, juridical precision and
moderation like an ideal consul, his epitaph called him the Consul
of God, but he also found a language suitable for those unfamiliar
with the traditions of classical Rome. He was a loyal subject of the
emperor, who nevertheless prepared the ground for Rome to break
with Constantinople. He had been nuncio in Constantinople, yet
perhaps his most momentous initiative was to send missionaries
to the Anglo-Saxons at the other end of the known world.

Author of a commentary on the Book of Job, at times he seemed
its protagonist, not only because of the many social crises he faced
but also because of chronic illness. Frequently in pain from one
ailment or another, Gregory spent long periods in bed, but rarely
interrupted his work. It has been suggested that rigorous fasting
ruined his health, but the cause may have been partly psycho-
somatic as he had been obliged to return to the public life he had
abandoned for contemplation. Constant stress must have taken its
toll: he noted that when the Lombard chief Astolf was "killing and
beheading at the gates of Rome . . . I was seized by such melancholy
that I fell into a bilious fever."

For someone who ate frugally it seems odd that, in his last years, he suffered gout. Perhaps it was due to the resinous wine he imported from Alexandria in the belief that it aided his poor digestion. He suffered frequent bowel pains, debility, and a recurrent fever.

Occasionally he was waspish as if his sufferings had got the better of him. He could give pithy rejoinders: when the emperor accused him of being a fool for crediting Lombard peace proposals, he agreed that he must be one to endure what he did. He admitted to enjoying small talk: "Because I too am a weak creature, being slowly drawn into the talk, I soon find myself enjoying the gossip to which I first lent an unwilling ear—and end by wallowing where I had first dreaded to fall."

Gregory's ninth-century biographer John the Deacon described him as of medium height with a slightly aquiline nose and swarthy complexion. He was balding, had a tawny beard, hair over his ears, and two curls in the middle of a high forehead. Gregory felt his appearance was so unprepossessing that people might smile at the contrast between it and his high office. He called himself an ape forced to play the role of a lion.

He was born about 540 into a Roman patrician family that had supplied civil administrators, a tradition he continued by becoming governor of Rome. The great-great-grandson of Pope Felix II, he was related also to Pope Agapitus. During his schooling he was able to take advantage of the library established by Agapitus near Gregory's family home on the Coelian Hill. Gregory's father, Gordianus, was a notary. On his death, his wife, Silvia, retired to a monastery near St. Paul's. Two of Gregory's aunts founded a convent and asked their sister Gordiania to join them there, but instead she eloped with the bailiff of the family estates.

Following his father's death, Gregory abandoned his post as governor of Rome, gave the family estates in Tivoli and Sicily to the church, and lived with friends as a monk in a monastery, St. Andrew's, which he founded in his family home. He also established six monasteries in Sicily. But after four years Pope Benedict, convinced Gregory's experience was needed, made him his deacon, or senior administrator, of socio-charitable work. The following year, 579, Pope Pelagius II sent him as papal representative to Constantinople.

Pelagius, who had occupied the post himself, said that it did not allow one to ever spend "more than an hour at a time away from the emperor's palace." On one occasion, in the emperor's presence, Gregory debated with Patriarch Eutychius, who argued that after the resurrection the bodies of the saved would be "impalpable and more subtle than wind or air." The strain on them was such that, on leaving the meeting, both Gregory and Eutychius collapsed. Feverish Gregory was gravely ill. The emperor decided in Gregory's favor and had Eutychius's books burnt. Before dying shortly afterward, Eutychius recoiled from a future in which he would be subtler than air and accepted Gregory's more orthodox view of the resurrection.

Gregory had not been sent to Constantinople to debate theology but mainly to plead for help against the aggressive Lombards. In October 584 Pelagius wrote him:

> So great are the calamities and tribulations we suffer from the perfidy of the Lombards despite their solemn promises that no one could adequately describe them.... The territory around Rome is completely undefended.... May God bid the emperor to come to our aid with all speed.

However, Gregory found the emperor more concerned with the traditional enemy, the Persians. The emperor advised the Romans to bribe the Lombards or to seek an alliance with the Franks. In fact, later, as pope, Gregory was to buy off the Lombards with a gift of five hundred pounds of gold; the emperor's cool reply might have also spurred him to look later for new allies in the West.

He was sponsor at the baptism of Theodosius, the son of Emperor Maurice. His friendship with members of the imperial family and leading generals survived subsequent Rome-Constantinople tensions. But Gregory remained convinced of the superiority of Rome, even though it seemed in irreversible decline in contrast to Constantinople, which was still powerful. From Rome he was to write to Boethius's granddaughter Rusticana, who had gone to Constantinople and did not want to return: "I cannot understand how anyone can be so entranced with Constantinople and so forgetful of Rome." He learned no Greek in Constantinople but acquired a taste for resinous wine.

After seven years there he returned to Rome and the monastic life but on Pelagius's death in 590 was elected its bishop. His rigorous lifestyle, theological competence, eloquence, and administrative experience would have been in his favor. He wrote to his friend the emperor Maurice begging him to withhold his consent, but the pope-elect's brother intercepted the letter. "I have taken charge," Gregory said, "of an old and grievously shattered ship."

He was to look back longingly to his years at the monastery of St. Andrew: "Now I have to bear with secular business and, after so fair a vision of rest, am fouled with worldly dust.... When I recall my former life, I sigh as one who looks back and gazes on the shore he has left behind." Again he wrote: "I have lost the deep joy of my quiet, and while I seem outwardly to have risen, I am inwardly falling.... I have fallen into fear and trembling for, though I dread nothing for myself, I am greatly afraid for those who are committed to my care."

The signs were everywhere and the signs were terrible. "As the end of the world approaches," wrote Gregory, "many unprecedented disasters occur: war, famine, plague, earthquakes." And he added: "Behold all the things of this world, which we heard from the Bible are doomed to perish, we now see destroyed. Cities are overthrown, fortresses are razed, churches are devastated, and tillers of the soil no longer inhabit our land."

The portents of the imminent end were patent in Rome itself, which had been terrified by the Lombards, ravaged by bubonic plague, and submerged by flood.

> See to what straits Rome, once mistress of the world, is reduced, worn down by her great and ceaseless sorrows, by the loss of her citizens, by the assault of the enemy, by the frequency of ruin.... Were not Rome's dukes and princes lions who scoured the world's provinces and by violence and murder seized their prey? It is here that the young lions had their feeding place, for hither children, youths, young worldlings hastened from all parts of the world to make their fortunes.... The eagle has lost all its feathers; it is completely bald.

Gregory sounded a doleful note but acted resourcefully, convinced that, if the end was nigh, there must be first a "great gathering in of souls." Although there were many refugees from the Lombards in Rome, including three thousand nuns, the population had dwindled to about ninety thousand. One of the scourges first felt at that time was conquered only in the 1920s: the fields, which were no longer drained, turned into swamps where malarial mosquitoes bred, making Rome a summertime deathtrap.

Gregory ordered forty processions through the empty streets of Rome: as the participants begged God's help against the plague and other afflictions, some fell dying. As one procession approached St. Peter's, Gregory saw the Archangel Michael on the top of Emperor Hadrian's mausoleum, sheathing his sword. The plague ceased, and a chapel was built where Gregory had seen Michael alight. The vision is commemorated in the building's name, Castel Sant'Angelo, and by a statue of the archangel atop it.

Interestingly enough, while restoring some Roman churches, Gregory built only one. He reorganized papal landholdings not only in mainland Italy (where the pope was the largest landholder), Sicily, Sardinia, and Corsica but also in Gaul, Dalmatia, and North Africa. He appointed efficient but humane farm managers directly responsible to him and insisted on meticulous bookkeeping. There are hints that predecessors such as Gelasius were also good managers, but detailed evidence exits only for Gregory.

One of his earliest biographers wrote that he "tenderly provided for the needs of all," whether the daughter of a patrician who had become a monk but then left to marry or an itinerant organ grinder with his monkey. "On the first day of every month" a chronicler recorded:

> he distributed to the poor in general that part of the church's revenue paid in kind. So, in its season, corn, and in their several seasons, wine, cheese, vegetables, bacon, meat, fish, and oil were with the greatest discretion doled out by this father of the Lord's table.... Moreover every day he sent couriers with cooked provisions to the sick and infirm in the streets. For those of high rank who were ashamed to be seen, he sent food to their homes, a dish from his own table as a present of St. Peter.

(Gregory accepted social hierarchy and the institution of slavery: more than once, to express gratitude, he gave people slaves. Most Christians wanted slaves treated fairly; they had an equal standing in liturgical rites but slavery itself, which was often a form of bonded labor, was accepted as a fact of life).

Food distribution was part of church assumption of what had been the responsibilities of the civil administration. A more striking example was that, at times, Gregory was also paymaster for the imperial army. Because the aristocracy was depleted and dispersed and the imperial provincial government weak, the pope, like bishops elsewhere in the Western empire, played an ever more prominent secular role. The last Latin-speaking emperor, Justinian, made bishops the overseers of local government, obliging them to report law infringements by imperial officials and bring people's complaints to the emperor. They had to supervise the treatment of prisoners, orphans, foundlings, and the mentally ill, civic expenditure, aqueduct management, public order, and the victualing of troops.

Gregory recommended dialogue between church authorities and the faithful: "Those who govern should freely say what they see to be true.... In their speech superiors should practice humble authority, and inferiors free humility." He considered himself not only *servus servorum Dei,* a servant of the servants of the Lord, or, to use another of his phrases, of the "people of God," but was also in constant dialogue with them. He acknowledged that he could learn from any of the faithful.

"If my audience or reader, who certainly can understand the sense of the Word of God in a profounder and truer way than I, does not like my interpretation, I will follow him tranquilly as a disciple follows his master," wrote Gregory. "I consider as a gift the things which he understands or feels better than I." The crucial issue, according to Gregory, was that both teachers and community "proceed with humility because the more one is full of truth, the more one realizes that one cannot understand the word of God alone."

He appealed to civil authorities for aid against the Donatists who survived in North Africa. This may explain why he referred to heresy as "the hot wind from the south," a description that brings to mind the enervating scirocco wind from the Sahara that to this day makes Romans edgy. He approved employment of troops against schismatics in Istria because he was convinced their motive was pride rather than conviction. He had little success against them or the Donatists.

He tried to convert Jews by persuasion rather than force. Judaism was permitted and its synagogues protected, but Jews were not allowed to make converts or marry non-Jews, own Christian slaves, hold public office, leave bequests, build new synagogues, or circumcise their slaves. But for Gregory Judaism had more of a future than classical Rome, which he depicted, using an image from Ezekiel, as close to collapse. He recalled a biblical prophecy that eventually the Jews would accept Christ: "It will be a feast precisely because in fully accepting Christ as a man, aware of his membership of their race, they will take pleasure in his divinity."

Gregory was the first monk to be pope, and some of Rome's clergy may have decided that he should also be the last. When elected, Gregory brought with him his family of fellow monks including Peter, his friend from schooldays; Aemilius, who took down Gregory's sermons in shorthand; Marinianus, whom he made bishop of Ravenna, which was the seat of the Byzantine governor (exarch) and which at times aspired to ecclesiastical autonomy; Maximianus, who was made bishop of Syracuse; Probas, who was sent to supervise building of a pilgrim hostel in Jerusalem; and Augustine, not be confused with the bishop of Hippo.

The monks formed a close-knit team of collaborators who took over many functions, such as administration of estates, formerly entrusted to clergy, who consequently lost considerable power and money. Some of the clergy must have resented the fact that monks, despite their unworldly vocation, had taken the levers of power. The clergy had a strong team spirit strengthened by the fact that, after the prolonged war, only the church offered career prospects. Their collective identity was reinforced by collegial decision making and customs such as excluding all non-Romans from ordination ceremonies. Among their jealously guarded privileges were the use of white, fringed, ceremonial saddlecloths, white stockings, and black slippers, all taken over from the Senate. Disgraced clergy were stripped of these privileges.

Gregory also broke the influence in the Lateran chancery of clerics in minor orders, who continued living with their families, and also that of prominent laymen. He wanted to free his administration from outside influences. Another measure probably designed to reduce careerism was abolition of the office of archdeacon. The archdeacon had been the previous popes' main administrative assistant, theological advisor, and likeliest successor. Instead, Gregory appointed a deputy known as videdominus, and, for the following two centuries there was no archdeacon. A Roman clergy backlash against Gregory was not surprising.

In September 591 in the Lateran the archdeacon Laurentius,

who had been passed over in favor of the younger Gregory in the papal election, was deposed for "pride and other crimes," which probably meant he had not accepted Gregory's extensive reshaping of the papal court.

As a shrewd administrator Gregory knew the importance of finding the right personnel and intervened successfully in the election of bishops in key Italian sees but had less success with Dalmatia and North Africa, which guarded their autonomy. He welcomed the conversion of the Spanish Visigoth kingdom from Arianism to the Catholic faith but had little contact with Spain. He collaborated with ruthless Queen Brunhild in a largely unsuccessful reform of the lax Gallic church.

Gregory found relations with Constantinople difficult despite his seven years there and the good will he had won on election by declaring his allegiance to the first four councils, which he had compared daringly to the four Gospels. He considered the patriarch of Constantinople's adoption of the title "ecumenical patriarch" arrogant and contrasted it with his own conception of the pope as "servant of the servants of the Lord." Gregory took "ecumenical patriarch" to mean worldwide patriarch, which he felt challenged papal prerogatives. "Those appointed to be generals in humility are raising the stiff neck of pride," he complained, seeing this as a presage of the Antichrist. He expected the patriarchs of Alexandria and Antioch to sympathize with him, but the patriarch of Alexandria thought that Gregory wanted the title for himself while Anastasius of Antioch warned him against "pride and envy." This answer stung, Gregory confessed, "like a bee." Emperor Maurice warned Gregory that he was making a mountain out of a molehill. The issue was unresolved at Gregory's death; the title is still used, implying the patriarch's concern for Orthodox communities in Western Europe, the Americas, Australia, and elsewhere.

In 593 Emperor Maurice, to stop the drain of talent from the civil service and army, decreed that no public servant could exchange his post for an ecclesiastical office or retire to a monastery, nor could soldiers become monks until their term of service was completed. Evidently when duties were too onerous, public servants and soldiers were finding a way out.

Gregory promulgated the ruling but told the emperor that it was unjust:

Christ answers through me, the lowest of his servants, and yours, "I advanced you from being a notary to be captain of your guards, from captain of the guards to be Caesar [commander of the army], from Caesar to be emperor, yes, and more than this, I have also made you the father of emperors. I have committed my priests to your charge, and you now withdraw your soldiers from my service." Reply, I pray you most pious lord; tell your servant what answer you will make to your Lord when he comes and addresses you on Judgment Day. I have transmitted this law to various countries. I have also informed my most serene sovereigns that the law is certainly not in accordance with the will of God.

Rather than send his letter through his representative in Constantinople, Gregory used the emperor's physician as a go-between. After long negotiation, the emperor changed the law. Public servants could be received into monasteries if officially released from their duties, and soldiers could be admitted after a careful enquiry into their previous life and a three-year novitiate.

Surprisingly Gregory congratulated the coarse centurion Phocas more effusively than was usual when he became emperor after his men had butchered Maurice's four younger sons before the emperor's eyes and then beheaded him. His eldest son, Theodosius, Gregory's godson and co-emperor, was executed shortly afterward. The news of the bloodshed may have confirmed Gregory's preference for troubled Rome over Constantinople.

– XIII –

New Angles

G REGORY admired a monk, who had died about the time he was born, whose combination of spiritual depth, sensible management, and responsiveness to new needs marked also his pontificate. The monk who became his model was St. Benedict. Gregory wrote his first biography and also encouraged the spread of Benedictine monasticism.

Benedict, born in Norcia, Umbria, about 480 in a well-to-do family, had studied in Rome but, reacting against the worldliness of other students, withdrew to live as a hermit in Subiaco. About 525 he moved to Monte Cassino to found a monastery, where he died some twenty years later. The monastic movement, which began in Egypt in the early fourth century, had acquired a Western form both with Augustine and a monk from Dacia, John Cassian, but Benedict gave it a further ordering through practical, balanced guidelines (the Rule). The aim was an orderly life built around work, study, and communal prayer.

In contrast to others, his Rule was not harsh: there were to be no hair shirts, scourgings, or starvation regimes. Monks followed a vegetarian diet but were allowed wine. They had warm clothes and bedding, shoes and stockings, and eight hours unbroken sleep daily. Humility and obedience to their abbot were exalted in a chaste, sober life during which monks were expected to remain attached to one monastery. The Rule countered the undervaluation of work by pagan Rome, where the ultra-rich were attended by a horde of parasites who were sopped-off with bread and circuses while slaves did the work. In contrast, monasteries were communities of equals where all worked under their elected leader (abbot). This work had three aspects: manual labor for sustenance, study to enable the monks to read devotional texts, and, most important of all, God's work (*opus Dei*), communal prayer: the liturgy. Monks gathered eight times daily to pray and chant together. Their communities were miniature cities, prefigurations of a society in which all activities would have a Christian focus. In a time of widespread anarchy Benedict went back to basics, insisting on the essentials for community through sharing (poverty) and cohesion (obedience) within a group modeled on a Gospel-guided family. What began simply as a method to enable Italians and Goths to live orderly, pious lives was adopted by many monasteries and shaped a religious order (the Benedictines) renowned for its learning and for rebuilding civilization after the barbarian invasion.

It was more difficult to sustain life than when the empire was at its height. In the five centuries since the second century A.D., the population of the empire is estimated to have decreased a third from forty-five million. There is no agreement about the causes, whether climatic change, plague, warfare, or a combination of these and other factors, but a consequence was weaker defenses and greater insecurity. The philosopher Alisdair MacIntyre sees parallels between the contemporary situation and Benedict's era when people ceased to "identify the continuation of civility and moral community with the maintenance of that [Roman] *imperium.*" As an alternative they constructed "new forms of community within which the moral life could be sustained so that both morality and civility might survive the coming ages of barbarism and darkness."

Gregory praised Benedict as "knowingly ignorant and wisely unlearned," a description that, in a way, applied to himself. Although heir to the scholarly culture of predecessors such as Gelasius, he recognized the need for something different in a world in which frequent calamities had induced chronic insecurity. As people felt the need of miraculous aid, Gregory presented near-contemporary holy men as heroes, pointing out that they were more efficacious than pagan shamans, who were still influential, particularly in the countryside.

Gregory rejected the strict rhetorical rules that Jerome, for instance, had respected, adopting a humble style in colloquial language. The balanced antitheses, the poise and polish of classical prose had suggested an imperturbable order, which by now had been broken. Scripture favored the changed approach, for it seemed to sacrifice style for message or, rather, had many styles outside the mold, the rhetorical rules that facilitated expression but also limited it. By Gregory's time the classical models were hackneyed. His abandonment of sophisticated style to speak directly to those unfamiliar with the high tradition was successful: his homilies, lectures, and *Dialogues* circulated widely. *Dialogues* is set in a garden where Gregory, weary with the cares of office, meets his old friend Peter. Gregory tells Peter of the saints who had lived in the Italian peninsula in the preceding century as if to convince him that God had not abandoned it. Some stories are based on Gregory's personal experience; for others he gathered written testimonies, but most derive from oral tradition. "To remove all occasions for doubt," he wrote, "in every passage I will give my authorities clearly."

They differ from martyrs' stories because their heroes do not die for the faith but live for it in a constant, if sometimes hidden, struggle against evil. Each episode has its point. For instance, that regarding an Arian Goth, Zalla, in the time of Totila, shows that those who serve God with great fidelity, sometimes "achieve prodigies" by the power God gives them. At other times, Gregory added, they do so by prayer.

Zalla, Gregory recounts, "persecuted Catholics with incredible cruelty": any cleric or monk who fell into his hands was killed. One day, driven by desire for gain, he tortured a peasant. Exhausted by his suffering, the peasant swore he had assigned himself and all his goods to the servant of God Benedict, hoping that his torturer would desist. Zalla tied the peasant's arms and pushed him forward in front of his horse: the trussed victim led Zalla to the monastery where Benedict was seated, reading. "With crazed and perverse" intention, Zalla shouted at Benedict, "Stand up! Give back the wealth you took from this peasant." As Benedict raised his eyes from his text to look at the Goth and the peasant, the prodigy occurred: "The cords were loosened more quickly than any man could have done it." When the previously crouching peasant was entirely free, Zalla took fright, jumped to the ground, and, bowing his head, begged Benedict's prayers. Benedict did not interrupt his reading but called a monk, ordering him to take Zalla inside and set a table for him. When Zalla returned, Benedict told him to desist from such cruelty. "Moving away humiliated, the Goth no longer dared ask anything of the peasant whom the man of God had liberated not with arms but merely with his glance." Gregory's account of the Zalla episode in his *Dialogues* was relevant to seventh-century conditions in which landowners still treated peasants cruelly.

Gregory's *Pastoral Care* was a seminal handbook for bishops. He had deplored the worldliness of some bishops, their abuse of power, their greed, their desire for praise and gossip. In *Pastoral Care* he proposed an ideal bishop but also looked at candidates' motives. It shaped a Western episcopate concerned with pastoral care more than theological speculation. Although Gregory described his writing as a mere "despicable trickle" compared to the "deep torrents" of Ambrose and Augustine, it made accessible complex theology in a variety of forms which not only influenced his contemporaries but also others throughout the Middle Ages.

Even though Gregory mourned the decline of Rome, he was alert to new possibilities. For him, history was not steady progress, which was disproved by Roman ruins, but a spiritual deepening as the salvation story unfolded. Consequently monks should not simply preserve what was precious from the ravages of the new peoples and restore the destroyed countryside but had to emulate the early apostolic community by taking the Good News to outsiders.

On September 10, 595, Gregory commissioned the purchase in Gaul of slaves from the British Isles so that they could be educated in Rome, perhaps with a view to future missionary activity. It suggests that there may be a basis to a tradition recorded by Bede:

> Before he [Gregory] became pope, there came to Rome certain people of our nation, fair-skinned and light-haired. When he heard of their arrival he was eager to see them; being prompted by a fortunate intuition, being puzzled by their new and unusual appearance, and, above all, being inspired by God, he received them and asked what race they belonged to....They answered "the people we belong to are called Angles." "Angels of God," he replied. Then he asked further, "What is the name of the king of that people?" They said "Aeli," whereupon he said, "Alleluia, God's praise must be heard there."

However, there are also pointers that Anglo-Saxon Christianity was not founded simply on a pun but because of a request for missionaries from the Anglo-Saxons, who did not want to accept the faith from either hostile Britons or the Franks. Whatever the case, sending forty of his fellow monks to the British Isles was one of Gregory's most fruitful initiatives. Bede claimed that the British king Lucius wrote to the bishop of Rome, Eleutherus (175–89), successfully asking to be made a Christian. At the Council of Arles in 314 there were two British bishops. In 429 Rome had commissioned Bishop Germain of Auxerre, Gaul, to root out the Pelagian heresy in Britain. Two years later, a deacon, Palladius, who had participated in the anti-Pelagian activity, was made Ireland's first bishop; he worked in southern Ireland. Shortly afterward Magonus Sucetus Patricius, who became known as Patrick the apostle of the Irish, returned to the island. The son of a Briton who was a town councilor and a deacon of the church, at sixteen he had been captured by Irish pirates and spent six years herding animals in the north of what is now County Mayo. In this situation he began to pray intensely and received inspiration to escape. He persuaded sailors to give him a passage to his native land. After adventures in which he felt divine assistance, he reached home and trained for the Christian ministry. Although he acquired a thorough knowledge of the Latin Bible, it did not compensate for his lack of a higher education. He went to Gaul before being sent from Britain "as bishop" to Ireland, where he probably established his episcopal see in Armagh. He brought Roman liturgy and organization but made them accessible to a nonurban people.

A few decades after the last Roman legions were withdrawn from Britain in 410 to strengthen defenses against the barbarians, Anglo-Saxon and Jute heathens arrived, driving Britons to the west. Many Britons maintained their faith and were influenced by the monastic movement that flourished in the Celtic areas from the mid-sixth century.

Gregory was attempting to spread Christianity through a mission to pagans who had not been part of the empire but were now living within its former confines. British Christians had not evangelized the newcomers as they were understandably hostile to the invaders. The newcomers had contact with the Merovingian kingdom of Gaul; a bishop had come from there with Princess Bertha when she married King Ethelbert of Kent.

To lead the mission Gregory chose Augustine, who had succeeded him as head of the St. Andrew community. None of the missionaries knew Anglo-Saxon, they did not have an interpreter, and they were anxious about traveling to "a people at the world's end" who venerated Wotan, the god of war, and Thor, the hammer-wielding thunder god, who daubed their bodies with blue dye, had ritualized curses, and cast runes. From Aix in Gaul the missionaries asked to return to Rome, but Gregory encouraged them to proceed. They landed at the island of Thanet off Kent.

By July 598 Gregory was writing to the patriarch of Alexandria that the mission was well underway:

> While the nation of the English, situated at the ends of the earth, remained up to this time unbelievers worshiping trees and stones, I decided, with the aid of your prayers and the inspiration of God, to send a monk of my own monastery to preach to them. And with my leave, he was made bishop by the bishops of Germany and with their encouragement he reached the nation at the end of the world. And now letters have just arrived telling us of his safety and of his work.

The letters had been borne by two of the monks who would have been able to recount King Ethelbert's arrival at Thanet and his meeting with the missionaries "bearing a silver cross and an image of the Saviour painted on a panel." Ethelbert allowed them to preach (it is not known in what language) in his capital, Canterbury, and hold services in the church of St. Martin, a renovated Roman building used by Queen Bertha. On Christmas Day 597, ten thousand people had been baptized. Exultant Gregory interrupted his commentary on Job to rejoice: "Look at Britain, whose language was barbarian: it now resounds with the Hebrews' Alleluia."

In a letter to Ethelbert, Gregory compared his conversion to that of Constantine:

> My most illustrious son, watch carefully over the grace you have received from God and hasten to extend the Christian faith among the people who are subject to you. Increase your righteous zeal for their conversion; suppress the worship of idols; overthrow their buildings and shrines; strengthen the morals of your subjects by outstanding purity of life, by exhorting them, terrifying, enticing, and correcting them, and by showing them an example of good works.

Gregory advised a second batch of missionaries not to destroy temples:

> Tell him [Augustine] that the temples of that race should by no means be destroyed, but only the idols in them. Take holy water and sprinkle it on these shrines, build altars and place relics in them. For if the shrines are well built, it is essential that they should be changed from the worship of devils to the service of the true God. When these people see that their shrines are not destroyed they will be able to banish error from their hearts and be more ready to come to the places with which they are familiar, but now recognizing and worshiping the true God.

Celebration of saints and martyrs, he added, should replace animal sacrifice. Gregory had decided to encourage conversion by conciliation.

Throughout Gregory's reign the Lombards were the most pressing military and political problem. At the time of his election, they were an immediate threat to Rome, whose only communication with the Byzantine enclave centered on Ravenna was by the Flaminian Way, which skirted Perugia.

In 592 Gregory appealed vainly for help from Ravenna against the Lombards and then coordinated the Rome duchy's defense. Eventually, he paid the Lombard leader Ariulf to withdraw. It is said that Ariulf then fell ill and sought Gregory's advice; with a sick man's interest in medicine, Gregory prescribed a milk diet, which cured Ariulf. In gratitude, he promised not to attack Rome again.

However, that did not mean other Lombards would hold back. The following year the Lombard king Agilulf besieged the city. From its walls Gregory saw tethered prisoners being sent to the slave markets of Gaul and smoke rise from burning farms. Soldiers who had been captured returned to Rome with their hands chopped off. There were stories of Lombards killing clerics and peasants who would not adore their beast-gods. With the backing of the military governor and city prefect, Gregory met Agilulf on the steps of St. Peter's and paid another tribute, this time a tribute of five hundred pounds of gold, which ensured the Lombards' withdrawal.

After two sieges in two years, Gregory sought the help of the archbishop of Milan as an intermediary between the Lombards and the Byzantines. After laborious negotiations, peace was concluded in 598.

Some Lombards were pagan, some Catholic, but the majority were Arian. Gregory had not sent missionaries to them, perhaps because the Lombards could well consider them imperial agents. He counted rather on the influence of Theodelinda, a Catholic princess from Bavaria who had married Agilulf. Paul the Deacon, a Lombard monk who was the historian of his people, wrote:

> By means of this queen, the church of God obtained much that was useful. For the Lombards, when they were still held in the error of heathenism, seized nearly all the property of the churches, but the king, moved by her [Theodelinda's] wholesome supplication, not only held the Catholic faith but also bestowed many possessions on the church of Christ and restored to the honors of their wonted dignity the bishops who were in a reduced and abject state.

Contrary to Paul the Deacon's affirmation, Agilulf did not convert from Arianism, but he tolerated the Catholic faith and even favored it. In 603, his son Adaloald was baptized a Catholic.

Theodelinda, however, was a schismatic Catholic. Like most Christians in north Italy at the time, she did not accept Rome's alleged ambiguity about the *Three Chapters* dispute: these Christians claimed to adhere more fully than Rome to the Chalcedon Council. Initially Rome had refused to condemn the *Three Chapters* but, when the fifth ecumenical council confirmed their condemnation, Pope Vigilius had assented. A letter by Pope Pelagius II, which is generally attributed to Gregory, justified Rome's changed stance: "If a position was held while truth was being sought, and a different position was adopted after truth had been found, why should a change of position be imputed a crime to this See? For what is reprehensible is not to change one's position, but to entertain fickle opinions."

This defense of flexibility apparently cut little ice with Theodelinda, but her relations with Gregory, who gave her a jeweled Gospel and a silver set of a hen with seven chicks, were excellent. By the end of Gregory's reign the Lombards were better disposed toward the papacy than at the beginning, but they stuck to their aim of establishing control over all Italy at the expense of the emperor.

The evil days of the beginning of Gregory's reign seemed to have returned. The Lombards were once more on the warpath against the Byzantine exarch. And famine so gripped Rome that the populace turned on the pope whose constant concern had been to feed them; just as well he had made a study of Job's suffering. On his death on March 12, 604, a mob that stormed the Lateran wanting to burn his books was dissuaded only by his monk friend Peter.

Gregory's epitaph "Consul of God" indicates that his classical heritage was put at the service of the faith. But his greatness was largely in finding ways to go beyond the heritage and bring the faith to the illiterate and to the new peoples within and beyond the empire's boundaries. He was the quintessential pontiff, or bridge-builder, and the bridge joined classical Rome to the Middle Ages.

– XIV –

THEOLOGY AND THUGGERY

IN 613 POPE BONIFACE IV received an impassioned, playful, and polemical letter from a monk in northern Italy that called on him to "remove the cloud of suspicion from St. Peter's chair" due to Pope Vigilius's (537–55) vacillating over Christ's nature. The letter writer, who described himself as a "greenhorn" and "bumptious babbler" from the "world's end," was Columban the Younger (so-called to distinguish him from the founder of Iona monastery, Columban the Elder.)

Born in Leinster between 543 and 550, Columban had felt the attraction of girls during his youth, but an aged anchoress convinced him to become a monk. On announcement of his intention, his mother threw herself across the doorway, but Columban stepped over her and left. His monastic studies took place on an island in Fermanagh county, where he received a solid grounding in grammar, rhetoric, and biblical studies, specializing in the Psalms. He taught in a monastery at Bangor and also wrote poetry that showed familiarity with Ovid, Horace, and other pagan authors. He was a product of the vigorous Irish monastic movement, which, stimulated by British Christians fleeing from Saxon invaders and other Christians from further afield, flourished in the sixth century.

After teaching for two decades, in the Celtic fashion Columban had set out as a pilgrim with fellow monks. They established monasteries in Gaul, which was divided into various subkingdoms among the heirs of King Clovis. On the invitation of King Theodoric II of Burgundy, Columban established a monastery in Luxeuil and then others in the Vosges mountains. As he found that pastoral assistance was inadequate, he undertook this work also. Columban was one of the first to introduce private, or auricular, confession, in contrast to public confession, and develop individual pastoral care. His lists of the penance appropriate for various sins had a wide diffusion. Eventually about a hundred monasteries were setup on the model of his community at Luxeuil, and many young aristocrats entered them. But he aroused hostility: Irish monasteries enjoyed autonomy, but the bishops of Gaul, who were used to exercising jurisdiction over monasteries, did not accept it, while the clergy chafed at Columban's reminders that they should be shepherds of souls.

About the year 600 Columban had written to Pope Gregory complimenting him on the success of his pastoral and expository writings and asking permission to continue to follow the Irish Easter calendar, which was different from that used in Gaul. He even joked about the name of Gregory's predecessor Leo, citing the scriptural text: a living dog is better than a dead lion (Leo in Latin). Although Gregory was a punster himself, he did not respond, and the Gallic bishops summoned Columban to a synod to discuss, among other things, his paschal calendar. He declined politely, explaining that he could not guarantee he would keep his temper.

The bishops were hostile, but Columban had the protection of King Theodoric, until he refused both to bless the king's illegitimate son and to allow Theodoric, because he had a concubine, to enter his monastery. If this were not enough, he threatened to excommunicate Theodoric. The king ordered that Columban be thrown into death row in Besançon prison, where the monk promised inmates freedom if they repented. Somehow he led them out of prison and convinced them to pray with him in a nearby church. The king insisted on expelling him: Columban and his monks were put on a ship at Nantes but, because of a storm shortly after setting out, it turned back and the monks disembarked.

This time Columban was welcomed by another son of Clovis, King Clothair of Neustria, and later moved to Metz, where he joined up with monks from Luxeuil. They rowed along the Rhine to Lake Constance, on whose banks they settled. On the way Columban composed a boating song. The pagans in the area were hostile, and after about a year a change in the political context convinced Columban to leave. This decision caused a quarrel with his closest companion, Gall, who decided to stay and subsequently converted the Alemans. The Swiss town of St. Gallen is named after Gall and on feast days displays banners showing him carrying a cross and blessing a bear.

In the late autumn of 611 Columban, who was in his sixties, with companions walked over the Alps and reached Milan. He was shocked by what he found. For one thing the Lombards, who controlled northern Italy and had duchies in central Italy (Spoleto) and southern Italy (Benevento), were mainly Arian. The theological basis of Arianism had been undercut by the Councils of Nicaea (325) and Constantinople (381), but it had acquired a new lease on life when an Arian bishop, Ulfila, created a Gothic script and translated the New Testament into it. By enabling the Germanic tribes (except the Franks) to become Christian without having to accept Roman-Hellenistic culture, it strengthened their identity.

In the seventh century Arianism had little influence in Gaul while the conversion to Catholicism of the Arian Visigoth King Recared in 587 had ended Arianism in Spain. But it was still powerful in north Italy, whose Christianity depended less on Rome than on the patriarchate of Aquileia, whose sway extended to Milan and what is now Austria.

Among the Lombards, as well as Arians there were pagans and Catholics who disagreed with Rome over the relationship of the human and divine natures of Christ. The schismatics, found also in Tuscany, Illyria, and North Africa, accused Rome of adopting, in the *Three Chapters* dispute, the Nestorian belief that Christ had two personalities.

After crossing the Alps, Columban received a letter from the bishop of Como saying that Boniface IV was slipping into Nestorianism. Columban was welcomed by the Arian Lombard King Agilulf, who asked him to write to Pope Boniface to resolve the *Three Chapters* dispute. Agilulf hinted that, if Catholics would only come to an agreement, he would convert.

Columban accepted the king's request, as he feared a great opportunity was being lost because of Roman ambiguity. Although he described himself as a "doltish Irish pilgrim," he was used to being heeded by kings as well as monks and could be authoritarian as well as breezy. His five-thousand-word letter mixed impatience with Boniface and respect for the papal office: "Follow Peter and let the whole church follow you." At the same time he dared redress the pope because the Irish valued a man's principles rather than his station. He was bouncy ("Keep vigil," he advised, "because it seems Vigilius was not very vigilant"), verbose, and confident, despite an imperfect grasp of the situation, partly because he was not familiar with the fifth ecumenical council.

It was a valiant attempt to improve Lombard-Roman relations

but there was no response. After his letter, perhaps to withdraw from the thorny issues of the schismatic Catholics and Arians, Columban took advantage of the king's offer of an abandoned church, St. Peter's, in Bobbio. At 820 feet altitude in the Trebbia valley of the Apennines, twenty-five miles from the Lombard capital, Pavia, Bobbio was the sort of wooded, watered, hilly retreat he preferred, and there was already a hermitage nearby. King Clothair of Neustria sent him chests of gold and requests for his return to Gaul. But Columban stayed in Bobbio, carrying beams for the monastery he built until a few months before his death on Sunday, November 23, 615. His last gesture was to send his pastoral staff to his fellow monk, Gall, who was still living near Lake Constance, as a sign of reconciliation and to let him know of his approaching death. But Gall announced Columban's death to his monks the morning it took place and before arrival of the staff.

Boniface IV (608–15) and Honorius (625–38) were both inspired by Gregory and like him turned their family mansions into monasteries. Both vigorously supported the fledgling English mission. Boniface had consulted in Rome with the first bishop of London, Mellitus, and furnished him with letters for King Ethelbert of Kent, Archbishop Lawrence of Canterbury, and the English people. Honorius congratulated King Edwin of Northumbria on his conversion and dispatched Birinus to evangelize the West Saxons. In 628 he granted the Bobbio monastery the first-ever exemption from episcopal control. By linking the monastery directly to the papacy, he freed it from royal pressure: within a few decades, the monastery had 150 monks and was a renowned center of learning. Honorius improved relations with the Lombards but, nevertheless, they remained difficult, which was an incentive to strengthen bonds with Constantinople.

Honorius accepted responsibilities that imperial officials could not handle, such as repairing aqueducts, maintaining the corn supply, and acting as army paymaster. A wealthy aristocrat from the countryside near Naples, he had given two thousand pounds of silver to the church. He managed the papal estates well and used the income to help the needy of Rome. An extensive church building and restoration program suggests that he was both confident and had resources. No substantial work on churches had been done in the almost four decades since St. Lawrence-Outside-the-Walls had been reconstructed. However, there had been an important "acquisition": in 609 Emperor Phocas had granted Boniface IV permission to turn the Pantheon, which was imperial property, into a church, which saved it from being quarried like other Roman monuments. Elsewhere many pagan temples had been made into churches, but, almost three hundred years after Constantine's victory, this was the first example in Rome, perhaps because of belief in idolatry's persistent negative influence. What had been the temple of all the pagan gods was dedicated to the Virgin Mary and all the saints, but it remains also a monument to impersonal, cosmic Stoic calm. In gratitude to the cruel usurper Phocas, a column, which was the last addition to the Forum, was erected there, where it still stands. Boniface had saved the Pantheon; Honorius likewise saved the Senate house in the Forum by making it the Church of St. Hadrian. He converted the halls of several mansions into churches: St. Martina, St. Lucia in Selice, and Quattro Coronati. He replaced sixteen beams in St. Peter's, covered its roof with bronze tiles from the Temple of Venus and Roma and its main doors with silver and inserted in the nave a gilded, coffered ceiling.

In taking over the army paymaster role, Honorius made himself vulnerable to criticism. Immediately after his death, Byzantine agents provocateurs convinced the Roman garrison that he had hoarded their pay. Fully armed, they marched to the Lateran, where papal officials were able to resist them for only a few days. The Byzantines took the offerings accumulated for centuries, "bequeathed to the blessed Apostle Peter by many Christian emperors, patricians, and consuls, for the redemption of their souls, the perpetual support of the poor, and the ransoming of captives."

Some of the loot went to Emperor Heraclius in Constantinople, who successfully asserted his authority throughout much of the Mediterranean, establishing the Byzantine empire in which there was no division between the East and the West. Instead of a Western emperor in Ravenna, there was an exarch, a governor or viceroy reporting to the capital on the Bosphorus. These closer relations with Constantinople increased the likelihood of head-on clashes if ecclesial-theological differences had political implications.

That is precisely what happened. In 634 Honorius had received a letter from Patriarch Sergius of Constantinople, who believed he had found a way to mollify those Christians of the East, mainly in Egypt, Syria, and Armenia, who had not accepted the Council of Chalcedon's formulation about Christ's fully human and fully divine nature. The Monophysites (from the Greek word for "one nature"), as those who did not accept the Chalcedon formula were called, were disaffected and some had even accepted Islam's expansion into their territories as a liberation.

Patriarch Sergius claimed that a formulation that referred to "two natures but only one will" in Christ (Monothelitism or "one will") had won over many Monophysites which, for civil authorities concerned about large-scale disaffection, was a persuasive argument. It seemed a way of placating the Monophysites without expressly denying Chalcedon but, in the event, did not satisfy either.

Patriarch Sophronius of Jerusalem criticized Sergius's formula as a disguised form of Monophysitism. In other words, the Christological dispute about the relationship between Christ's divine and human nature, which had seemed settled at Chalcedon, had reemerged with explosive implications.

Honorius regarded most theological disputes as fit only for grammarians, but for many Easterners theology was the grammar of the universe. In this case, Honorius agreed enthusiastically with Constantinople, where Emperor Heraclius, in his *Ecthesis* of 638, ordered that all must profess that there was only a single will in Christ.

This led to a dramatic pope-emperor conflict when Martin I was elected pope in 649. Born outside Todi in Umbria, Martin had probably come to live in Rome as a youth with his family fleeing the first Lombard incursions. He may have attended a kind of junior seminary established by Gregory the Great in his residence, at the Lateran. It is certain that, like Gregory and several other predecessors, he was the papal representative in Constantinople before becoming pope himself. It became a hardship post as emperors grew more insecure about the loyalty of the West and more embroiled in theological disputes. In 647 the papal representative, Anastasius, had been exiled to the Caucasus.

In Constantinople Martin observed the court personalities, the inroads of Monothelitism, and the violence that could accompany theological conflicts. On his election he did not seek its ratification by Constantinople. That could take three months, but by that time energetic Martin had summoned a synod in the Lateran attended by 105 Western bishops and also by exiled Greek-speaking theologians. They had stiffened Roman resistance to Monothelitism, which was endorsed by the boy-emperor Constans in an edict known as "Typos."

Prominent among these Eastern dissidents at the Lateran Synod was Maximus, of a well-known Constantinople family, who had been secretary to the preceding Emperor Heraclius before entering a monastery. After fifteen years there, in 630 when Persian forces threatened Constantinople, he sailed for Carthage. Here he entered another monastery, led by Sophronius, who was to be a doughty defender of Chalcedon when he became patriarch of Jerusalem.

Maximus agreed with Sophronius that all attempts to water down Chalcedon were insidious because, if its affirmation of the fully human and fully divine nature of Christ was fudged, his salvific action could not be properly understood. Moreover Maximus saw affirmation of the difference between the human and divine as a guarantee of human autonomy and of the positive values in creation, whereas the Monothelite version implied pessimism about human possibilities. Maximus looked to Rome to defend orthodoxy because it was St. Peter's burial place with "the keys of the faith," he wrote, "and of the orthodox confession." He maintained that in endorsing the doctrine of Constantinople Honorius, like Liberius before him, had been ambiguous rather than in error.

The Lateran Synod convoked by Martin condemned Monothelitism and the emperor's edict "Typos," which endorsed it. Martin excommunicated the bishop of Thessalonica for rejecting the synod's decisions. He forwarded a copy of them to Constans but provided a way out for him by blaming the patriarchs of Constantinople for the condemned doctrine. But Constans believed he was being censured by one of his subjects and may have suspected that Martin, who had not requested ratification of his election, was subversive.

Constans sent the chamberlain Olympius as exarch, or governor, to arrest Martin and bring him to Constantinople, but, after a failed attempt to assassinate Martin during Mass at St. Mary Major, Olympius deserted Constans and declared himself sovereign of Italy. Constans next sent a former exarch, Theodore Calliopas, with troops from Ravenna to silence the pope. Roman clergy greeted him on his arrival at the imperial palace on the Palatine Hill on Saturday June 15, 651, but explained that Martin was too sick to attend. In fact, Martin had been gravely ill for months. Seeing a crowd gather at the Lateran the next day, Calliopas suspected that Romans were preparing to defend their bishop. On Tuesday his men searched the Lateran for arms, but Martin assured them that rumors of resistance were groundless.

Martin later described what happened next:

> I had my bed set up in front of the altar in the church and there slept, but just after midnight soldiers burst in fully armed with drawn swords and lances at the ready—an unspeakable act. Just as leaves are torn from trees in winter storms, they sent candlesticks crashing thunderously. The moment they entered an order from Calliopas was read to the priests and deacons containing much abuse of me: that I had illegally and uncanonically seized the bishopric, was unworthy of the Apostolic See and must be taken to Constantinople.

A crowd that had gathered shouted to the troops that Martin was orthodox. Theodore Calliopas answered that he had not been arrested for doctrinal reasons, and indeed he was to be charged with political crimes such as supporting the exarch Gregory of Africa (cousin of the preceding emperor, Heraclius, who was thought to have designs on the throne) and convincing Olympius to betray the emperor. The entanglement of the political and ecclesial makes it unlikely that this was simply a pretext but also that the doctrinal aspect was irrelevant.

After ordering the clergy not to resist, Martin was taken to the imperial palace on the Palatine Hill. His clergy, together with the laity, surrounded the palace, insisting that they leave with Martin for Constantinople and received promises that they could do so. But after they dispersed, before dawn on the following morning to prevent any attempt to rescue Martin, the aged and still weak pontiff was carried on a litter down the Palatine Hill accompanied by only six clergy. The litter with guards skirted the Circus Maximus, where Christians had once been killed, but under pagan emperors, and passed through the southern gates near the still extant Caius Cestius pyramid. Martin, who had no time to prepare for the trip, and his six companions embarked on a sloop near St. Paul's.

At Cape Misenum outside Naples, where units of the Byzantine fleet were stationed, he transferred to a ship where he had to bunk on a mat in a hold. He suffered repeated attacks of dysentery but was able to have a bath only after six weeks when the ship was delayed by a storm at the island of Naxos. Some of the islanders tried to bring him food, but guards drove them away from the alleged traitor.

After three months he arrived in Constantinople. An eyewitness, perhaps one of the accompanying clerics who could also have sent the reports on the eventual trial, described Martin as subject to prolonged verbal abuse on board the day the ship berthed. He was kept in solitary confinement for ninety-three days before the trial began, presumably to allow witness against him to be brought from Italy.

On the morning of December 19, 653, he was taken to the tribunal where the Senate was to judge him. Too weak to stand, he was not allowed to sit; the president of the tribunal ordered that he be held upright. One of the witnesses, Dorotheus, formerly governor of Sicily, said Martin "ought not to live because single-handedly he has subverted and overthrown the entire West by raising it in rebellion; he has been like a brother to Olympius, a murderous enemy of the emperor and the empire."

Soldiers who had served under Olympius gave anti-Martin evidence, which he considered rehearsed. "They are well drilled!" he commented dryly.

Several of the witnesses were compromised with the opposition to the emperor but saved their skins by putting the blame on Martin. He turned the tables by referring to their past misdeeds, but the president of the court told the interpreter not to translate these comments from Latin to Greek. And he foiled Martin's attempt to discuss the theological issues raised by "Typos"; he was to be tried as a traitor, not as a theologian. To underline that it was a rigged trial, Martin suggested that witnesses be released from taking the oath on the Bible so that they could tell the necessary lies without damning themselves. Although convinced he was defending the truth from those he considered "thieves of the treasury of faith," he knew he would be condemned.

He was put on display in the courtyard between the tribunal and the emperor's palace to be heckled by a huge crowd that spread all the way to the race track. Then he was transferred to the loggia of the palace, where the emperor could see him from his dining room. There the president of the tribunal ordered that the papal insignia be stripped from Martin and that he be sliced to pieces.

Preceded by the executioner bearing a sword and shackled in chains, Martin was dragged through the street to the magistrates' offices. An hour later he was dragged through the streets again to prison, leaving a trail of blood from his legs and wrists.

The executioner was called away and the wife of the prison commander let Martin sleep in a bed for some hours. When he awoke, he found that the prefect Gregory had sent him food and a message that he was not to be executed but exiled for life: his martyrdom was to be prolonged.

His sentence had been changed because the emperor had told Patriarch Paul II, who proposed the doctrines condemned by Martin, of the treatment meted out to the prisoner. Paul, who knew he was near death, which came two days later, said such punishment could not be inflicted on a pope. He feared it would weigh against him in God's judgment.

Martin spent a further eighty-five days in prison before he was put on a small ship. He gave the kiss of peace to the clerics who had accompanied him from Rome, but they lamented his departure until he protested, "Is this the peace I asked for?"

The vessel crossed the Bosphorus, then hugged the coast of what are now Bulgaria and Romania, passing the estuary of the Danube, which once had been Rome's frontier against the barbarians, before setting him down at Cherson, near what is now Sebastapol in Ukraine.

"There are few inhabitants and they are pagans," Martin wrote in one of his letters from Cherson, "without even the compassion of the barbarians."

He was in exile, but was he imprisoned? He complained of hunger, which suggests he was not in prison, where he would have received some sustenance. "Bread is mentioned, but we do not see it." He pleaded for wheat, wine, and olive oil and recorded his disappointment when, a month after his arrival, a letter came from Constantinople, presumably from one of the clergy whom he had bid farewell, without any of these things.

One of Cherson's few products was salt, which, when rare ships arrived, was exchanged for wheat. Did Martin gather salt and wait desperately for a ship? Shortly before he died on September 16, 655, he wrote that he had only been able to buy some bushels of wheat from a ship seeking salt.

"I have been saddened" he confessed, "by the lack of interest and sensibility of my friends and relatives who have forgotten me and do not want to know if I am dead or alive."

Worse still were those of the church of Rome who "look after their members but do nothing to ease my suffering."

Against his wishes, the church of Rome elected a successor while he was still alive. After his death, Martin was soon venerated as a martyr by the Latin-speaking church and, since 1969, by the Greek Church. He was the last pope so honored and the first to be martyred by a Most Christian Emperor.

On receiving a full report of his trial and imprisonment, Romans were indignant. When the new patriarch of Constantinople, following the customary practice, sent a letter to the successor of Martin, Eugenius, with assurances of orthodoxy, many Roman lay people considered it unsatisfactory regarding Christ's dual will. They besieged Eugenius and his clergy at Mass at St. Mary Major and would not let the pope leave until he promised to reject the patriarch's letter.

The monk Maximus, who had provided acute insights on the subject of Christ's nature accepted by the anti-Monothelite Lateran Synod, was arrested in Rome and tried in Constantinople about the same time as Martin. He was exiled to Thrace but, in 661, was brought back to Constantinople with two of his disciples. Despite the privations of Thracian exile, they refused to budge from reaffirmation of Chalcedon. To prevent them from propagating their views, their tongues and right hands were cut off. They were exiled to a town near the Black Sea, where Maximus the Confessor died that August.

Constans, who had tried and exiled Martin and Maximus, paid Rome a twelve-day visit in July 663. Pope Vitalian and his clergy went out to greet him to the sixth mile on the Appian Way. The next day, on foot, Constans came to St. Peter's, where he presented jeweled and gilded copies of the Gospels for its treasury. The day after, Constans with his twenty thousand troops, many of them Asiatic, visited St. Mary Major. Constans's name was cut into the stairwell of Trajan's column, probably by one of his entourage. Treating the city as his property, he stripped buildings of metal parts, bronze tiles, and the clamps with which they were bonded. Ancient Roman buildings were resistant because standards were stricter than they are today. Quicklime, which provides more durable binding the older it is, could not be sold until it had aged six years, which is longer than is now customary. However Constans's removal of clamps, leaving holes still visible today, left the buildings vulnerable to the weather. He wanted the metal to make armaments, but the ship carrying it was intercepted by Arabs off Syracuse. Constans went to Sicily himself because he was considering transfer of his capital to the island for defense purposes, but in Palermo he was murdered in his bath by one of his officers.

Vitalian's conciliatory policy seemed to have brought nothing in return, but nevertheless he mobilized the Byzantine army in Italy, with African and Sardinian units, to support the assassinated emperor's son Constantine IV against a pretender. Perhaps Vitalian's policy contributed to reestablishment of good Rome-Constantinople relations during the reign of Pope Agatho (678–81).

The Byzantine government informed Agatho, a Sicilian monk proficient in Greek, that it had abandoned Monothelitism and proposed a council to reestablish full unity. Agatho first held a preparatory synod in Rome and then sent to Constantinople an important delegation, including two future Popes: John V and Constantine. The council, the sixth, which was held in the imperial palace, reaffirmed the Chalcedon doctrine and anathematized Monothelitism. In the council's concluding address it was acknowledged that the true faith, written with God's hand, had been given to the church by Old Rome and that Peter had spoken through Agatho. The emperor was described as collaborating with God himself.

But if Agatho was right, so was Martin. And if Martin was right, had not Honorius been in the wrong? The logic was inescapable. In condemning Monothelitism, the council had condemned Honorius. Constantinople withheld ratification of the election of Agatho's successor, Leo II, an exceptionally cultured Sicilian, until he accepted the council's condemnation of a pope (Honorius). As was the custom, Leo had the council's decisions translated from Greek to Latin before sending the text to church leaders and rulers of the West asking for their acceptance. When Leo wrote to Emperor Constantine IV, in the Latin version of the letter he said that Honorius had attempted to "subvert the pure faith by his profane betrayal," but the Greek version softened this to "by his betrayal he allowed the pure teaching to be sullied." Writing to the Spanish episcopacy, Leo simply said Honorius had failed to stamp out the flame of heresy. Leo was lenient about un-repentant Monothelite bishops and clergy: he dispersed them in monasteries. (Honorius's endorsement of a heretical doctrine presented a difficulty for proponents of papal infallibility at the First Vatican Council. He was defended on the grounds that he had been not heretical but merely hasty).

For the moment theological problems with Constantinople had been settled, but papal elections remained an occasion for destructive conflicts, particularly since in some way that remains obscure the military participated. On the death of John V in 686 the Roman clergy elected an archpriest, Peter, but the militia preferred a priest, Theodore. Eventually the clergy presented as a compromise candidate an elderly, ill priest, Conon. After eleven months Conon, who was not even strong enough to carry out ordinations, died, leaving all the tensions unresolved.

As archdeacon under Conon, a certain Paschal had written to the exarch in Ravenna, John, offering a hundred pounds of gold if he would ensure his election. On Conon's death John had dutifully instructed Byzantine officials in Rome to ensure the election of Paschal. But instead Sergius, a Sicilian whose family had come from Syria, was chosen. Paschal wrote again to John renewing his promise if only the exarch would come to Rome and make him pope. John did come but found Sergius had wide support; nevertheless the exarch still wanted a hundred pounds of gold. He delayed ratification of the election until Sergius stripped that amount of gold from St. Peter's to counter Paschal's bribe. Paschal was tried, found guilty among other things of witchcraft, and subsequently imprisoned in a monastery.

While Paschal was a disgrace to the church, John was no honor to the imperial government. However Emperor Justinian II's only concern seemed to be to have a submissive pope. In 692 he convoked a synod that issued 102 canons ignoring Western norms and, among other things, declared that Constantinople was the second patriarchal see. The nuncio signed the deliberations but, when they were forwarded to Rome, Sergius refused to endorse them.

It seemed there was to be a replay of Pope Martin's Calvary. Justinian dispatched an army officer, Zachary, to bring back either the pope or his signature. Zachary led troops from Ravenna toward Rome but, when word of his intentions leaked out, they rebelled.

Fleeing for his life, Zachary sought refuge in the Lateran under the pope's bed. Sergius reassured him and then tried to demobilize the troops, but they insisted on mounting guard for him all night. It showed there was a pro-papal element even in the Byzantine forces, who probably shared the populace's resentment against heavy taxes.

Byzantine brutality in dealings with the church in Rome also caused disaffection. In 710 Pope Constantine, a Syrian, accepted an invitation to visit Constantinople and was received with great honors by the noseless Justinian II. (In 695 Justinian had been deposed, his nose was sliced off, and he was exiled to the Crimea, but a decade later he regained the throne. He was nicknamed "No Nose"). On meeting Pope Constantine, Justinian had kissed his feet and received communion and absolution. Constantine stayed for a year, during which time newly-arisen disciplinary and ritual disputes were resolved. (The agreement served no purpose, however, as a fortnight after Constantine returned to Rome, Justinian's troops revolted and this time they were not content with mere nose-slicing). While the pope was being treated handsomely in Constantinople, the new exarch of Ravenna had arrived in Rome and, for unknown reasons, had slaughtered Constantine's vicar and other senior officials. Constantine had not let the massacre upset his negotiations but it could only have increased the Romans' diffidence.

In this period Eastern religious dissidents flocked to the city, where they established many monasteries. In 645 a monastic community from the Judean hills settled in a house said to have belonged to the family of Gregory the Great. The walls are part of the extant San Saba church. Rome benefited from the influx of Greek-language theologians but was wary of their possibly heretical opinions. When it was found that Syrian monks who settled as a community in Rome were Nestorian schismatics, they were dispersed between various monasteries.

Some refugees brought relics, such as what was claimed to be the manger of Christ, which was installed in St. Mary Major, and the heads of St. Anastasius, a Persian martyr, and of St. George. They were two of the many Eastern saints who began to be venerated in Rome. Three feasts of the Virgin, the Nativity, the Annunciation, and the Dormition, were introduced there from the East as was the use of the Agnus Dei in the liturgy. Gregory the Great had fended off a Byzantine empress's request for martyrs' bones with stories of the dire consequences of disturbing them but, under Eastern influence as well as barbarian sieges, the Roman church began to transfer relics from the catacombs to churches within the city walls.

A few of the icons introduced at this time have survived and are striking: the Virgin and Child in the Pantheon, St. Sebastian in St. Peter's-in-Chains, the Virgin in St. Francesca Romana, and the Virgin flanked by angels in St. Maria in Trastevere.

Pope John VII, the son of Plato who was the curator of the Byzantine palaces on the Palatine, was a patron of Byzantine-style art. Shortly after his election in 703 he built a papal residence on the Palatine, confirming the suspicions of those who thought he was in the Byzantines' pocket, whereas other suspected he was asserting papal sovereignty in an area reserved for imperial authority: in the San Cesario chapel there the reigning emperor's portrait was always on display.

Below the hill on the Tiber bank was the church of Santa Maria in Cosmedin, which would not have been out of place in Constantinople. It dominated what was called the "Greek" quarter. Attached was a food distribution center, one of a network throughout the city. Vessels from the East berthed close by, and there may have been fear their crews and passengers would bring the Monophysite contagion from Alexandria. The Greek or Byzantine influence was also felt in papal liturgy, which at this time acquired much of the magnificence of Byzantine court ceremony with the use of ostrich feather fans, incense, jeweled vestments, and other means to present the pope as a demi-God.

Dissidents from the religious policies of Constantinople were one source of the increased Eastern influence; another was those who had fled from the warriors of a new religion that had swept up from the Arabian peninsula: Islam. It was monotheistic but not trinitarian, which made it immune to the disputes that had fragmented Christianity. In 635 Islam conquered Syria. In 640 Jerusalem fell as did Egypt the following year, including of course the apostolic see of Alexandria.

Still more refugees came to Rome when Constantinople banned representation of human figures in art, which may have been due to Monophysite prejudice against attributing human characteristics to the Trinity. Ostensibly it was an application of the biblical injunction against adoring graven images. But that was quite a step from venerating icons. The policy was introduced by an able emperor Leo III who came to power in 717 after a series of inept rulers had failed to halt advancing Bulgarians and Islam. Leo encouraged a free peasantry in Anatolia, which provided the troops who swept the Arabs out of Asia Minor. He punished the monasteries that opposed iconoclasm, confiscating their lands and also preventing them from draining away potential army recruits.

He also threatened Gregory II, who had done much of the negotiating during Pope Constantine's year-long stay in Constantinople in 710, that if he did not approve the prohibition of images he would be deposed. Of wealthy Roman stock, Gregory, who was the first locally born pope after several of Greek or Syrian background, refused. He told the emperor his iconoclastic campaign was heretical. Leo wrote him claiming absolute power: "I am both king and priest." Gregory cast doubt on Leo's kingly claims by saying that once he (Gregory) was three miles from Rome, which suggested this was the limit of Byzantine control, he would be safe because the whole West revered Peter's successor. His was a proud declaration of papal autonomy:

> [The whole West] relies on us and on St. Peter, the Prince of the Apostles, whose image you wish to destroy, but whom the kingdoms of the West honor as if he were God himself on earth. . . . We are going to the most distant parts of the West to seek those who desire baptism. Although we have sent bishops and clergy of our holy church to them, their princes have not yet received baptism, for they wish to receive it from ourselves alone. . . . You have no right to issue dogmatic constitutions, you have not the right mind for dogmas, you are too coarse and martial.

As if to prove the last statement, in response there were vain Byzantine attempts to kill Gregory. When the Byzantine Exhiliratus, who had a duchy near Naples, tried to raise a force to seize Rome and arrest the pope, Romans marched south and put Exhiliratus and his son to death. They also blinded Peter, a Byzantine appointee as the first-ever Roman duke, whom they suspected of planning to betray the pope.

To cow Gregory, the Byzantines even allied with their traditional enemies, the Lombards. The exarch Eutychius and King Liutprand led armies to Rome, but Gregory convinced Liutprand, who was the first Catholic Lombard king, to come to St. Peter's to pray. Peter was too powerful: before his tomb, the Lombard offered his cloak, gilded sword, scabbard, breastplate, baldric, and crown.

The church of St. Maria Antiqua in the Forum dates from this century. Its most interesting feature is badly faded frescoes, believed to have been painted by refugees from the iconoclasts. They resemble those of the rock churches of Cappadocia and honor Eastern saints whose images were being destroyed in the East such as St. John Chrysostom, St. Gregory Nazianzus, St. Basil, St. Athanasius, and Sts. Quiricus and Julietta. The portraits of three popes, Zachary (741–52), Paul I (757–67), and Hadrian (772–95), with the square halos of the living, allow dating of the frescoes, which influenced Western art. There is a scene of a donor kneeling, instead of standing as was customary, and detailed scenes of martyrdom, which were both innovations for the West, whose art was profoundly influenced by the papacy's support for images.

In the Italian peninsula, people protested not only against the iconoclastic decree but also against tax pressure. Gregory forbade tax payments, which would have sharply reduced income from papal holdings. In reprisal, Emperor Leo confiscated all the papal estates in southern Italy and Sicily, whose annual income is estimated at 252,000 scudi. From the time Emperor Constantine had made these endowments, they had provided much of the papal income and more recently had been the main source of Rome's food supply. Leo also put southern Italy and Sicily under the Constantinople patriarchate, cutting off territories that had supplied many of the church of Rome's leaders, scholars, and contacts with the East.

Despite this, when Ravenna was seized by the Lombards in 733, Gregory III (731–41) helped the Byzantines to regain control. This demonstration of loyalty led to a truce, but Roman disaffection continued to grow as theological and political motives were often inextricable in Constantinople, and, moreover, increasingly it was punitive toward Rome rather than protective.

It tried to gain assent to high-flown theological argument by bludgeoning tactics that ran the gamut from humiliation, kidnapping, torture, and rigged trials to exile and murder. The creation of Constantinople had saved the bishop of Rome from the pressure of a resident Christian emperor but had also meant another center of power that was religious as well as political. The cultural differences between East and West resulted in different concepts of the church. Eastern theological flair enabled Christians to hone understanding of the Triune God but could run to hair- and headsplitting. Rome's interest in the definition of rights could seem empire building: the papacy's preeminence based on Peter was widely acknowledged, but when this was gradually embodied in traditional Roman juridical terms, there was resistance in the East. The tensions were enough in themselves without the emperors trying to yoke the church to their social aims or, worse still, determining doctrine rather than simply protecting it. There were periods of harmonious relationship between Rome and Constantinople but also many acrimonious episodes.

The papacy tried hard to maintain harmony. Paul of Tarsus had recommended respect for emperors when they were pagan and Gregory the Great affirmed that even wicked lay rulers must be obeyed. But the popes' obligation to preserve pure doctrine meant they were often torn between their duties as Romans and Christians.

"As a Roman-born, I love, honor, and revere the emperor," said Pope Gelasius, "and as a Christian, I desire that he who has a zeal for God shall have it with an accompanying knowledge of the truth." In Rome's view, some of the emperors lacked knowledge of the truth. Several rocked the barque of Peter and did not hesitate to threaten its captain. Eventually the emperors made the links with Rome tenuous although without their formal severance. To the Byzantines, the Romans may have seemed simply to make a crescendo of claims about Peter's spiritual suzerainty. And, to their surprise, by sleight-of-hand the Ravenna exarchate was to end in St. Peter's pocket. For their part Romans, reflecting on the long relationship, might well have asked which was more tiresome, Constantinople's theology or its thuggery.

– XV –

HOBBLING
THE PAPACY

A s Rome's ties with the Byzantine empire loosened, those
with the Franks grew stronger in defense against the Lombard attempt to control all Italy. Lombard pressure was
such that Gregory III (731–41) sought help from Charles Martel,
the dominant figure in the Merovingian kingdom in Gaul. Using the only language that Charles would understand, Gregory
lamented that the Lombard armies had destroyed "all St. Peter's
farms and carried off the livestock." He voiced suspicion that
Charles was allied with the Lombards: "From you, most excellent son, whom we had appointed our refuge, we have received
no consolation: we observe that since you have not actually given
the order to march against these kings, you have believed their lies
rather than our truth."

Gregory's suspicions were well-founded. The Lombards had
helped the Franks repel the Muslims who, after crossing the Pyrenees, had reached the Rhône, and their help could be needed again.
Charles did not come to the pope's aid.

Gregory's successor Zachary, born in Calabria of Greek stock,
is depicted in St. Maria Antiqua as slight, small, and balding. It
seems that he was also likeable and politically shrewd; at least
he charmed the Lombard king Liutprand, who was threatening
Rome. Zachary went on foot to Terni, sixty miles northeast of
Rome, to meet Liutprand. Deeply impressed by his celebration of
Mass, Liutprand accepted the bishop of Rome's invitation to a
banquet and found it the most enjoyable he had ever attended. He
agreed to return some towns already occupied in the duchy and
sign a forty-year peace treaty. Zachary seems to have acted as the
elected representative of a duchy with a long legal-social identity.
The empire was its vague context.

153

The following year, Liutprand attacked the Byzantine exarchate centered on Ravenna. Zachary went to its aid and in the Apennine mountains was welcomed by refugees from Ravenna as "the shepherd who leaves his sheep to rescue those that perish." Zachary convinced Liutprand to hand back the cities he had taken.

No sooner had Zachary been welcomed triumphantly on his return to Rome than Liutprand died. His successor, Ratchis, seized Perugia and towns near Ravenna, but once again Zachary saved the situation because Ratchis accepted his offerings and heeded his pleas. He knelt at the tomb of St. Peter, divested himself of his regalia, and later, with members of his family, entered a monastery. It may have been better if he had remained king because his successor, Aistulf, was two-faced and aggressive.

Stephen II, a Roman aristocrat who succeeded Zachary, concluded a forty-year peace treaty with Aistulf. It seemed to be customary for Lombard kings to propose decades of peace only to resume hostilities almost immediately: after only four months, Aistulf advanced on the Rome duchy threatening to slaughter all its inhabitants. Stephen inaugurated processions from the Lateran to St. Mary Major, St. Peter's, and St. Paul's in which he, the clergy, and populace, barefooted, with ashes on their heads, carried an icon of Christ "not made by human hands" and chanted prayers for divine intervention against the Lombards. In despair, Stephen sent a secret message through a Frankish pilgrim to Pepin. Pepin had succeeded his father, Charles Martel, who in 733 at Poitiers had inflicted the first European defeat on the Muslims, as the key figure of the Merovingian Kingdom. Pepin dispatched envoys to Rome to accompany Stephen. On October 14, 753, with his Lateran secretariat and the Frankish escort, the pope left Rome.

Some Romans, fearful that Stephen would be halted or even killed, accompanied him forty miles to the border of the duchy. He was allowed to proceed to the Lombard capital, Pavia, where Aistulf ignored his peace pleas and was angry that he intended to continue his journey. Subsequently Aistulf, to bring pressure on Pepin, forced his brother Carloman, who had entered Monte Cassino monastery, to leave it, but the tactic was not successful. In late November, for the first time ever, a papal party crossed the Alps: in inclement weather, it passed through the Aosta Valley and over the Great St. Bernard Pass. It was a momentous crossing because it meant the papacy was moving beyond the Mediterranean world.

Pepin sent envoys to the papal party at the St. Maurice monastery, Agaune, and then his eldest son, Charles, to meet it at Langres a hundred miles south of his royal residence at what is now Châlons. When the party reached his residence on the feast of the Epiphany (January 6, 754), Pepin took the papal horse's bridle like a groom just as Emperor Constantine was supposed to have done with Pope Sylvester. The following day, dressed in sackcloth, Stephen prostrated himself before Pepin, who helped him to rise, thus accepting the role of protector. He invited the papal party to rest at the monastery of St. Denis; indeed, Stephen, exhausted by his journey, spent the whole winter at Pepin's court.

Stephen needed help from Pepin, while Pepin, for his part, was indebted to the papacy: protection was granted in exchange for recognition of legitimacy. On the death of Charles Martel in 741, his sons Pepin and Carloman had succeeded him as joint governors of the Merovingian kingdom. They were well disposed toward the Catholic Church. In 747 Carloman had resigned, come to Rome, received the tonsure from Pope Zachary, and entered the Monte Cassino monastery. Pepin had written to Zachary that he had kingly power but no title and asked for the pope to approve a change of dynasty. Zachary assented and the sickly, weak Merovingian king Childeric had been sent to a monastery.

No wonder, then, that Pepin, mindful of the papal acquiescence in the smooth coup d'état, received Stephen handsomely. This may have encouraged the pope to present during his stay a notorious document known as the Donation of Constantine, although there is dispute about the exact date it emerged and, indeed, about almost every aspect of it. Tradition mistakenly held that Pope Sylvester had converted Emperor Constantine, baptized him, and cured him of leprosy, and that the emperor, in gratitude, had left him Rome and other territories. Drawing on this tradition, someone prepared what was purported to be a document written by Constantine on March 30, 313, in which the emperor recognized the preeminence of the Roman see and conferred on Sylvester, as Peter's successor, dominion over Rome, Italy, and the West. "It is not just" said the document, "that the world emperor has powers where the celestial emperor has decided that the head of the Christian religion and of the priesthood has his see."

The document was couched in crude Latin and made clamorous mistakes such as talking of the see of Constantinople before it existed. It was not a case of forging a tradition but, nevertheless, it was a momentous historical forgery. Sylvester had existed but, probably because of the Lombard threat, it was found necessary to reinvent him. Some historians claim that the false "Donation of Constantine" was fabricated not by the papacy but by the Franks as a defense against the Byzantines who were irritated that Pepin transferred what had been their possessions to the papacy.

Before departure, Stephen repeated the anointing of Pepin and his two sons as kings of the Franks, which a papal legate had performed two years earlier, but also added a new title: Patricians of the Romans. This entitled them to wear Roman clothes appropriate to the rank; doubtless Stephen also hoped it would encourage them to protect other Romans. Subsequently Stephen always referred to Pepin and his wife, Bertha, as his spiritual co-parents and to their sons as his spiritual sons; he had become their godfather.

Although Stephen tried to avoid Lombard-Frank fighting, eventually the Franks routed the Lombards in the Alps, and Aistulf successfully requested peace. He did not fulfill any of the terms and, within three months, marched again on Rome. Stephen sent envoys by sea to beg desperately for Pepin's help, reporting Aistulf's ultimatum to Romans: "Open the Salarian gate and I will enter the city; hand over your bishop and I will spare you; otherwise I will flatten your walls, I will slay you with my own hand, and then we will see who can save you from my clutches." Stephen described the Lombards' rampage:

> Far and wide outside the city they ravaged all the farms with fire and sword, burning and leveling to the ground all buildings. They burnt the churches of God, impaled saints' images on their swords and threw them on the fire; they desecrated the sacred vessels that carry the Body of Our Lord Jesus Christ by eating from them, bloating themselves with huge meals of meat.... Those of God's servants, the monks, who had stayed behind in their monasteries to perform the divine office, they beat up and severely injured; they abducted and most savagely misused the nuns and cloistered women, some of whom were murdered as well as raped. They burnt all St. Peter's estates and those of the Romans as well, it is

reported; they have burnt all houses on the city outskirts, removed the livestock, torn down the vines to the roots, torn up the crops, and devoured all. . . . They yoked together the servants of St. Peter and of the Romans and led them off; innocent babes were snatched from their mothers' breasts, the mothers raped, the babes sold by the Lombards. For certain they did more evil in this Rome province than any pagan race has ever done; so that one could say that the very stones weep at our desolation. For fifty-five days they have besieged afflicted Rome, day and night fierce battle has raged beneath the city walls.

In response to the appeal, Pepin's armies swept through the Alps and trounced the Lombards. A representative of the emperor arrived from Constantinople to negotiate return of the exarchate from the Lombard Aistulf only to find in charge Pepin, who believed it was rightfully St. Peter's—he had the pope's word for it. Pepin's representatives placed the keys of the twenty-two reconquered cities, and a document stating that they and their territories were the pope's perpetual possession, on the altar above St. Peter's tomb.

Not all central Italy rejoiced. There must have been raised eyebrows about the alleged document of Constantine assigning everything to the bishop of Rome, which had taken 440 years to surface. In Ravenna in particular, the founding bishop St. Apollinarus and the archbishop had as much title to governing the territory as St. Peter and the bishop of Rome. The church of Ravenna was wealthy with vast possessions, and the archbishop often played a civic role: it had a better claim than Rome to act there as a residual legatee of imperial authority. Despite such objections, Rome had "the patrimony of St. Peter" and would hold it for eleven hundred years.

Byzantium began to court the Franks: Emperor Constantine II gave an organ, a lavish gift, to Pepin and a marriage was proposed between his son Leo and the daughter of Pepin, Gisela, but it did not take place.

After Aistulf's death in a hunting accident, the papacy aided the duke of Tuscany, Desiderius, to obtain the Lombard throne. Stephen, who died in 757, considered Desiderius to be peace-loving, but he began to extend his power throughout the peninsula, and Pepin was disinclined to intervene. Stephen's successor, his younger brother, Paul, was in a bleak situation because, although Constantinople's support had been jeopardized, that of the Franks was not forthcoming.

The fragility of Paul's situation is indicated by the fact that some Roman clerics who disapproved of the alliance with the Franks were found intriguing with the Byzantines. In 767 Paul died after taking ill in St. Paul's basilica, where he had sought refuge from excessive midsummer heat. Division in the clergy over the best alliance for Rome was the background to an intricate series of coups after Paul's death. It was a many-sided conflict with double double-crossing so that some involved were confused as to who were their allies and who were their enemies.

First Duke Toto of Nepi seized the Lateran and proclaimed his brother Constantine, a layman, as pope. By threats he also obtained Constantine's consecration. Toto's intervention indicated that the aristocracy of the countryside near Rome wanted to influence the papacy now that it had become a temporal power.

Christopher, head of an influential family of papal office holders, avoided swearing loyalty to Constantine and did not attend the consecration. As his support was crucial, Constantine applied pressure to obtain his allegiance, but Christopher and his son Sergius, another important papal official, took refuge in St. Peter's. They convinced Constantine that they wished to become monks in a monastery outside Rieti. Constantine provided safe-conduct for the dissembling duo. But Rieti was in Lombard territory; from there they went to the capital, Pavia, and gained King Desiderius's support. With Lombard troops, Christopher and Sergius marched on Rome, Toto was stabbed in the back by one of his supporters, and Constantine, who had sought refuge in a church, was arrested.

Desiderius's men took a priest, Philip, from a monastery and proclaimed him pope. But now the Christopher-Lombard alliance broke down: Christopher would not accept the Lombard's man, and Philip, surely more than a little bemused, was returned to his monastery. The next day Christopher assembled clergy, army, and laity and held a regular election of a priest named Stephen, a mild Sicilian who was a sound Scripture scholar. A horrendous purge of those who had been responsible for Constantine's election followed: eyes were gouged out and tongues cut off. Blinded Constantine, brought before a synod in the Lateran in

769, begged pardon but also irritated the participants by trying to justify himself. He was consigned to a monastery for lifelong penance. A decree was emitted which excluded laymen from future elections.

It seemed that Christopher, his son Sergius, and their supporters, the dominant Lateran officials, now controlled the papacy because they had defeated the Lombards and the lords of the Roman countryside. But the Lombard king Desiderius, who had not forgiven Christopher's betrayal, had the backing of a papal chamberlain, Paul Afiarta, who was even more of a fox than Christopher. Desiderius came to Rome ostensibly to discuss Lombard reparations for the church with Pope Stephen. While Stephen met Desiderius near St. Peter's, Afiarta unsuccessfully tried to rouse Romans against Christopher. On Stephen's return to the Lateran, Christopher, Sergius, and armed followers, including Franks, burst in on him and demanded Afiarta's arrest. Stephen, however, mistakenly thought they aimed to murder him. He got away to St. Peter's and then told Christopher to join him there or to enter a monastery.

When Christopher, who was too cautious to cross the Tiber to St. Peter's because Desiderius and his troops were stationed nearby, refused to join the pope, some of his followers deserted him. His son Sergius tried to reach the sanctuary of St. Peter's, but the Lombards arrested him; then Christopher surrendered. Christopher and Sergius were taken to Stephen in St. Peter's. He ordered that they be given the tonsure and the monastic habit and left them in the basilica, planning to have them brought from the basilica into the city itself under the cover of night.

But, as a later investigation ascertained, Afiarta with Lombard troops took Christopher and Sergius from St. Peter's and blinded them. Three days later Christopher died. Sergius was strangled in Via Merulana near the Lateran, where he was buried while still breathing.

Shortly afterward, Stephen died. Afiarta, confident he could control the new pope, Hadrian, who had been one of Stephen's deacons, went to the Lombard capital, Pavia, and promised that he would bring Hadrian there to consecrate Carloman's sons, who were under Desiderius's protection, as kings of the Franks. (Pepin's sons, Charlemagne and Carloman—not to be confused with his uncle of the same name—had been at loggerheads after his death in

768. If Carloman's sons were made kings, it would weaken Charlemagne, the enemy of the Lombards.) All the dominoes were falling in favor of Afiarta and the Lombards who were close to controlling the papacy and the West. Pope Hadrian would come to Pavia, Afiarta promised, "even if I have to hobble him." But he did not know his man.

– XVI –

Knocking at
Heaven's Door

THE ROME THAT PAUL AFIARTA aimed to bring under Lombard control was attracting ever more pilgrims. From the second century, souvenirs with the effigy of Peter and Paul had been made for pilgrims. Hegesippus, probably a Hellenistic Jew, visited Rome in 155 or 156 as part of a pilgrimage that led to his conversion. St. Augustine pointed out that kings made pilgrimages to Peter's tomb but not that of Emperor Hadrian. The seventh-century pilgrims came mainly from the West, which showed that Peter had sired spiritually a number of churches—and nations. As well as being the seal and guarantee of the faith, he exercised a magnetic attraction as gatekeeper of heaven.

Pilgrimage, a physical journey to enact a spiritual quest, was a rite of passage that combined elements of penance, after-death insurance, and tourism. Some came by ship, many crossed the Alps by packhorse, or on foot, risking frostbite and attacks by brigands. For a time, Saracens were an additional threat. The only defense against rapacious innkeepers was accommodation in monasteries or hostels run by religious who were obliged to see Jesus in every wayfarer. Shingles or St. Anthony's fire plagued many pilgrims but some hostels provided an ointment as a remedy. Contrite murderers made their pilgrimage wearing an iron collar. Some merchants were denounced for pretending to be pilgrims to avoid paying tolls and customs duties. Wars and unrest modified routes but did not stop pilgrimages altogether. In pilgrim towns in Gaul and Italy, English prostitutes promised a shortcut to paradise.

Some Anglo-Saxons wrote to the monk Boniface complaining that they had lost many relatives and friends who had gone to seek Peter and Paul. They asked if it were better for Christians to live in their own land or go into exile on pilgrimage. Some of the pilgrims intended to stay in Rome to be at the head of the queue for the heavenly gate.

Many pilgrims came from the British Isles. Celts had a taste for penitential pilgrimages while the Anglo-Saxons were grateful to Peter for giving them the faith. There were notable feats of endurance. At the age of seventy Abbot Wilfred walked to Rome, a journey that took a year. With his companions he returned to England on horseback bearing relics, vestments, and silk hangings for churches. After forty-seven years as a priest and thirty-five as an abbot (he was the abbot of the historian Bede), Coelford decided at the age of seventy-four to go to Rome with eighty companions but, on September 25, 716, died at Langres. Between 653 and 798, sixty-four recorded English pilgrimage groups went to Rome. Routes varied according to where they landed in continental Europe, but most passed through Lyon and then Siena or Bologna. It was all done for love of Peter, one pilgrim wrote, "not for love of sea or mountains." (Because of the Muslim conquest of Jerusalem, from the seventh century, even more than previously, all pilgrim roads led to Rome.)

But at times Rome could prove nasty: a woman friend of Boniface was imprisoned, and Bishop Amandus of Maastricht, who visited Rome in 627, 630, and around 650, and who named foundations in his diocese after Peter and Paul, fell foul of a sacristan: "One day, toward evening," his biographer recounted, "this holy man was sitting in a small church after everyone had left for he wished in his devotion to pray through the night; but one of the custodians, finding him there, ejected him with contemptuous words and blows."

The first Germanic king to come on pilgrimage to the tomb of the apostles was Sigmund of Geneva at the beginning of the sixth century. Three years later the deposed Duke Harald of Acquitania came to live close to the Gatekeeper's tomb. The Anglo-Saxon kings Ine, Offa, and Caedwalla (baptized by Pope Sergius I) also moved to Rome. Like Paul, each could say *civis Romanus sum,* but in a different sense, for they were citizens of another Rome, the Rome of Peter and Paul rather than of the Caesars.

The influx helped Rome continue its cosmopolitan tradition: when Irish envoys arrived about 633 to discuss the date of Easter, they found themselves staying with a Greek, a Syrian, a Scythian, and an Egyptian, and they celebrated Easter together in St. Peter's.

Inevitably there were shady dealings: Pope Zachary found that Venetians were buying male and female slaves in Rome for re-sale to pagans in North Africa. Zachary bought the slaves and set them free.

Although initially Rome had objected to the Eastern practice of moving saints' bodies and providing relics, later it transferred remains from the catacombs to inside the city walls to save them from barbarian looting. Once the Franks became protectors of the church, their requests for relics could hardly be denied. At the request of King Pepin the remains of Petronilla, mistakenly believed to be St. Peter's elder daughter, were moved from a shrine by one of the consular roads to a mausoleum near St. Peter's. By authenticating relics, the church in Rome tried to exclude crooks from the growing trade that included grills on which Lawrence was allegedly roasted and arrows supposed to have pierced Sebastian.

Most pilgrims wanted simply to touch relics, but some robbed them. Bishop Gregory of Tours described what to expect to a deacon he was sending to Rome:

> [St. Peter's] sepulcher, which is placed under the altar, is very rarely entered. However, if anyone wishes to pray there, first its gates are opened, then a little window; the pilgrim inserts his head, and makes his requests. Nor is the result delayed, if only his petition be a just one. If he desires to carry away with him some blessed souvenir, he throws inside a small handkerchief which has been carefully weighted and then, watching and fasting, he prays most fervently that the apostle may give a favorable answer to his devotion. Wonderful to say, if the man's faith prevails, the handkerchief when drawn up from the tomb is so filled with divine power that it weighs much more than before; and then he who has pulled it up knows that he has obtained the favor. Many also make gold keys to unlock the gates of the blessed sepulcher; then they take away those previously in use as a sacred treasure, and by these keys the infirmities of the afflicted are cured. For true faith can do all things.

Bishop Gregory also explained how to obtain the much-desired filings from the chains worn by St. Peter in prison: "A priest stands by with a file; in the case of some seekers a portion comes off so quickly from the chains there is no delay." But for others, presumably of less worthy intentions, it was found impossible to obtain any filings at all.

Mid-seventh-century tourist guides did not mention the monuments of the pagan emperors because they were considered adorers of false gods and persecutors of Christians. Their itineraries moved around the city perimeter from one martyr's site to another on the radial consular roads.

Pilgrimages helped Rome to be a cultural clearing house. Partly because of them, Roman practices, some of which it had absorbed from the East, were transmitted to northern Europe, both shaping the churches there and binding them to Rome. Before printing, forgeries were often used in historical and doctrinal disputes, which made the Lateran archives and library of the greatest importance. They drew scholars to Rome, which also had other libraries in Latin and Greek, particularly in the late seventh and the eighth centuries when many exiled Greek-speaking scholars worked in the city. Gregorian chant enchanted. (Some scholars claim it dates from the time of Pope Vitalian or Gregory III rather than Gregory the Great). It was one aspect of the stational processions through the streets of Rome by the pope and his "family" that so impressed pilgrims. In the mid-760s King Pepin's brother, Bishop Benedus of Rheims, sent his monks to Rome to learn chant at the Lateran Choir School. Books of Roman Mass texts were in great demand beyond the Alps.

Papal hostels in Rome provided not only food and beds for pilgrims but also medical care and insisted on frequent washing. Certain national groups, such as the Anglo-Saxons, Lombards, Frisians, and Greeks set up their own hostels and churches in compounds known as scholae. They formed contingents that were part of the militia and army of the Romans, used not only for defense but also on ceremonial occasions.

The Anglo-Saxons had one of the largest of these compounds between the Tiber and St. Peter's, approximately where the hospital of Santo Spirito in Sassia now stands. The *burgus Saxonum* gave its name to the whole quarter now known as the Borgo. Its foundation is usually attributed to King Ine of Wessex, who abdicated in 726 to take up residence in Rome. The Borgo linked St. Peter's to the city on the other side of the Tiber, but the two remained distinct: Lombard kings, unwelcome in the city, could visit St. Peter's without entering it. Although separate, St. Peter's and the city sometimes drew strength from one another.

There were damaging fires in the Anglo-Saxon zone, perhaps because the foreigners built wooden houses, as at home, in the city of bricks and marble. Nevertheless the pilgrim presence took permanent form in this St. Petersburg-by-the-Tiber.

The bulk of the pilgrims were barbarian peoples who had been converted to Christianity. Shortly before Gregory the Great was elected, the Arian King Recared converted to Catholicism. He brought the whole Visigoth nation with him as proclaimed at the first national council of the Spanish Visigoth church held in Toledo which, like Constantinople, was both a royal and ecclesiastical capital. The bishops acclaimed Recared as another Constantine.

At the Council of Pavia in 698, the Lombards were won to the Catholic rite, and with Liutprand (712–44) the Lombard monarchy became Catholic. He influenced episcopal nominations, and, for a period, bishops were bound to military service. But as the Lombard sees of Emilia belonged to Ravenna and those of Tuscany, Spoleto, and Benevento to Rome, no fully national Lombard Church was formed.

The Catholic Visigoth kings "wedded" Spain, but the Lombard kings did not manage to make Italy their bride as she was already partly committed: the Lombards did not achieve control of all the territory, and, moreover, Rome was still loyal to the empire, which seemed more consonant with the idea of a universal church. The suffragans of the Lombard sees under Roman ecclesiastical jurisdiction swore to work for peace between the empire and the Lombard kingdom. But there was nothing similar tying the Holy See to the Lombards; in fact, it was negotiating for Frankish support against them. The latent conflict of allegiance ended only with the end of the Lombard kingdom.

Christianity had reached Gaul by the second century: the martyrs of Lyons, Hilary of Poitiers and Martin of Tours, were among its outstanding representatives. The son of a pagan, Martin became a Christian after a vision, traveled in what is now Hungary, Croatia, and Italy, and clashed with an Arian bishop in Milan. On return to Gaul he founded the first monastery there and in 372 became one of the first monks ever to be made a bishop.

Most of the remainder of the episcopacy seemed the local Roman senatorial class at prayer: they were drawn from the ranks of the elite of Gaul whose destination previously was the Senate. Because of his profound religious impulses, Martin was an exception to the customs that leaders of civil society became leaders of the church. As bishop he was zealous in evangelizing pagan peasants and established a rudimentary parochial system. After his death in 397 his tomb became a goal for pilgrims.

Some eighty years after Martin's death, the last Roman emperor was deposed. Subsequently Gaul was no longer divided into three, as Julius Caesar had noted, but into seven because of tribal, dynastic, and political conflicts. Most of the Germanic tribes that had overrun the Western empire were Christians, but heretical Christians, Arians who recognized the king's authority even in church matters.

When the barbarians crossed the Danube and the Rhine, they entered an empire that was becoming Catholic. To a degree, the church in these territories took the place of destroyed civil structures and, for many of the new arrivals, was a point of contact with a civilization to which they aspired. The newcomers managed to bring the Burgundians and Spanish Sueves, formerly Catholic, to Arianism and established regimes hostile to Catholics.

Catholic missionaries worked among the newcomers: the Irish monk Killian conducted a mission to the tribes east of the Rhine, and in Mainz, where he was stabbed to death, he is still remembered even in the name of food stores; another monk, Pirmin, converted the Germanic peoples in the Lake Constance area.

The first Germanic chieftain to accept Catholicism rather than remain pagan or become Arian was Clovis of the Salic Franks, who had moved westward from central Germany. They were *foedetari,* that is, a people that had settled within the boundaries of the empire where they were granted land in exchange for military service: Clovis, or Hlodwig as he was called in Frankish, continued this tradition of fidelity to Rome but was to extend it to the religious sphere.

One of Clovis's sisters was pagan, but the other was an Arian who for a time was married to the Ostrogoth king Theodoric. There were plans also for a marriage between one of Theodoric's sisters and Clovis but it did not take place. Clovis's reign, situated largely in what is now north-central France, was overshadowed by the Arian kingdoms of the Visigoths in Burgundy and the Vandals of Provence and Spain backed by the Vandals of North Africa and the Ostrogothic kingdom of Italy centered on Ravenna.

Clovis could well have become an Arian but his wife, Clothilde, was a Burgundian, a people that had become Catholic about 428–29. She tried to convince him of the truth of her faith. In 496 a Germanic tribe attacked the Franks along the Rhine. They appealed to Clovis for help, but he arrived late with his troops and was on the verge of defeat until he invoked Clothilde's god, vowing that if victorious he would be baptized.

On Clothilde's prompting, he took instruction from Bishop Remy of Rheims but did so in secret to avoid rebellion by his troops, who believed in the god of war, Wotan, a winner, rather than in an apparent loser such as Christ. Still not convinced that he should be baptized, Clovis consulted with a former soldier, Vaast, who had become a hermit and mystic, and for a time made him a traveling companion.

After being defeated twice by Visigoth forces near Bordeaux in 498, Clovis arrived at Tours on the feast of St. Martin. There he was impressed by the many pilgrims, the cures that took place, and his discussions with the priests of the sanctuary. After seven years examining the faith, he finally decided to be baptized.

He wrote to all the bishops of Gaul that he was entering the second phase of the catechumenate; the first was that in which the catechumen listened to explanations; the second required a written request for baptism. Usually baptism took place at Easter, but his was arranged for Christmas Day (probably in 498 or 499) to signify the birth of a Christian king. One of the bishops who could not come to the ceremony because he was living under Arian-Gothic domination wrote to Clovis that "your faith is our victory."

Clovis's sister was baptized with him after publicly renouncing her pagan beliefs; his Arian sister also became a Catholic. Her baptism as an Arian was valid, but she received Confirmation when Clovis became a Catholic. To ensure Clovis's safety, his three thousand personal guards were baptized with him, but the bulk of his troops preserved their pagan beliefs. Clovis established his capital in Paris and built there a church dedicated to Peter and Paul, which was evidence of his attachment to Rome (Peter the Gatekeeper was much cited in polemics against the Arians).

For some, Clovis's delay in choosing Catholicism was due not to prolonged reflection but to political opportunism. They noted that after his baptism he killed male relatives to ensure his son's succession. Clovis on the rampage wielding a double-headed axe has been compared to Terminator; there was a point of similarity with

Constantine. Whatever the motives for Clovis's decision, it did not mean baptism for his people but, as a result, their subsequent history was to be intertwined with that of the church.

Although the British Isles were further away, Rome had a more direct role in the conversion of the Anglo-Saxons than of the Franks because it was effected by missionaries sent by successive popes. As a result, a strong tradition of pilgrimage from the British Isles built up. The withdrawal of the Roman legions from Britain in 410 to strengthen defenses when Rome itself was under attack had laid the islands open to the invasion of Saxon and Jutes a decade later. The Britons, who were partly Christian, retreated to the west, leaving the east in the hands of the heathens whom Augustine and his fellow monks found.

Soon after Gregory's envoys reached Britain, Rome began to receive reports of conversions in some of the Anglo-Saxons' many small kingdoms. But there were other reports, about missionaries from Ireland, which caused concern. Christianity had probably been brought to Ireland by returning prisoners of war, but in 429 Rome had dispatched there Palladius, a deacon who was later made a bishop. Patrick arrived in Ireland first as a slave but returned as a missionary bishop. About the same time, Ninian and David were evangelizing in what are now, respectively, Scotland and Wales. Columban the Elder, who left Ireland in 563, established a monastic community on the island of Iona off the Scottish coast, which, through its ascetic practices and missionary zeal, was to influence North Britain. King Oswald called on Aidan, a monk of the Lindisfarne island community that was an offshoot of Iona, to organize the church in Northumbria.

Augustine landed in Kent thirty-four years after Columban reached Iona: Christianity was being propagated in both the north and south. That was the good news about the Good News. From Rome's viewpoint, the bad news was that they were differing styles of Christianity: the Celtic variety did not have a classical context, although by the sixth century the Celts had adopted the Latin alphabet. Rome may have feared that the Celts could disseminate a distorted form of the faith as had the Arian Goths. Or at least that the different styles of Christianity would lead to confusion and friction because the spheres of influence overlapped.

Different dates were used for the major feast of Easter; there were differences in discipline such as the cut of tonsure. (The

Roman style was a shaved crown with a circle of hair above the temples to recall the crown of thorns. Celtic clergy shaved the front of the scalp, allowing hair to grow at the back, which Romans claimed had been the style of the magician, Simon Magus.) Roman ecclesiastical organization was diocesan whereas that of the Celts was predominantly monastic. But the basic issue was whether such questions should be decided in Rome or Lindisfarne.

Rome did not forget the mission. Mellitus, a Greek who was the first bishop of London, brought letters from Rome to Archbishop Lawrence of Canterbury and to King Ethelbert of Kent and his subjects. Boniface V (619–25), a Neapolitan, showed particular interest in the mission, among other things asking how anyone could prefer paganism to Christianity: "How can people be so deluded as to worship as gods objects [idols] to which they have given the likeness of a body? Accept therefore the sign of the Holy Cross, by which the whole human race has been redeemed, and exorcise from your heart the damnable crafts and devices of the Devil." He wrote to King Edwin's Catholic wife, Ethelberga, because he had heard that Edwin "still serves abominable idols," advising her "not to avoid the duty imposed on us in season and out in order that...the king also may be added to the Christian fold."

After discussions with the missionary Paulinus, a vision, and prolonged reflection, Edwin decided to become a Christian but held a council with his chieftains to discuss Christianity. One of the participant's contributions would have pleased Boniface:

> Your majesty, when we compare the life of men on earth with that time of which we have no knowledge, it seems to me like the swift flight of a single sparrow through the banqueting-hall where you are sitting at a dinner on a winter's day with your thanes and counselors. In the midst there is a comforting fire to warm the hall; outside, the storms of winter rain or snow are raging. This sparrow flies swiftly in through one hall door and out another. While he is inside, he is safe from the winter storms, but after a few moments of comfort, he vanishes from sight into the wintry world from which he came. Similarly, man appears on earth for a little while; but of what went before this life and of what follows, we know nothing.

Therefore, if this new teaching has brought any more certain knowledge, it seems only right that we should follow it.

Pope Boniface's successor, Honorius, wrote to congratulate Edwin on his "ardent faith" and also sent missionaries to the West Saxons. But the tension between Roman and Celtic versions of Christianity had not disappeared and, indeed, was sharpened when Colman became bishop of the Northumbrians. In 664 King Oswy of Northumbria convoked a synod at Whitby, presided over by his relative Abbess Hilda, to decide which was the more reliable tradition.

Abbot Wilfred of York, who had been on a pilgrimage to Rome eleven years earlier and whose deepest aspiration was to live near Peter's tomb, presented the case for Rome. According to the historian Bede, he said that the Roman dating of Easter was followed by different nations and languages throughout the world wherever the church had spread. "The only people," he continued, "who stupidly contend against the whole world are these Scots [as the Irish were then called] and their partners in obstinacy, the Picts and the Britons, who inhabit only a small portion of these two uttermost islands of the ocean."

When Colman replied that he was following the tradition of the Apostle John, Wilfred argued that the calculations used were mistaken. Conceding that Colman's predecessors were holy men, he asked what did their authority count against that of the universal church: "Do you imagine that they, a few men in a corner of a remote island, are to be preferred to the universal church of Christ throughout the world? And even if your Columban—or, may I say, ours also if he was a servant of Christ—was a saint potent in miracles, can he take precedence before the most blessed Prince of the Apostles?"

Bede did not say what effect this "what-good-can-come-out-of-Nazareth?"-style argument had on King Oswy, who had received Christianity from the Celts, but Wilfred's citation of Matthew's "You are Peter and upon this rock I will build my church, and the gates of hell will not prevail against it, and I will give you the keys of the kingdom of heaven" constituted a clincher. Oswy asked Colman if these were really the Lord's words. When the reply was affirmative, the king said: "This is the gatekeeper whom I will not resist; rather I want to obey his orders in every way according to my knowledge and ability, lest, when I come before the gates of heaven, there may be no one there to open them, because he who holds the keys turns his back on me."

Rome, or rather St. Peter, had won. Another episode crucial for the Anglo-Saxon church took place in Rome shortly afterward. Northumbria had chosen an Anglo-Saxon archbishop of Canterbury, but he died in Rome where he was to be consecrated by Pope Vitalian. As a replacement the pope chose a Greek, Theodore, who went to Canterbury in 669. In the twenty-two years until his death he gave the Anglo-Saxon church a shape that would last for centuries. He was the first archbishop of Canterbury recognized by the whole church, whose synods legislated for several different kingdoms.

Ground for the attachment to Rome had been laid by people such as the cultured nobleman-monk Benedict Biscop, who visited it in 653, 665, 667, and 671 and brought back "paintings, books, and relics of every kind" plus John, the archcantor of St. Peter's, to teach fellow monks liturgical chant. Pope Vitalian had to convince Biscop to return rather than remain in Rome.

A drab port on the Tyne near Newcastle, with its heaps of coal, moored freighters, electrical power lines, and oil storage tanks is the site of the remains of one of the monasteries Biscop founded. Part of the walls of the monastery church, St. Paul's, still stands outside Jarrow, but it is difficult to imagine the establishment once had 250 monks. A child born on the monastery lands was entrusted, from the age of seven, to its abbot and spent the remainder of his life there. "My chief delight has always been study, teaching and writing," confessed this stay-at-home savant, Bede, who taught biblical exegesis, grammar, poetry, chronology, and historiography. Among the authors he cited were Virgil, Pliny, Ovid, and Horace. His love of learning and of Jesus is evident in his prayer: "I pray You, noble Jesus, that as You have graciously granted me to imbibe the words of your knowledge with joy, so You will also in Your bounty grant me to come at length to Yourself, the Fount of all wisdom, and to dwell in Your presence for ever."

Although he did not travel, Bede had wide interests. His small collection of Middle Eastern objects suggests that he was on a monastic cultural exchange circuit; as he lay dying in 735, he distributed treasures such as pepper, linen, and incense. At a time when Anglo-Saxons built almost exclusively in wood, his monastery imported stonemasons and glaziers from Gaul and requested a harpist from continental Europe. For Bede's *History,* Nothelm, an English priest in Rome, obtained documents on the reign of the contemporary pope.

Bede and the Anglo-Saxon bishops were responsible for the development of Christian dating. Early Christians had wanted to prove their faith's antiquity relative to secular history. Their time scale started in the Garden of Eden and stretched toward the Second Coming. This was Anni Mundi (A.M.) dating. But for secular events Christians used pagan or Jewish chronologies such as the regnal year of the emperor or the four-year cycle of the Olympics. There were many different local uses.

In Rome a monk, Dionysius, had calculated future celebrations of Easter and concluded that it was the 525th year since the Incarnation. This made A.D. dating possible (and, as a corollary, B.C. dating, which could recede endlessly).

Dionysius's description of how to convert A.M. dates to A.D. dates was welcomed by Cassiodorus at his Vivarium monastery in Calabria. When it closed, some of the manuscripts and incunabula went to the Jarrow monastery. There Bede dated his *Ecclesiastical History of the English People,* completed in 731, by the Anglo-Saxon kingdoms' regnal years but also by years dating from the Incarnation. When the bishops from various Anglo-Saxon kingdoms met in conferences, they dated from their shared point of reference, the Incarnation, rather than by diverse regnal years. In Britain, ecclesiastical unity long preceded political unity and fostered it just as Bede's idea of an English people tended to create them out of a melting pot of Saxons, Jutes, and Britons.

After the example given by Bede and the bishops, dating from the Incarnation spread throughout northern Europe, although in Rome, despite Dionysius Exiguus's discovery, secular-based dating continued to be used. It had taken centuries for Christians to establish a fairly wide consensus on dating from the Incarnation, but, within a decade of Mohammed's death, Islam had begun to date from his flight from Medina to Mecca as it still does. Islam was more decisive about its founder's experience being a new start for history or, at least, in imposing this on society's calendar. Christianity and Islam began their new dating practices within approximately a century of one another but, of course, the Christian starting point was many centuries earlier.

As well as fostering the faith in the British Isles, Rome sponsored Anglo-Saxon missionary enterprises in continental Europe. On November 27, 695, at St. Cecilia in Trastevere, Sergius I consecrated the Northumbrian monk Willibrord as archbishop of Utrecht. A few days later Willibrord set out on his mission to what is now the Netherlands.

In the spring of 718 another Anglo-Saxon monk arrived at the Lateran seeking a papal audience. Gregory II was well disposed toward the emaciated, blond, pale-complexioned monk in a black Benedictine habit who, after leaving his monastery in Wessex, had traveled through London, Caen, Rouen, Le Mans, the Alps, and Lombardy. The monk bore a letter of presentation from Bishop Daniel of Winchester, but the pope already had a high opinion of Anglo-Saxons because of visitors such as Biscop, the scholar Adelm, and Willibrord.

The new arrival, called Wynfrith, had entered Exeter monastery at the age of seven. He had become an eminent monastic teacher, author of a Latin grammar, of poetry, and of innumerable riddles, but, at the age of forty, conscious of his Saxon descent, he felt called to a mission to the Saxon pagans in their homeland. However his first mission had been to the Frisians, where Willibrord had been working for years with little success, partly because the Catholic Franks warred against them. After a few months, Wynfrith had decided little could be achieved and returned to his monastery, Nursling, in Wessex. Bishop Daniel had told him he needed the pope's backing for missionary success and provided the letter he had brought to Rome.

Although Gregory welcomed Wynfrith's proposal, rather than assent immediately he lodged the monk near the Lateran and throughout the winter they discussed the proposed mission. Gregory probed Wynfrith's scriptural learning but also his political knowledge of central Western Europe, where Charles Martel could be an important defender of the church's interests.

Finally Gregory made Wynfrith a member of the papal household. Wynfrith was to be the pope's man in Thuringa, Hesse, and elsewhere in Germany. As it would mean a new life for the slim monk, Gregory gave him a new name, Boniface, and a to-whom-it-may-concern letter of support dated May 15, 719. A revealing detail was the papal court's insistence that, as legate, Boniface be accompanied by servants.

Boniface returned to Rome four years later, but in the meantime he had sent frequent scrupulous reports and requests for advice. He had returned to Frisia, where he resisted Willibrord's attempt to make him his auxiliary, and then made converts in Thuringa and Hesse. Missionaries such as the Irish Killian had preceded him in some of these territories, but Boniface complained to Rome about the low standards and ignorance of the priests he met, many of them Anglo-Saxons. Some sacrificed to the pagan god Thor, while others lived openly with concubines. Almost all were ignorant about the faith, some even baptizing in the name of the Fatherland, the Daughter, and the Holy Spirit.

The reports were detailed, but Gregory asked Boniface to return to Rome himself. With companions he sailed along the Rhine and then on horseback crossed the Rhine Valley, baking in late summer heat.

After receiving Boniface cordially, Gregory asked him to write a profession of faith. While Boniface's companions visited catacombs and churches, he spelled out his beliefs, affirming his fidelity to the Roman liturgy and his commitment to the unity of the universal church. On receipt of the profession, Gregory made him bishop for all Germany responsible directly to the pope. The following day, November 30, Boniface, who was fifty, the minimum age for episcopal consecration, was consecrated bishop and swore fidelity to the pope at St. Peter's tomb. Significantly, unlike oaths taken by other bishops directly dependent on the pope, it did not include a promise to fight the enemies of the empire. Emperor Leo had been more or less happily reigning in Constantinople for seven years, but Boniface would be working beyond the empire's boundaries and owed allegiance only to Gregory and Christ. (Gregory had warned the icon-smashing Leo that he was behaving like a barbarian while Christianity was civilizing the barbarians.)

Snow blocking the Brenner Pass prevented Boniface's departure until the spring. When he did leave, he took with him a present from Gregory: a collection of conciliar canons and thirty-eight papal decrees as guidance to church law. Boniface had a papal letter that asked all Germany to give him every assistance and threatened those who hindered him with eternal damnation for themselves and their unfortunate descendants. He also had a letter from Gregory to "his beloved son in Jesus Christ," Charles Martel, which explained that Boniface was sent "to preach the

Gospel to the Germans living east of the Rhine who persist in the errors of paganism and are lost in the darkness of ignorance." In Frisia Boniface had learned that evangelization was virtually impossible when the temporal power was hostile, while Gregory saw the possibility of building an alliance with Martel, who recently, at Poitiers, had defeated Islamic forces threatening western Europe.

Boniface was well received at Martel's court in Trier but was shocked by the soldiers' crudeness and brutality and, still more, by the avaricious, immoral court prelates. More interested in hunting or fighting than in priestly duties, they sometimes celebrated Mass in hunting garb. By exploiting the poor and church property, they managed to live sumptuously, were gluttonous and drunken, played dice, which was expressly forbidden for clerics, and even had mistresses and illegitimate children. Boniface reported the sorry state of affairs to Gregory, who decided not to tackle the problem head-on but build good relations with Martel; Boniface would have to restrain his desire to reform the Frankish church.

Shortly after, Rome heard of a striking gesture by Boniface designed to convince pagans that the gods they worshiped were false idols, merely the forces of nature personified, and their heaven, Walhalla, an illusion that did not justify the sacrifice of children. Pagans were prostrate before a sacred giant oak on Gudensberg mountain in Hesse when Boniface and his companions arrived. While two monks hacked at the tree, the missionary from Wessex stood holding high a cross. The pagans protested, warning of Thor's terrible wrath, but a strong wind rose and toppled the oak, smashing it into four parts; Thor's revenge did not eventuate. With the wood, Boniface built a chapel dedicated to St. Peter. Later he built a monastery nearby at Buraburg, one of a series throughout the German lands that were centers of learning and instruction but also important to the economy because of the monks' agricultural know-how used, for instance, to make marshes fertile land.

All the time Rome was supplying Boniface with authoritative answers to his queries about issues such as the remarriage of widows, the sale of slaves, the grades of relationship that prevent a marriage, whether a sickness of a spouse affected marital rights, what was to be done with food offered to idols, and what was to be done with "unworthy bishops and priests full of vice." Pope Gregory advised him that "if a wife is too sick to perform her wifely duty, it is best that her husband practice continence but, if this is impossible, he might have another wife provided he take care of the first."

After a pontificate of sixteen years, Gregory II died on February 11, 731. His successor, Gregory III, made Boniface archbishop of all Germany with the right to create dioceses and appoint bishops. This strengthened him against bishops who were hostile because he was a foreigner or too rigorous. Boniface still tormented himself over bishops, such as some in Bavaria, who bought their way into office and then enriched themselves by selling church treasures, sacraments, and lands. He felt he should consult directly with the new pope.

Boniface arranged to meet in Rome his Anglo-Saxon friend Abbess Bugga and her daughter Eangith and took them to catacombs, churches, and tombs of saints, particularly that of Petronilla. The story was that Petronilla, a consecrated Roman virgin believed to be St. Peter's daughter, had refused to marry a nobleman. Denounced as a Christian, she was condemned to be thrown to wild beasts but died after a three-day fast. Boniface was excited to hear that her remains were to be shifted near to St. Peter's tomb. Gregory gave Boniface power to convoke synods: it was a green light for reform of lax clergy.

On his return trip Boniface took with him many saints' relics for the altars of the churches and monasteries he was establishing, but also two noble Anglo-Saxon brothers, Wunnibald and Willibald. The first had been a monk in a Roman monastery, while the second had recently returned from a pilgrimage to Jerusalem. They were to be joined by their sister Walburga, one of the many Anglo-Saxon consecrated virgins who assisted Boniface.

Shortly after Boniface's departure, Gregory III died. His successor, Zachary, received a letter from the missionary archbishop, asking permission to hold a synod of the Frankish church, because "in many places episcopal sees are assigned to greedy lay men or corrupt clergy. There are so-called deacons who from youth have lived in adultery and take four or more concubines to bed every evening.... There are bishops who are drunken, lecherous warriors who spill the blood of both pagans and Christians." He also told Zachary that there were reports of "pagan processions, singing sacrilegious songs in Rome and women who, in the pagan style, sold amulets or told fortunes." The subtext was: look to your own backyard, which needs reform, and don't block it elsewhere. Boniface was criticizing customs that the church in Rome evidently accepted as harmless: rowdy New Year celebrations and fortune telling. But for the monk Boniface there was no harmless middle ground.

Perhaps there were knowing smiles in Rome when Boniface held his synod, and others in subsequent years, which emitted severe warnings against persistent pagan practices and scandalous clergy, but, nevertheless, many of the deplored practices continued. Ignorant priests still baptized in the name of the Fatherland, the Daughter, and the Holy Spirit. Several bishops, such as Gerold of Mainz, remained hostile to Boniface. Gerold, more a warrior than a priest, had claimed jurisdiction over half of Boniface's territory, but Zachary replied that a bishop who was too lazy to preach the word of God could not have another's diocese.

Zachary had other reasons to be concerned about Boniface's missionary territory. On the death of Charles Martel, his heirs had divided the realm, which made the Frankish area unstable and potentially chaotic. Charles had been the effective Frankish leader, but the throne of the Merovingian dynasty was occupied by inept King Childeric III. Charles's heirs, Pepin and Carloman, divided the realm but were threatened by Guiffred, Charles's son by a second marriage. He was defeated in battle and Carloman withdrew to a monastery at Monte Cassino near Rome, which left Pepin in control.

It was at this time that Pepin asked Zachary if he would condone a bloodless coup d'état: claiming that Childeric III would not face his responsibilities, Pepin proposed to join charisma with clout and replace the Merovingian dynasty. Zachary assented, and Childeric was packed off to a monastery. Perhaps he recalled the lament of his predecessor Chilperic: "We remain poor but our riches are transferred to the churches; only bishops rule and they steal our dignity." On his return from a meeting with Zachary, where the substitution had been discussed, Bishop Burchard of Würzburg reported to his mentor Boniface.

In November 751, in the capital, Soissons, near Paris, a papal legate, whom a minority of historians claim was Boniface, poured oil on the head of Pepin to show he was king of the Franks "with the Lord's aid." Pepin was the first Westerner to receive such a consecration. Even if Boniface was not the celebrant, he had contributed to the event by establishing good relations with Pepin and by gaining his collaboration for church and missionary endeavors. As he had deplored the dissoluteness of Charles's court, he may have had misgivings about the event, but the new dynasty assured the church a firm, well-disposed power in the area from the Atlantic to the Elbe and from the Pyrenees to the Danube.

By this time Boniface was archbishop of Mainz; he had wanted the Cologne see but had been opposed by the local clergy, perhaps inspired by a long-standing enemy, Bishop Milone, whom he had deposed at Rouen. To compensate Boniface for missing out on Cologne, Rome raised Mainz to archdiocesan status forever. Boniface continued to seek guidance from Rome on questions such as the treatment of lepers, on what conditions those under the normal age of thirty could be ordained priests, and what should be done about a new people who had arrived at the frontier asking to live in Christian lands: the Slavs. Slavs? Zachary responded that he needed time to think about the matter.

But Zachary did not have much time left: he died on March 15, 752. His successor, Stephen II, received a tardy letter of homage from Boniface, who explained that he had been unable to write earlier as thirty churches and monasteries had been burnt or sacked by barbarians. Perhaps after the consecration the previous year of their enemy Pepin, the barbarians could not distinguish between the church and civil authorities.

Stephen had more urgent political issues in mind: because of Lombard pressure, he begged Pepin to invite him for a visit and ensure safe conduct. Pepin sent his brother-in-law and Bishop Chrodegang of Metz with troops as escorts for the pope on a trip through the Great St. Bernard Pass. Stephen consecrated Pepin, as had the papal legate, but with lesser authority, in 751. In this way Stephen gained his military protection and recognition of what were to become later the Papal States.

On return to Rome Stephen may have spared a thought for Boniface, who had made an essential contribution to the alliance with the Franks. He would have known that eighty-year-old Boniface, instead of retiring to await his death in a monastery he had established at Fulda, had set out again along the Rhine with fifty-two men: priests, monks, deacons, novices, servants, and ten soldiers. After forty years as a missionary, he wanted to complete the conversion of the Frisians and the Saxons: he was nothing if not tenacious. He arranged a meeting of converts near the Zuidersee, but just before they arrived, Boniface's camp was overrun by brigands who slaughtered him and many of his companions. It was the seal on his willingness to give his life for the faith.

Collaboration between Anglo-Saxons and Rome continued through people such as Alcuin, a monk from York who had studied under a pupil of Bede and had paid his first visit to Rome in 767. As head of the Carolingian Royal Palace School he ensured that it absorbed not only patristic and classical learning but also Roman liturgy and ecclesiastical practices. At the end of the eighth century the papacy would have reason to be grateful to Alcuin.

– XVII –

ANOTHER CONSTANTINE,
ANOTHER ROME

A s LOMBARD PRESSURE on Rome persisted, it again sought
help from the Franks, who had a new leader, Charlemagne. His earliest biographer, Einhard, described him
as powerfully built with russet hair, bull neck, long nose, and a
high-pitched voice. Although Einhard does not mention a moustache, some scholars say that he wore one, which would have been
unusual at the time. He was an intrepid warrior and a tenacious
commander. War and prayer were not at odds: he saw the expansion of his territories as a Christian triumph over paganism.
Once he gave five thousand defeated pagan warriors a choice between baptism and death: only five hundred chose baptism. He
was to have five wives, four concubines, and nineteen children.
Born between 742 and 748, he came to power before he was thirty,
evolved into a statesman, and, although illiterate, understood the
importance of education in uniting his kingdom.

The new leader of the Franks dealt with a new pope, Hadrian,
who was to rule for twenty-three years, half the period Charlemagne was in power. Affection grew between the two leaders.

When Hadrian was elected in 772, the Lombards seemed on
the point of dominating the papacy. Paul Afiarta, who had master-
minded the bloody episode which had put Hadrian's predecessor,
Stephen, in his hands, promised King Desiderius that he would
bring the new pope to the Lombard capital even if he had to
hobble him. Instead it was Hadrian who hobbled Afiarta. He had
the schemer arrested, but the archbishop of Ravenna tried him.
Afiarta was condemned to death; Hadrian released those Afiarta
had imprisoned.

Nevertheless Desiderius marched on Rome and retreated only
when Hadrian threatened excommunication. Hadrian appealed to

Charlemagne, who only a few years before, when he had married Desiderius's daughter, had seemed on the point of allying with the Lombards. However, the following year, on the grounds that she was too sickly to give him an heir, he repudiated her, which offended her father.

Now, in response to Hadrian's plea, Charlemagne besieged Pavia, the capital of the kingdom of his former father-in-law. During the siege, at Easter 774, he made a surprise visit to Rome and was welcomed outside the city by clerical and municipal authorities accompanied by local militia with their banners, lay patrons, and children chanting his praise as a patrician and therefore protector of Rome. His meeting with Hadrian, the first, was momentous: the pope greeted him at St. Peter's, where they prayed together at Peter's tomb; then Charlemagne and his entourage were given permission to enter the city proper. At St. John Lateran they witnessed the traditional Easter Saturday baptism of catechumens. During Charlemagne's five-day stay he renewed in writing the pledges his father, Pepin, had made to Pope Stephen. Even independent Istria was promised to Rome, but Charles later made it clear that he did not intend to give northern Italy to the papacy. Although he did not abandon Frankish dress and other customs for Roman ways, Charlemagne took his patricianship seriously. On his way back from Rome he occupied Pavia; Desiderius was taken to France, and Charlemagne added "King of the Lombards" to his title of King of the Franks.

With peace and security assured, Hadrian could make long-term plans. An orphan of a noble Roman family whose mansion stood near the present Palazzo Venezia, he was raised by his uncle Theodatus who had been an important city official. When a deacon, Hadrian won a reputation as a preacher but was also engaged in helping the needy, an activity he continued as pope. As the countryside had been ravaged by the Lombards and the Byzantines had cut off Sicily, the papal granary, he expanded the church's mainland agricultural estate system, whose tenant farmers served also as a militia. The estates, which linked many farms sold or bequeathed to the church, had oratories and resident clergy, perhaps as supervisors.

In the 1960s one of the five estates Hadrian established was excavated fifteen miles from Rome where there are now apartment blocks. The Capracorum estate consisted of farms Hadrian had inherited plus others he acquired. Daily it provided wine, bread, and condiments, distributed to a hundred poor people from the steps of the Lateran Palace. Moreover, the extensive estate produced wheat, barley, and vegetables, which were sent to papal storehouses in Rome, as was meat from its pigs.

It has been suggested that such estates, as well as enabling a reorganization of farming methods, served against local warlords who could challenge the papacy, as happened in 768 when one of them, Duke Toto, made his brother anti-pope.

On the estate Hadrian built a large church dedicated to St. Peter, which was lavishly decorated with a red and green marble floor, and endowed it with precious relics. In addition, he transferred the bodies of four of his sainted predecessors: Cornelius (251–53), Lucius I (253–54), Felix I (269–72), and Innocent I (401–17). For its dedication at the end of the 770s, he invited the whole of the Roman clergy and Senate. He could not have underlined its importance more emphatically.

He also opened new welfare centers for pilgrims and the Roman poor. Unusually, the one near St. Peter's required beneficiaries to take a weekly bath. Three more welfare centers were established in buildings in the Forum, where churches had been installed. In the wake of Lombard attacks, Romans had moved to live near the remaining aqueducts. Hadrian rebuilt the arches of the destroyed Sabbatina aqueduct so that water again fed the fountain in St. Peter's atrium, the baths for pilgrims nearby, and wheat mills on the Janiculum hill. Other aqueducts, such as the Acqua Vergine, which supplied most of the city, were also repaired.

Hadrian rebuilt towers along the city walls and an embankment to protect the colonnade that ran from Castel Sant'Angelo by the Tiber to St. Peter's. Sometimes he supervised the work personally; he also led a fire-fighting operation. Many churches were repaired and refurbished. Charlemagne supplied thousands of pounds of lead for St. Peter's roof. Thirty-five huge beams, some from the forests near Spoleto, strengthened the roof of St. Paul's, fifteen that of the Lateran, fourteen St. Peter's. Metal clamps were installed in the apse of the Holy Apostles Church, and its mosaics were renewed. Much reconstruction was done outside the walls as churches there, such as St. Paul's and San Pancrazio, had been the most vulnerable to Lombard attacks. In fact, when the church of San Silvestro and monastery were completed in 761 on the grounds of the family mansion of Paul I, he had brought there from the catacombs "innumerable saints' bodies." (A church for English-speaking Catholics still functions on the site, but the monastery has become the central post office). Likewise when Hadrian rebuilt Santa Maria in Cosmedin, he brought there saints' remains.

Pilgrims were dazzled by the results of this incessant construction work. The shimmering mosaics, the icons, the spacious frescoes, the veils between classical columns, the gold and silver ornaments and plate, the glowing oil lamps, the large crosses and bejeweled liturgical books suggested that although the political clout of Constantinople had diminished, its artistic influence remained strong. And pagan Rome was being accepted more readily now that it was receding in time: guide books began listing Christian and pagan monuments without distinguishing between them.

Reconciliation with Constantinople came closer at the Seventh General Council in Nicaea in September 787, when Hadrian's statement against iconoclasm, which specified the proper use of images, was applauded. This rapprochement, however, upset Charlemagne, who had not been invited to the council. In a conciliatory gesture acknowledging the importance of the Frankish church, Hadrian sent him the proceedings. But in Rome they had been badly translated from Greek to Latin. Although the council had decreed that images could be venerated but not adored, the text Charlemagne received said images could be adored.

Charlemagne, who resembled Constantine in his intellectual curiosity as well as his military prowess, had attracted scholars from his realm but also from other places such as Northumbria and Ireland. For instance, Alcuin of Northumbria, who was recruited after teaching in Parma, was influential in many ways but especially for championing a revival of the Christian empire of Constantine. Some of the scholars became imperial administrators or bishops. The Carolingian think tank fostered the extension of A.D. dating and use of a uniform, legible miniscule script, which is still in use. The widespread adoption of Latin, introduction of good administrative structures and methods, and rigorous educational standards united the Frankish part of the promontory of Asia, which now began to be called Europe. Franks had been Catholic for almost three centuries, and good relations with the clergy strengthened the kingdom.

Charlemagne's theological advisers were incensed by what they learned of the Nicene Council from the faulty translation made in Rome. A synod of the Frankish church presided over by Charlemagne in 794 denied validity to the "inept" council. As there had been consultation among the churches of the West on controversial issues since the time of Martin I, the unconsulted Franks were not prepared to accept the council's dictates. Moreover, by now, three of the Eastern patriarchates (Alexandria, Jerusalem, and Antioch) were under Islamic control, which weakened Eastern Christianity. The Franks also objected to the emperors' customary claim that they "reigned with God," preferring Charlemagne's title as "defender of the faith." They were cutting Constantinople down to size but also making it clear to Rome that they could make theological assessments.

Despite such occasional friction between Charlemagne and Hadrian, on the pope's death on Christmas Day 795, Charlemagne grieved "as if he had lost a brother or a child." Throughout his realm, he organized Requiem Masses. The words inscribed on a black marble slab in the atrium of St. Peter's testify to his affection: "I, Charles, write these words while crying for your death, Hadrian. I was bound to you, a venerable father, by great and sweet affection. And I want our names to be joined forever: Charles and Hadrian, King and Father." Composed by Alcuin, they are also a fine example of Carolingian lettering.

That same year Charlemagne, whose sway already extended to the Byzantine frontier in central Europe, began work on a canal to join the Rhine and the Danube, which would have enabled him to transport troops and goods more quickly to what is now Hungary. (A canal that finally fulfilled Charlemagne's plan was inaugurated on September 25, 1992).

Hadrian's successor, Leo III, a Roman of humble origin, was accused of perjury and adultery. These charges may have arisen because he was threatening the power of lay nobles by extending the landholdings of the church at their expense and because he had dismissed Hadrian's nephews Paschal, the chief notary of the papal administration, and Campulus, the papal treasurer. They hired a gang, which in the central Piazza San Silvestro seized Leo as he rode in procession to Mass on April 25, 799. The mob threatened to gouge out his eyes and cut out his tongue. Leo was deposed and confined to a monastery, but his chamberlain lowered him from the monastery wall by a rope. He fled to Spoleto, then headed north, was escorted over the Alps, and sailed along the Rhine to Paderborn, Saxony, where Charlemagne received him with honors. Leo desperately needed Charlemagne's support, which was forthcoming: after two months, he returned to Rome with a military escort and the Frankish archbishops of Cologne and Salzburg who investigated the charges against Leo. Judgment was deferred until Charlemagne arrived in Rome.

On his election, Leo had informed Charlemagne, sending him a set of the keys to St. Peter's tomb, a gift sometimes made to important figures, Rome's banner, and a request for an envoy to receive the citizens' oath of loyalty. Although pliant with Charlemagne, Hadrian had never asked the citizens to take such an oath. In his response, Charlemagne said his task was to promote the faith and defend the church while Leo's was to pray for him: "For the king's task is the effective reinforcement, consolidation, propagation, and preservation of the faith; the pope's is to support the king in this duty by praying for him like Moses with outstretched arms." Charlemagne was claiming the senior role in the partnership; he advised Leo, whom he was treating as his chaplain, to combat simony. Leo had continued Hadrian's vigorous building program: some murals executed during his pontificate, such as one in the Lateran palace, depicted Charlemagne as another Constantine.

Constantinople was in no position either to defend Rome or oppose the creation of a Western empire because, since the death of Emperor Leo IV in 780, Empress-Regent Irene had been struggling with grave internal problems and Islamic pressure continued. It is estimated that in this period, for the first time, the number of Christians in Western Europe topped those in Eastern Europe and the Middle East.

On November 23, 800, Charlemagne, who ruled most of these Western Christians, returned to Rome for the fourth time. He was nearing sixty and mourning his fifth wife. His abundant russet hair had turned white; he was heavier but still a vigorous, imposing figure. He had just visited ailing Alcuin, now bishop of Tours, whose opinion that no earthly power could judge the apostolic see seems to have been crucial in subsequent proceedings. Charlemagne was conscious of the aura of Rome and the papacy, but he had seen several popes pleading for help since the time he had gone as a youth to meet Stephen, who had crossed the Alps to reach his father, Pepin. In the decade since his previous visit, Charlemagne's power and prestige had increased, but recently that of the papacy had shrunk.

Four years before Charlemagne had given his previously itinerant court a permanent capital in what had been a small Roman bathing place, Aquae Grani (now Aachen, Aix-la-Chapelle) in Germany near what is now the Belgian border. For the first time since ancient Rome, a palace was built with baths incorporated. Ancient columns were brought from Rome for the palace chapel, which had the largest dome north of the Alps. It was all of a piece with Charlemagne's policy of copying ancient texts and the superscription on his coins: *Renovatis imperii*. But despite the lavish embellishment of his capital, it was still wildly ambitious of the Franks to call it Roma Ventura (the Future Rome).

Alcuin reminded Charlemagne of Augustine's advice that conversion must be voluntary and not imposed. In 796 the Frankish bishops condemned the methods used in the thirty-year war against the Saxons: not just the violence used to force them to convert but also the tithes demanded for sustenance of their parish priests. Terror and taxes, the bishops realized, were not the way to win hearts. They intended to influence him in his war against the Avars, a group of white Huns, Mongols, and other peoples in the Danubian basin. Some did become Christian, but most were simply wiped out, inspiring the Russian expression for anything that vanishes as gone the way of the Avars. Charlemagne sent some of the war booty to Rome. By the time of his fourth visit there, Charlemagne ruled over much of present-day France and Germany, Benelux, northern Spain, what is now Austria, and northern Italy. He had relations with the Byzantine Empire, with which there were common borders in certain regions, and the Caliphate of Baghdad. He was more than a king. Leo, the clergy, militia, and populace came twelve miles from Rome to greet Charlemagne, who later dined with the pope. The following day Leo greeted Charlemagne on the steps of St. Peter's, and inside they prayed together.

Exactly a month after Charlemagne's arrival, a synod of the Roman church, together with Frankish bishops and nobles, reviewed the charges against Leo. Charlemagne may have had sympathy for the accusers as relatives of his beloved Hadrian, but they failed to prove their specific charges and insisted, instead, that Leo had denied the rights of Romans, presumably meaning the rights of lay nobles like themselves. But Charlemagne saw himself as the sole protector of these and would have been sure they were in good hands. He decided that the accusers were motivated by hatred rather than a desire for justice. After citation of the cases of Pope Pelagius I and other pontiffs, about which there were legends rather than documentation, papal juridical exemption was claimed. From the altar, Leo gave an oath: "Since I have no knowledge of the untrue charges which the Romans, who unjustly persecute me, have laid, I affirm that I have not committed these crimes." His accusers were condemned to death, but Leo had the penalty changed to exile in a Frankish monastery.

Two days later, at a crowded Christmas Eve Mass in St. Peter's illuminated by a thousand candles, Leo placed an imperial crown on Charlemagne's head and then knelt at his feet: it was the first and last time that a pope abased himself before a Western emperor. Charlemagne knelt for the coronation on a circular slab of porphyry near the altar. Today it is in the nave pavement only a few steps from the central door.

"The venerable and gentle pontiff crowned him with his own hands, with a most precious crown," recounts the *Liber Pontificalis,* a compilation of papal biographies. "Then all the loyal Romans . . . acclaimed 'To Charlemagne, most pious Augustus (Majesty) crowned by God, mighty and powerful emperor, long life and victory!' "

Einhard gave a different version:

Charlemagne really came to Rome to restore the church, which was in a bad state, but in the end he spent the whole winter there. It was on this occasion that he first received the title Emperor (Augustus). At first he was far from wanting this. He made it clear that he would not have entered the basilica that day at all, although it was the greatest of all the feasts of the church, if he had known in advance what the pope intended.

Controversy has never ceased about the episode, which took place 324 years after the fall of the last Roman emperor in Italy. With the coronation, the Roman empire acquired the adjective

"Holy," but it lacked much of the original empire from the East to North Africa, southern Italy, Dalmatia, and the British Isles. Did Leo have a rush of blood to his head? Is it feasible that Charlemagne was taken completely by surprise: "Why me, whatever made you think of such a thing?" Was the acclaiming chorus improvised? Leo had reasons to be grateful to Charlemagne, but his obeisance may also have been an act of appropriation.

It was the obverse of what had occurred when Theodosius I had abased himself before Ambrose of Milan to show repentance after impulsively ordering a massacre. For Augustine, that had been an example of a new Christian order in which even rulers would acknowledge a higher law and power would be tempered by "pious humility."

The crowning of Charlemagne was a replay of an incident that had not taken place between Pope Sylvester and Constantine but had been invented in the fake Donation of Constantine to symbolize an ideal pope-emperor relationship. It created a precedent; it was a template to shape events. Much about the crowning is obscure, and the fact that it took place only two days after the conclusion of Leo's trial suggests it was arranged before that verdict or took place in the wash of it. It meant that Rome, still convinced of the need for an alliance with a temporal power, after five centuries had substituted Charlemagne for Constantine.

In the same period another, arguably more important, substitution had taken place: the church in Rome had succeeded pagan Rome as law-giver and sacred symbol. The Christian movement, which began in a distant province, had targeted the capital of the empire: the Acts of the Apostles, usually attributed to St. Luke, drew an implicit parallel between Jesus going to Jerusalem to spread his message and the Gospel reaching the universal city, Rome. Paul, a Roman citizen, was convinced the city had a providential role in the spread of Christianity. He was martyred in one of the intermittent persecutions that inspired the contrary viewpoint that Rome was an evil power.

But some Christians had found aspects of pagan Rome congenial. The writings of Minucius Felix, a third-century Roman lawyer, indicate an easy cohabitation between the Christian faith and Roman culture; for him, one's culture could remain classical even when one's religion was Christian. An early fifth-century mosaic in the Roman church of St. Pudenziana, which depicts the apostles in senatorial togas, is another example of Christian-classical osmosis.

Humility is not a virtue usually associated with pagan or Christian Rome. But both pagan Rome and Roman Christianity were culturally humble while, at the same time, sharing an awareness of a universal mission. Pagan Rome respected Greek culture while Christian Rome, despite reservations, respected pagan culture as a whole. It accepted most of pagan culture's laws and sociopolitical institutions, and did not oppose its literary culture indiscriminately. Rather than destroy classic pagan texts, it encouraged their preservation, enabling them to become a constant source of reference and renewal.

The church of Rome had reference points beyond itself: it looked back to Jerusalem, and it did not claim to be the origin of the truths it conveyed. This disposed it to modify, rather than simply oppose, Roman civilization. Pope Damasus completed the replacement of Greek by Latin in the liturgy and insisted that early Christians had obtained Roman citizenship by martyrdom. The church in Rome had acquired a local habitation and a language. Jerome showed that Christians could use Latin as incisively as any pagan and that their Sacred Books had style.

However, as Christians became more sophisticated, some were anguished by their divided cultural allegiance. Eventually the pagan connotations of classical literature lost vitality and the class that identified Rome's greatness with it disappeared. Christians appropriated the classical but at different times in different spheres; in architecture it occurred as early as the fourth century, but it was not until the seventh that a Roman temple (the Pantheon) became a church; churches were installed among the ruins of the Forum, and guide books brought the pagan monuments, as well as the martyrs' tombs and churches, to the attention of pilgrims.

To judge by a reproof from the prickly missionary Boniface, practices such as fortune-telling and ribald New Year celebrations continued in Rome until the seventh century. Pope Gelasius's protests against the persistence of the Lupercalia festival suggest that his predecessors either had not managed to suppress it or did not think it necessary.

On that occasion Gelasius spoke out during an exchange with a senator who said the pope should discipline lax priests. In fact, as the moon of the church waxed in the light of Christ, a darker side also became visible: already in the fourth century, Jerome had scarified the comfortable, conformist Christians of the capital.

Had Rome conquered the church or had the church conquered Rome? Did it simply take over from pagan Rome rather than transform it? In pagan accounts at least, the Grand Guignol associated at times with obtaining the papacy was worthy of notorious emperors. Shifts in terminology suggest that Rome had conquered: in 381 the emperor's title of Pontifex Maximus, which indicated he was both king and priest, became exclusively that of the pope, while the word for the emperor's visit to the provinces, "parousia," was applied to the second coming of Christ. The word for the territories of the civil administration, "dioceses," was adopted for ecclesiastical districts.

However none of the pagan leaders had seen themselves, like Gregory the Great, as a humble servant of the servants of the Lord. Saints had replaced the shades of the pagan afterlife, giving Christians a new perspective on the present. Certain Christians' behavior showed that the stronger God who replaced those in whose name pagan Rome conquered had, as his secret weapon, compassion. This was reflected fitfully by legal provisions such as those that discouraged abandonment of children and ensured that the unmarried were no longer disadvantaged. Some laws were made more humane, but Christians were expected to live up to their precepts without the law necessarily reflecting them.

When the church, through force of circumstances, took over functions formerly exercised by pagan administrators, it provided relief for all the poor and not just, as previously, for citizens, and did so through anonymous donations rather than by donors who expected recognition. They had been wealthy (and were not taxed) but all Christians were called to fast and give alms. Christians opened new possibilities to women by considering spiritual pursuits worthy of their lifelong vocation. Their belief that God created the body in his image and likeness was one reason that eventually they opposed the previously accepted institutionalized cruelty of gladiatorial shows.

Once the church in Rome acquired cultural prestige similar to that which pagan Rome had enjoyed, it was in danger of becoming as hermetically closed in its traditions as were Symmachus and the Pagan Party. Various factors saved it: it was not elitist, had a different reference point, had spawned an extensive ascetic movement against the allure of conformism, and reacted creatively to the arrival of new peoples.

Ambrose of Milan had gone a long way and even too far in identifying Catholicism with the empire, but Augustine, after outgunning pagan Romans in erudition, pointed the way beyond it. Perhaps the impassioned debates on the Trinity reminded church leaders that the Spirit blows where it wills and that the smugness that had affected the Pagan Party would be out of place. As the empire crumbled, Leo the Great was quick to point out that the see of Peter had become Rome's standard bearer, but it would have had a shrinking audience unless Gregory the Great forged a language for those unfamiliar with the high style and sent out missionaries.

Here two factors helped Christians. Once they learned to look beyond the empire and see barbarians as other than a threat, they reaped the benefits of the prestige attached to the civilization they inherited because many of the new peoples were keen to accept the urban order identified with Rome, the administration, the roads, the law, and the plumbing. Acceptance of the faith was also acceptance of a culture, a socioeconomic upgrading.

At the same time, the church benefited from the humility that it had displayed in relation to Roman culture. Ultimately it saw its task not as defending what it had engendered but transmitting an inheritance from elsewhere.

The church in Rome not only absorbed the pagans' culture after drawing its religious "poison" but inhabited the city of the emperors. Here also a substitution took place: Peter and Paul replaced Romulus and Remus, historic founders of a spiritual realm instead of legendary founders of an imperial power.

In the words of the Irish monk Columban, Peter and Paul were "fiery steeds" drawing God's chariot. And while pagan Rome was turned to the past, Christian Rome embraced also the future, both in this world and the next. Its myriad churches pointed beyond the city to heaven, of which Peter was the Gatekeeper.

The fortunes of the church in Rome were linked to the non-Roman Peter, who had been crucified ignominiously upside down in Emperor Nero's chariot racecourse within sight of the obelisk that now stands in St. Peter's Square. Kings ignored Emperor Hadrian's tomb in favor of that of Peter: the Lombard Liutprand laid on Peter's tomb the arms he had intended to use against Rome;

Oswy of Northumbria chose the Roman form of Christianity to be on good terms with the Gatekeeper.

Peter embodied the continuity of the church of the martyrs with the more comfortable recognized church, and many papal documents were issued with the formula *Data Romae apud Sanctum Petrum:* given in Rome at St. Peter's (tomb). He was a resource, moreover, against Charlemagne after the Frank had become the first Holy Roman emperor in St. Peter's basilica on that momentous Christmas Eve.

Even after the end of persecution, the Roman see often seemed not only built on a rock but situated between a rock and a hard place; it battled to preserve the autonomy that would enable it to develop its precious heritage. The episode of Charlemagne's coronation was but the latest in this struggle for survival: it entailed ambiguities but looked likely to ensure safety for Rome as long as the Holy Roman Empire remained powerful and the emperor kept his distance.

Aquae Grani, wherever its location, would never have Rome's charisma. It aspired to be the future Rome, but with the church's absorption of the city's traditions and prestige and its acceptance of the new peoples, Peter represented both the past and future Rome. Charlemagne overshadowed Pope Leo but Peter overshadowed both. Moreover, Charlemagne would pass away as would Leo, but could the attrition of Time wear away the rock that was Peter?

CONCLUSION

T
HE ROCK HAS RESISTED: continuity with the period from Constantine to Charlemagne is tangible in sites such as Castel Sant'Angelo fortress beside the Tiber close to St. Peter's. Its base is the mausoleum of Emperor Hadrian, who, as punishment for a Jewish rebellion in A.D. 135, buried Christ a second time by deliberately covering over his tomb in Jerusalem. The angel surmounting the fortress, which was a bulwark against Gothic invaders, commemorates the vision of Gregory the Great while he led a procession imploring God's aid against plague: as the angel alighted, it sheathed its sword, foreshadowing an end to the epidemic. Castel Sant'Angelo is a reminder that, as well as martyr's tombs, Rome has other evidence of the faith persisting despite desperate circumstances.

The presence of the past explains why the twin fountains in St. Peter's square are nicknamed Scripture and Tradition. Since Vatican Council II, while Scripture has acquired new vigor, Tradition has been downplayed because of concern about encrustations.

Although some scholars want to look from the peaks of classical Greece and Rome directly to the Renaissance, as if nothing significant happened in between, it is harder to understand why Christians ignore centuries in which the church underwent decisive changes while salvaging a culture and shaping society. Both the energy and anxiety of late antiquity and the patristic period should strike chords today.

The contemporary relevance of the church in Rome from Constantine to Charlemagne can be found in episodes such as its refusing to be cowed by imperial support for Arianism and affirming that expelled bishops, such as Athanasius, had a right to appeal to Rome. With some exceptions, its popes had a good record in withstanding overbearing rulers; in particular, Martin I, the last pope-martyr, showed not only courage but also style.

Rome was the seal and guarantee of sound doctrine; it fostered unity and became a finishing school for converted barbarians and a cultural clearing house. The colony of Greek exiles in Rome gave Paul I works on grammar, geometry, and orthography and writings of Aristotle and Dionysius the Aeropagite, which he presented to Pepin of the Franks. They were one basis for the Carolingian renaissance. Rome ushered Christians through the downfall of the Roman empire and the disruption that followed, and then it seeded a new society. Although tempted to identify completely with the empire that was Rome without limits, the church saw beyond it, took over civil functions in the devastated city when no one else could fulfill them, repaired the social fabric, and recognized its missionary responsibilities.

Today it is the same church, but the times have changed profoundly. Once again society and the church face the shock of the new: not only did the Berlin Wall fall unexpectedly, but limits in all fields from biology to economics to communications seem to melt into air. Once again society and the church need firmness and flexibility, avoiding both political correctness and ideological obsessions. The church must adjust to the demise of the church-state relationships that it earlier devised in the wake of the empire's collapse. One consequence was the Papal States, whose defense made the Catholic Church oppose modernity indiscriminately. The resulting cultural lag persists despite the Second Vatican Council, which was partly a catching-up revolution and partly a response to two World Wars that brought a collapse of a form of Christian civilization and of a civil order almost as total as the fall of the Roman empire.

The cultural lag complicates responses to the current problems of sexual relations, the family, genetic manipulation, dizzying social-technological change, and economic inequalities as well as intra-church problems such as the role of women, ministries, mission, and participatory structures.

It would be a mistake to rely on answers devised in late antiquity to solve new problems, but attitudes displayed then can point the way forward. It is encouraging that Gregory the Great competently handled even more daunting problems in both church and society. Although he feared an imminent end to the world, he prepared the future. When some invoke a John Wayne–pope, he shows instead the virtues of confidence in the laity and dialogue, pastoral flexibility, and tact in building on neutral cultural practices. Like other major figures of the Constantine-Charlemagne period, Gregory speaks directly to today.

The insights and energies that enabled their achievements suggest what is needed if the current shock of the new is to be transformed into a rejuvenation of faith and culture. For that to happen, there has to be a conversation between faith and culture as daring and profound as in the centuries between Constantine and Charlemagne.

SELECT BIBLIOGRAPHY

Overviews

Brague, René. *Europe, la voie romaine*. Paris, 1992.
Bynum, Caroline Walker. *The Resurrection of the Body in Western Christianity*. New York, 1995.
Chadwick, Henry. *The Early Church*. London, 1971.
Eno, S.S., Robert B. *The Rise of the Papacy*. Washington, D.C., 1990.
Herron, Judith. *The Formation of Christendom*. Princeton, 1987.
Hibbert, Christopher. *Rome: Biography of a City*. New York, 1985.
Jedin, Hubert, Editor. *History of the Church*. Vol. 11. London, 1980.
Kelly, J. N. D. *The Oxford Dictionary of the Popes*. Oxford, 1988.
Krautheimer, Richard. *Rome: Profile of a City 312–1308*. Princeton, 1980.
Llewellyn, Peter. *Rome in the Dark Ages*. London, 1971.
Schimmelpfenning, Bernard. *The Papacy*. New York, 1984.

Monographs

Barnwell, P. J. *Emperors, Prefects and Kings*. London, 1992.
Brown, Peter. *Augustine of Hippo*. Berkeley, 1967.
———. *The Body and Society*. New York, 1986.
Bonner, Gerald. *St. Augustine of Hippo*. Norwich, 1986.
Caruso, Antonio. *Cassiodoro*. Catanzaro, 1998.
Chadwick, Henry. *St. Augustine*. Oxford, 1986.
Christer, Neil. *Three South Etrurian Churches*. London, 1991.
Granzotto, Gianni. *Carlomagno*. Milan, 1978.
Heather, P. J. *Goths and Romans, 332–489*. Oxford, 1991.
Kelly, J. N. D. *Jerome: His Life, Writings and Controversies*. London, 1975.
Martin, Joseph. *Doors to the Sacred*. New York, 1991.
Mazzolani, Lidia Storoni. *Ambrogio Vescovo*. Milan, 1992.

————. *Sul Mare della Vita*. Palermo, 1987.

Meer, Frederic van der. *Augustus the Bishop*. London, 1986.

Pagnotta, Don Elvio, and Margherita Chiaramonti Caporali. *San Martino I: Papa e Martire*. Todi, 1991.

Richards, Geoffrey. *Consul of God: The Life and Times of Gregory the Great*. London, 1980.

Romain, Willy-Paul. *Bonifacio*. Turin, 1991.

San Martino I: Papa e Martire. Documenti e iconografia locale. Todi, 1991.

Stock, Brian. *Augustine the Reader*. Cambridge, Mass., 1996.

Primary Sources

Ammianus Marcellinus. *Writings*. London, 1971.

Augustine, St. *The Confessions*. London, 1984.

Bede. *A History of the English Church and People*. London, 1967.

Claudius Rutilius Namatianus. *Il Ritorno*. Turin, 1992.

Einhard and Noter the Stammerer. *Two Lives of Charlemagne*. London, 1969.

Gregorio Magno, S. *Benedetto da Norcia*. Subiaco, 1967.

Jerome, St. *Letters*. Oxford, 1893.

Macrobius. *Oeuvres Completes*. Paris, 1863.

CHRONOLOGIES

Popes

311–314	Melchiades
314–335	Sylvester I
336	Mark
337–352	Julius I
352–366	Liberius
355–365	Felix II*
366–384	Damasus I
366–367	Ursinus*
384–399	Siricius
399–401	Anastasius I
401–417	Innocent I
417–418	Zosimus
418–422	Boniface I
418–419	Eulalius*
422–432	Celestine I
432–440	Sixtus III
440–461	Leo I
461–468	Hilary
468–483	Simplicius
483–492	Felix II
492–496	Gelasius I
496–498	Anastasius II
498–504	Symmachus
498–505	Lawrence*
514–523	Hormisdas
523–526	John I
526–530	Felix III
530–532	Boniface II
530	Dioscorus*
533–535	John II
535–536	Agapitus I
536–537	Silverius

*a rival pope, often called anti-pope.

537–555	Vigilius
556–561	Pelagius I
561–574	John II
575–579	Benedict I
579–590	Pelagius II
590–604	Gregory I
604–606	Sabinian
607	Boniface III
608–615	Boniface IV
617–618	Deusdedit
619–625	Boniface V
625–638	Honorius I
640	Severinus
640–642	John IV
642–649	Theodore I
649–653	Martin I
654–657	Eugene I
657–672	Vitalian
672–676	Adeodatus
676–678	Donus
678–681	Agatho
682–683	Leo II
684–685	Benedict II
685–686	John V
686–687	Conon
687	Theodore*
687–692	Paschal*
687–701	Sergius I
701–705	John VI
705–707	John VII
708	Sisinnius
708–715	Constantine
715–731	Gregory II
731–741	Gregory III
741–752	Zachary

752–757	Stephen II (or III)
757–767	Paul I
767–769	Constantine*
768	Philip
768–772	Stephen III (or IV)
772–795	Hadrian I
795–816	Leo III

Byzantine Emperors

306–337	Constantine I
337–340	Constantine II
337–350	Constans I
337–361	Constantius II
361–363	Julian
363–364	Jovian
364–375	Valentinian I
364–378	Valens
375–383	Gratian
383–392	Valentinian II
379–395	Theodosius I
395–423	Honorius
395–408	Arcadius
408–450	Theodosius II
423–425	John
425–455	Valentinian III
450–457	Marcian
457–474	Leo I
474–491	Zeno
475–476	Basiliscus
491–518	Anastasius I

518–527	Justin I
527–565	Justinian I
565–578	Justin II
578–582	Tiberius II
582–602	Maurice
602–610	Phocas
610–641	Heraclius
641	Constantine III
641–668	Constans II
668–685	Constantine IV
685–695	Justinian II
695–698	Leontius
698–705	Tiberius III
705–711	Justinian III
711–713	Philippicus
713–716	Anastasius II
716–717	Theodosius
717–740	Leo III
740–775	Constantine V
775–780	Leo IV
780–797	Constantine VI
797–802	Irene

General Councils

325	Nicaea I
381	Constantinople I
431	Ephesus
451	Chalcedon
553	Constantinople II
681	Constantinople III

INDEX

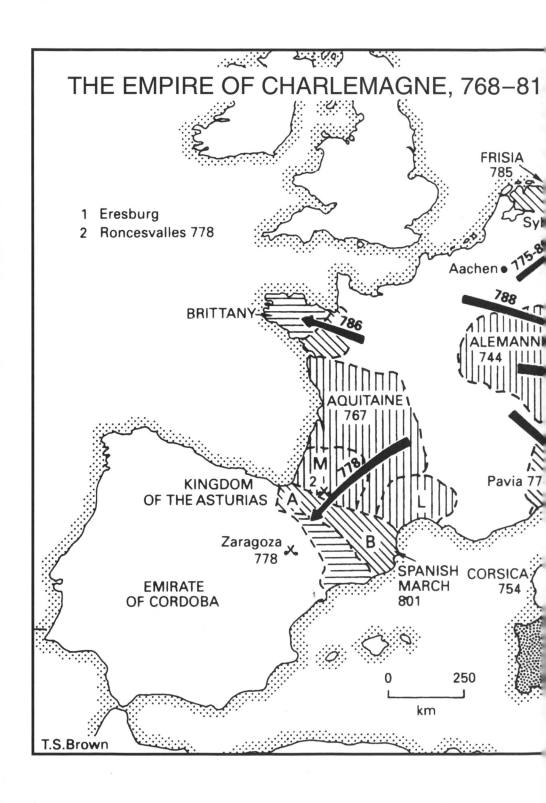

THE EMPIRE OF CHARLEMAGNE, 768–81

1 Eresburg
2 Roncesvalles 778

FRISIA
785

Sy

Aachen ● 775-8

788

BRITTANY 786

ALEMANN
744

AQUITAINE
767

M
2
A

L

Pavia 77

KINGDOM
OF THE ASTURIAS

Zaragoza
778

B

EMIRATE
OF CORDOBA

SPANISH
MARCH
801

CORSICA
754

0   250

km

T.S.Brown